Praise for *Offered In Secret*:

"Connelly takes us on a poignant, disarming, and often funny literary journey exploring loss, family loyalty, and the buried roots of the parent-child bond."

—Eric Lichtblau, Pulitzer Prize-winning New York Times journalist, author of *The Nazis Next Door*

"For anyone who has ever had a mother... Part family memoir, part investigative odyssey, Offered in Secret is the story of one son's reluctant quest to find the ideal final resting place for his mother's ashes. Connelly's humorous and heart-wrenching narrative brings readers along for the ride for his often uneasy adventures as he confronts old family friends, leery strangers, and, ultimately, himself. Finely wrought and affecting, Offered in Secret reminds readers that in seeking to honor the memory of those who are gone, we might just unearth a little redemption for ourselves."

—Denise Kiernan, New York Times bestselling author of *The Girls of Atomic City*, *The Last Castle*, and *We Gather Together*

"Stuart Connelly's ability to string words together is much like the person he is – candid, real, honest and interesting."

—Crystal Zevon, author of *I'll Sleep When I'm Dead: The Dirty Life and Times of Warren Zevon*

"Much more than a memoir, this is a sweet, wry, clear-eyed retelling of a story that will resonate with just about anyone who's taken a road trip with family. I can only hope it encourages all of us to consider our loved ones with as much honesty and care."

—Celeste Headlee, NPR anchor and author of *Speaking of Race*

OFFERED
IN
SECRET

Stuart Connelly

REDHAWK
PUBLICATIONS

Redhawk Publications
The Catawba Valley Community College Press
2550 U.S. Hwy 70 SE
Hickory NC 28602

ISBN: 978-1-959346-46-3
Library of Congress Number: 2024930383

Design by Modoc Spring

Library of Congress Cataloging-in-Publication Data
    Connelly, Stuart
        Offered in secret / by Stuart Connelly
            p.   cm.
        ISBN-13: 978-1-959346-38-8
    I. Title

FIRST EDITION

Printed in the United States of America

For Whom It May Concern

It's a warm late summer day. I'm a man driving a top-down convertible, wind in his hair, heading to points unknown. In the passenger seat sits a plastic box with a cheap shiny plaque glued down on its top. Less than three pounds of powder inside – what any of us can be boiled down to, it seems.

Meet Carolyn. Or what remains of her, anyway. Though she's joining in on the journey, she won't be coming this direction again. It's a one-way trip. I'm the escort. I'm the delivery boy.

I'm the son.

BY WAY OF INTRODUCTION...

As DIFFICULT AS IT IS to know oneself, how much more so to truly know another? Particularly when you've already assigned to that person all the salient traits you believe define them, the depth of character you imagine they possess, and which actions you're certain they are and are not capable of taking. You can't cut them open to see what makes them tick, so you're left analyzing from the outside and coming to your own conclusions.

I can recall, when trying to get away with whatever things I wanted to get away with as a boy, that the structure of my thinking was stable, built upon this singular foundation: my mother was never a child. She has no way to figure out what I'm putting over, because she was never down here in the trenches like me. Yes, I knew biologically, mathematically, and logically that this wasn't the case, but on a deeper level, the level of developing human instinct, I wasn't so convinced. I felt sure that anyone who was capable of being a mother would not have previously behaved in any kind of childish way. She may have been young once, but that youth would have been only the temporary casing, a years-long holding pattern for this otherwise fully developed mother within. Her childhood was all chrysalis – her eventual motherhood simply her natural butterfly state.

This pattern of thinking presumes two facts not necessarily in evidence: one; that the traits and abilities and emotions tiny children project upon adults have any correlation to objective reality, and two; that Carolyn Black Connelly *was* capable of being the kind of mother who makes it look easy and natural.

It turns out neither of these things are true.

It turns out that my mother had quite an extensive if not impressive career as a human being before I showed up, new-appendage-like, just days after her thirty-sixth birthday. In a world before me and my two siblings, Carolyn was not simply marking time. Quite the opposite; all indications suggest that she was a more successful child and adolescent than parent.

And yes, the "oh, Mom and Dad were *real people!*" epiphany is something all children come to at some point as they begin to co-occupy adulthood with their parents. But in my experience that sense, for the most part, still remains a hazy hypothetical in the offspring's imagination. All soft focus, not delineated and nailed down. It might well have stayed in that gossamer realm for me, too.

But I've shifted my thinking on all of this in the face of recently unearthed and irrefutable proof. The evidence now in hand is black and white – photographs, telegrams, jaundiced newspaper clippings, and letters of both the love and hate variety. They blend together to form a portrait of a woman having all manner of fun and decadence, consuming suntan lotion and cigarettes and men in equal measure. Action in which the younger me could not have imagined her engaged. Armed with this slowly clearing vision (version?) of my mother, I am confronting if not a life well-lived, then at least: a life... well, *lived*.

I've come late to these quicksilver mementos of her time on earth, which ended September of 2015. It is now late August of 2018, and I've organized the papers left behind, most likely never meant for anyone to read. I've built my mother's timeline out of the detritus, a map of her existence. Seeing when and where it superimposes onto mine, how it diverges. And now I'm off to follow this map. See where it leads. The journey is an investigation in the spirit of a YouTube unboxing video. But rather than the latest gaming console or collectable figurine, what I'm unboxing is a person, a life, and that life's place within my own.

As in all endeavors, Newton's First Law applies: a body in motion remains in motion, a body at rest remains at rest. My body's feverish motion will cover more than eighteen hundred miles in just over a week. And after nearly three years in the back of a closet, my mother's remains will be put to rest.

If all goes according to plan.

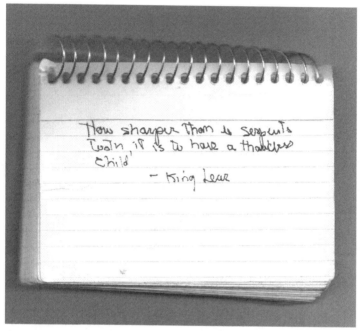

The first page of a spiral bound index card notebook found among my mother's belongings:

> How sharper than a serpent's tooth
> it is to have a thankless child.
> — King Lear

The second page lists the names and phone numbers of her three children.

I feel I must interject here
You're getting carried away
Feeling sorry for yourself
With these revisions and gaps in history

So let me help you remember
I've made charts and graphs
That should finally make it clear
I've prepared a lecture on why I have to leave

– The Postal Service
"Nothing Better"

ONE

∞

FIRST STATE

SOME DOORS REMAIN CLOSED

THE CELLAR DOOR was right there, tantalizingly close but, like the past itself, completely out of reach. In some ways, I should've expected as much. Should've expected this and worse, really. Within arm's reach of the basement? Right out of the gate? I had no right to have gotten as far as I had. And so quickly. Not a bump in the road. The bar had been set high, needing to get inside a stranger's home; but when I pulled up across the street from this totally unfamiliar Wilmington, Delaware, house in the middle of a workday, I found the front door propped open a full ninety degrees. It was opportunity beyond anything I had the right to hope for as I played amateur sleuth. But once it became apparent that I would be able to get inside number twenty-five, naturally that bar was reestablished. Zeroed out.

And so now I felt a debt owed to me, payable on demand by the universe. What do you mean no access? This cellar should be mine to explore because… well, it was my tale, my telling. So it should go the way I've planned, right?

And though this is my story, or more specifically my story of *Carolyn*, this certainly wasn't my basement. Or hers. Not anymore.

It belonged, or nearly so, to a young woman named Cachet. Who was now saying: "We can't go down there, because of the floor."

Uh-huh. The tiny kitchen's yellowed linoleum flooring was all torn up, in a state of mid-replacement. The minefield between me and the door. I wasn't going to get into the basement. First bump in the road.

Maybe it was just as well. Maybe I wasn't ready to descend quite yet.

I'D WOKEN UP at home three hours earlier, the morning of what would've been my mother's ninety-first birthday, less than fifty miles away. It was a horse farm tucked into the near-Amish countryside outside of Philadelphia. I'd settled in there and put down roots – including the occasional tomato and basil seedlings – so close to my mother's birthplace by sheer coincidence. The Connellys are not "born and bred" people. I was not from Wilmington because my mother, unlike most Americans, had no problem leaving her hometown for new horizons. I did, however, marry a woman, Mary Jo, whose extended family, two generations into the American experience, mostly hewed to the Philadelphia area. So when it was our turn to think about having a family, it made sense to my wife that we move close to her parents. In order to share the wonder... and perhaps get a little help, too. (Since we wound up with twins and I, the youngest of my family, had absolutely no experience with babies, this turned out to have been a brilliant move).

I wasn't that keen on leaving our place in the hills of San Francisco, but I had been harboring a writerly obsession with owning a quiet piece of land and a rambling old house in which to hole up and scribble away. My romantic version of the writer's life skewed more Sam Shepard than Lord Byron, and the open sky ranch life loomed large in my thinking of what kind of environment could work as writer fuel. But I came to realize I could handle becoming a Pennsylvanian under the right circumstances. We found a dozen-acre spread in Chester County with an old fieldstone house a mere twenty minutes from Mary Jo's parents and never looked back.

So I didn't end up living quite close to the place where my mother was born because that's where she was. She wasn't. My mother still lived in Syracuse, New York. Syracuse was my hometown, but a city my parents settled into in the 1960s, a place to which neither one of them had any familial connection. By the early 2000s, all those years later, my mother was getting a little long in the tooth, the notorious Central New York winters were getting harder on her, and those few friends she'd made after the divorce were drifting away into retirement along America's sunbelt.

I never gave Carolyn's situation any thought at all – her life, her call, I figured – but Mary Jo gave it a lot of thought.

"Carolyn should move to the area," she started suggesting a few years after we'd arrived back east. "We could see her more often. She could have dinners with us."

This idea wasn't unpalatable to me on its face. What was unsettling was the thought of choosing and directing the decisions and moves of another person. Even a family member. "If she wanted to move, she'd move."

"Maybe she doesn't know it's a choice," Mary Jo said. "If she knew she were welcome, it might be a different story."

I reminded her that I didn't like getting involved in other people's stories, that I was much more comfortable letting folks make their own decisions.

"But it's your *mother*," Mary Jo said.

That didn't change the calculus for me. Though I didn't grow up with money, I am as WASP-y as they come in terms of philosophy. Stiff upper lip and all that. I tend to approach most situations clinically, in a way that I would call rational but could probably be more accurately described as repressed.

This point of view may not make me sound like a fun date, but it has at least one upside: it keeps me out of other people's affairs. So when I shared with Mary Jo that I wasn't that interested in moving my mother anywhere, I didn't feel badly about it. Particularly since I'd derived this *laissez faire* attitude from the same well where we all dredge up most of our personality traits, the environment created by my parents. My mother had made her bed as it relates to the kind of man I was, and should have grown accustomed to lying in it.

But Mary Jo is no Protestant. She was hardwired to worry about 'her clan, perhaps even to put their interests ahead of her own (a concept that was fresh to me when we first met). It took a couple weeks of discussion until it became clear to me that Mary Jo's thoughts on what was best for my mother made a kind of sense. We opened the discussions with Carolyn and over the next year she started seeing the value in a change of address.

My mother found an apartment in West Chester, a small college town about fifteen miles from our place. She had a car and a spot in the parking lot but could walk into town on nicer days, get groceries and shop at little boutiques. She had a part-time job to add a little gravy on top of her fixed income. Now living less than thirty miles from her sister and brother-in-law, they could meet for lunch or the early bird dinner specials. And Carolyn would occasionally come out to the farm to try to help out. This mainly consisted of her fumbling to work the riding mower and cut the grass, but it was sweet and perhaps even a little useful.

For a few years that system hummed along pretty well, but eventually Carolyn began researching retirement communities. This took the family by surprise, but it probably shouldn't have. She'd been winding up for it for at least a quarter of a century. My mother had a self-sufficiency streak in her that ran deep and wide. It didn't match up to her earning power or investment strategy – she'd come up short on fuck-you money – but the streak was there nonetheless.

She knew that the older and more infirm one gets, the harder it becomes to find an affordable option. She didn't want to force her children into financing her final years, so while still relatively robust she struck out to make the best third-act decision she could with the cards she'd been dealt.

Carolyn's desire to avoid burdening others may sound selfless, but I didn't read it that way. Self-reliance can be wonderful, but in my experience my mother's strategy was a manifestation of her stubborn insistence on complete freedom. At any cost. Be in no one's debt, and therefore be in no one's service. Her organizing principle for life would have read something like: *If I'm paying for it, you don't get to have an opinion about it.* A type of philosophy that sounds more reasonable coming from someone with deep pockets. Carolyn was trying to live that mantra on social security checks and a dwindling pension.

From the moment the ink was dry on the 1973 divorce decree, Carolyn knew that it was up to her to make her own way in the world. My father, the plastic surgeon, didn't want the social blemish of a divorce and tried to use the "doctor's wife" lifestyle as leverage to keep the marriage going (at least by outward appearances). And though he was right – she was terrified of giving it all up and going out into the wilderness – he severely underestimated her pride. She probably believed that a fair alimony payment would ease the transition, yet she had no way of anticipating just how deliberately and vindictively my father would hide his assets and work the courts. A less trusting woman would have devised some sort of exit strategy before asking for a divorce; gathered incriminating evidence on her husband, stashed money secretly. Not my mother, she just wanted out. A critical misstep, that; by the time it was all over, Carolyn had little more than a roof over her head, tiny and infrequent child support payments, and three young mouths to feed.

She made it work the best she could. From doctor's wife

to broke in six months. Selling circus tickets was her first gig, not as glamourous as it sounds. Finally, after a hard year, what eventually proved to be her failsafe was her graduate-level degree in education, something she'd said she'd undertaken primarily in an attempt to become more interesting to her increasingly distant husband. That degree landed her a job at Syracuse University. Still, she was beginning to build a retirement nest egg more than two decades after most professionals start. It had been rough going, and at the end of the day she didn't have what most financial advisors would consider much economic wiggle room.

So Carolyn hit the jackpot when she visited Foulkeways, a Quaker-based not-for-profit retirement community about forty miles from our farm. Their admissions process featured two key components. First, applicants had to be interesting enough to be considered culturally valuable to the other residents, i.e.; if you're boring, live somewhere else. Additionally, actuarial reports were required on all applicants, a full assessment of their physical and financial health. The Foulkeways management team had to determine if the potential resident could afford the rent for the rest of what they estimated would be their life. This was critical, because admission to Foulkeways amounted to a compact between the parties. After the hefty non-refundable buy-in, someone like Carolyn would pay her monthly costs until she either died or ran out of money. In the event of the latter, Foulkeways committed to letting her stay for the rest of her life, paying for it all. This was gambling the same way insurance companies roll dice – the risk pool. Over time it has to work out in the aggregate, but any particular resident could be a money loser without the entire enterprise going down. For every resident who overstays their bank account's welcome, there's someone else who drops dead a year after writing their buy-in check. The scales always balanced out.

The Foulkeways people liked Carolyn. The savings account was on the borderline, but she had an interesting background that could be a good fit with the other residents. The admissions people fought for her, and in the end Foulkeways accepted Carolyn as a member of their community. A feeling of security, elusive to her since the mid-70s, was finally in hand. She would live there ten years, and die in the third, and nicest, apartment they provided for her.

My mother was a softy in a couple areas of life (animals and humans with no place to sleep spring to mind), but she came at most situations with a dollar-and-cents practicality that inures in people who live so close to the bone for so long. So it was with her death, pragmatism to the last. It wasn't that she didn't believe in the afterlife. She was quite a devout Christian – born again, much to my annoyance. No, it was simply that she saw through the rigmarole surrounding the burial industry as a not-so-artful way of separating the bereaved from their or their loved one's money. The concept of a burial plot didn't matter to Carolyn in the slightest. No view, no *who you'll be lying next to for eternity*. No silk-lined coffins with only the finest brass fittings. Screw all that. As with retirement, she made her own arrangements, wanted to minimize the cost, wanted to pay for it herself.

That all made sense to me... not because Carolyn made sense, but because, as Cheap Trick put it, "I'd known her all these years." Her choices on what to do upon her death fit precisely within the frame I'd constructed for her. At some point along the way, in planning for her death the same way she planned out the last third of her life – which is to say, with great focus and an eye towards footing the bill herself – she'd signed up for a kind of insurance package that locked in her discounted funeral costs if she made a full pre-payment.

> **Funeral Consumers Alliance of Greater Philadelphia**
> *1906 Rittenhouse Square, Philadelphia, PA 19103-5793*
> *215-545-9210*
>
> This card certifies that
>
> Ms. *Carolyn Connelly*
>
> is Member No. *6138* of this association
> and is entitled to all its privileges.
> In case of death, please notify this funeral
> director: _____

When Dead, Present This Card

This program was put out under the Funeral Consumers Alliance of Greater Philadelphia,[1] and had been thought through poorly. The whole program went out of business sometime after my mother signed up, and more importantly, ponied up. She was one of at least 6138 people to join, one of the apparently too few early adopters. RIP Funeral Consumers Alliance of Greater Philadelphia.

When I crossed the county line for a visit to the Huff & Lakjer Funeral Home to finish the paperwork and fetch whatever remains remained, I didn't feel any of the pressure usually associated with this meeting. I knew what Carolyn wanted. Whatever money she had left in this world, whatever was saved putting her to rest would be better spent on the living. Even if it was just taking my kids out for ice cream.

At the funeral parlor, where I was informed that the Funeral Consumers Alliance had folded up the tent, I was told something else, in the most solemn of tones. That there had been some back and forth among the powers that be, but after due consideration it had been decided that Huff & Lakjer would honor the terms of my mother's membership in the defunct Alliance.

Sounded fair to me; I'm no lawyer, but the paperwork I'd looked over made it seem very much like this Alliance had

---

[1] If that hourglass logo is any indication, it likely was not the most professionally thought-through organization.

entered into a contract with Carolyn, and now had a legal obligation that had come due.[2]

Two funeral parlor employees sat me down with a clipboard. One look at it and I knew they were going to try to run me through the wringer. I ticked every single box on their "arrangements checklist" that aligned with what Carolyn had previously been led to believe would be covered by the expired insurance concern. I selected not a single upgrade or extra, with the exception of ordering a couple additional copies of Carolyn's certificate of death that might come in handy. The check I wrote to the funeral home totaled twenty-nine dollars. Not a stellar day for the old sales team. I refused to even look at any of the urns or boxes that from my perspective might as well have had the word "upcharge" laser etched on their surfaces.

I drove home with a shit-brown plastic box on the seat next to me, vibrating with the turnpike beneath my wheels. *Carolyn B. Connelly*, the fake brass plate announced, *1927 – 2015*. My mother. Not a single misgiving on the funeral home negotiations. I knew her.

But in the intervening three years, I've been beginning to wonder how well I knew her after all.

MY WIFE Mary Jo was born and raised Catholic, is an active and practicing Catholic to this day. And whatever else that entails, it certainly means she has some pretty foundational ideas on the rituals surrounding the death of a loved one. Carolyn's box sat in the back of a slide-out shoe rack in Mary Jo's walk-in closet, and as the days turned into weeks, it began to become apparent to her that I was not working on any funeral arrangements. Nor would I be.

---

[2] As far as this particular funeral home's involvement was concerned, details were sketchy. It may be that Foulkeways had a standing agreement that all their dead were processed through Huff & Lakjer. At a retirement facility of that size, death would seem to be common enough to warrant some kind of umbrella contract with a practitioner of the "funereal arts."

Life as we knew it kept on.

But for that shit-brown box.

A tell-tale heart.

Can I imagine one of Mary Jo's parents burned up and stuffed in a carton in the back of the closet for several years? Not a chance. The Catholics have a solid system in place for dealing with life's hardcore transitions like this. Locked and loaded, echoing up through the centuries with the warming comfort only tradition can provide. Everyone in that club is and will always be on the same page. From Mary Jo's perspective, there was a playbook for dead parent, and the plays weren't getting called here with Carolyn. She knew I wasn't Catholic, but I was human, wasn't I? And where were my older brother and sister in all of this? The idea of my mother's remains festering and forgotten in a closet was eating away at Mary Jo and she kept asking, "When are you going to do something about your mother?" and "What will make this make sense for you?"

To me, the *when* was immaterial (Carolyn wasn't getting any more dead) and the *what*, well... the *what* I couldn't figure out. Does that make me cold? Hard? I don't know. But I do know who taught me how to look at the challenges of life. No one who knew me, least of all Carolyn, should've been surprised.

Mary Jo wanted closure; a ceremony, a wake, a way for all parties afflicted by Carolyn's passing to observe, reflect, have their say. In short, she wanted for Carolyn what ninety-nine percent of Christians in America expect and receive. A funeral.

That didn't interest me. Nor did it seem of any importance to my older siblings Lisa and David, who hadn't managed to gather in the wake of the death to go through Carolyn's belongings, clean out the apartment, try to settle up with the retirement facility.[3] So there was a disconnect here, with the

---

[3] In this particular case, the wheels in Foulkeways' actuarial slot machine didn't spin in their favor. By the time my mother died, they had provided

no-frills box of ashes representing one thing to the children and a very different thing to the daughter-in-law.

And Mary Jo kept asking the question: where could Carolyn's ashes go that would make her happiest? To me, the question didn't make any sense. I was clear on my mother's religious views on the matter: that she was gone. On to heaven, and those ashes weren't her any more than the bat guano piled up on her belongings out in our barn were. My perspective: same thing, minus the heaven. What was in the brown box was biochemical residue, a nuclear blast shadow of the woman at best. Throw 'em out for all it means to me. I said just that once to Mary Jo, not trying to be shocking or seem cruel, but just to try to cut through the assumptions and make sure my honest feelings registered. "If it were up to me, we could dump them in the trash and be done with it."

I didn't want to upset my wife, but I also didn't want to go through some *pro forma* ceremony for which I was bereft of feelings. My honor for my mother's life extended at least that far. The problem was, how was one supposed to devise an alternative, meaningful solution to a problem when the very fact that it wasn't urgent meant it was barely considered? It didn't warrant the front-burner attention that the actual problems in my life demanded. Like a movie just barely intriguing enough for one to add it to their Netflix queue, my take on what to do for my mother's funeral was eternally getting bumped for something more interesting, and it never made it to the top.

But after more than two years of ignoring the situation, what finally got me were the pictures. My mother's belongings, a two-room apartment's worth of the things

almost $200,000 to cover Carolyn's living expenses, though not cash but rather in credit against her monthly bill there. They put me though a reasonable due-diligence interview to ensure she wasn't siphoning her money to her children and crying poor, which is apparently something that happens.

she was able to hang onto as she moved into ever smaller accommodations, were stacked up in our barn mostly tucked under a protective sheet of painter's plastic. I started thinking there were some items in the jumble that might not stay intact much longer under such conditions, and I thought it was worth a few hours to try to salvage whatever might be delicate and important.

That turned out to be things made of paper.

I'm just old enough now and my mother was just old enough when she had me that I'm one of a relatively small number of my generation whose parents' family photographs evoke the Civil War collection at the Smithsonian. Yes, we have shots from the '70s, '80s, and '90s. I grew up connecting with those. This batch, though... this batch was something different. The pictures were filled with a girl grabbing life with both fists. She loved the beach – her beach, Rehoboth – the way American teenage girls have always loved the beach. She loved dances, she loved mixed drinks and cigarettes, she loved going on dates with men who she knew had less than chivalrous intentions. The woman had a goddamn *lust* for life.

Looking at these shots, I started to get the idea that I didn't have any kind of handle on my mother as anything other than my mother. It's not that our adult relationship was the same as the one we'd shared when I was little. But I'd never given a thought to any aspect of her life that wasn't filtered through her "job" as my mother. I'd known she wasn't great at that job, but it's still exclusively how I thought of her. And as that sunk in, rather than a feeling of guilt that should probably accompany it, I was instead hit with an intense curiosity. One that hooked in nicely with the problem of the box in the back of my wife's closet.

Because, in looking at the pictures, I had flashed upon the answer to the question of the ashes. I realized where they could be disposed of meaningfully. I should've known all along. What kept me from seeing it earlier was my utter lack of ability in processing things – anything, not even her ending – from my mother's perspective.

But now that I knew where to put the ashes, I immediately faced another hurdle, this one worse than the first. Why the hell would I want to make that trip?

Because it wasn't close by.

"EVERYTHING IS COPY," Nora Ephron once proclaimed, as tight and accurate an expression of a writer's guiding principle as you're ever likely to come across, a bit of gospel to us ink-stained correspondents. It's a polite way of announcing yourself as a thief. I steal from life all the time. Say it in front of me, and if it's interesting, some version of it is going to show up in a book or screenplay sooner or later. Sorry about that.

But oddly, I had never written about my mother.

There is, of course, a long tradition of writing about the deceased. It's called a eulogy, and it's customarily presented at the event I'd steadfastly refused to arrange on my mother's behalf. But a eulogy wasn't what I was envisioning. I have memories at the ready, of course. Stories I could trot out. They're all rehearsed, road-tested and good to go at any social gathering, including wakes and memorial services. They hit the right heartwarming notes. But they have no depth, they don't even have the depth of her old photographs, and those damn things are two-dimensional…

So no. Not the four-to-six-minute greatest hits speech with the soft laugh-line and the bittersweet tears at the tail end, but a real exploration. An honest one.

Who she really was.

A quirk of the family calendar started me thinking about a framework for something that would have meaning to me, and perhaps could bring meaning to Carolyn's death. August 22nd was coming up, the day that would have been my mother's ninety-first birthday. My own birthday would be following on the 30th. The summer had always wrapped up with a birthday party for her, then one for me. These were small affairs, but nevertheless taken together as birthday bookends, the week had an annual rite-of-passage comfort to it.[4]

And so… what if this pattern were superimposed on a research trip? A road trip into the past? What if I were to leave home on Carolyn's birthday, start with a visit to the house where she grew up, and then wend my way day-by-day through the places I suspected meant something to her, and the places I knew meant something to us both? The trip would end on my birthday, a little more than a week later, in Syracuse. My hometown.

I pitched it to Mary Jo, and she loved the idea. She seconded my plan for the final destination, too. "You're going to write about her, aren't you?"

She knew the answer.

"Yeah, I guess so. I'm going to write about her. And me… our relationship." So there it was. The conceit wasn't really about putting my mother to rest at all, it was about the ol' career, was that the lay of the land? Nevertheless, Mary Jo had been asking me to come up with a meaningful way of disposing of my mother's remains, and despite my belief there was no way for me to do this, I'd figured something out. Right, wrong or indifferent.

"I think that's a great idea." Mary Jo shared what she considered good news: unlike the public school district, the twins' first day at their new private school started after Labor Day, so Callie and Wesley were free and clear.

---

[4] Once she started doing admissions work for Syracuse University's College of Nursing, her duties surrounding old timey paper and pen class registration would dominate that week before Labor Day, and Carolyn would be MIA for my birthdays ever after. In place of a party, I'd come downstairs to find a hastily scrawled birthday note and an empty house.

This reaction of hers threw me. I was going this alone, I'd figured. Silent communion with the ghosts of parents past, that didn't go hand-in-hand with worrying about others' comfort. Looking for places that served milkshakes. Playing the license plate game. Solitude would be central to my ability to access whatever feelings I'd have on the road. If they were to be translated into a book, I would need focus. There was going to be no guided tour, no explanations. The trip would be built out of quiet reflection. A reconnecting, and possibly rewiring, of a mother-son relationship. That sounded like a prescription for flying solo if ever there was one.

"I think this is something I have to do by myself," I said.

My wife cocked her head. "The drive around the country, yeah. Sure. But the burial —"

"— It's not a burial."

"The ceremony, then," Mary Jo said, exasperated. "Whatever you want to call it."

I didn't want to call it anything. I barely wanted to *do* it. I said, "I'll just take care of it and come home." That seemed the simplest.

But it did not fit Mary Jo's preconceptions of how Carolyn Connelly should be put to rest. Family means everything to my wife. When she married me, she was all in to take on the problems of my family as her own. From her perspective, this was the funeral of our twins' grandmother. Burying my mother? The final chapter of a close family member's life? By myself? The last week of summer before the twins started high school? C'mon.

Mary Jo tried to hide her hurt, something she's never done well. "I don't have any intention of getting in the way of your pilgrimage or your writing," she said.

"I didn't mean —"

"The kids and I can meet you when you get there."

She wanted to meet me in Syracuse for the ceremony?

Seriously? "I can just do it myself," I said. Thinking that I was thinking about her.

Instead, I made her cry, my not realizing I was talking to her like she'd offered to help with the trash. Some unpleasant task I figured didn't require two people wasting their time.

I DO HAVE EMPATHY, but it's a peculiar brand. The emotional version of negative space. It doesn't operate by helping me feel how others feel. Not really. It works more like me trying to preempt others from experiencing those feelings.

I didn't want Mary Jo and the kids to drive all day for the dumping of some ashes because if someone asked me to do that, I'd consider it a tremendous inconvenience. I would want to get out of it, and so I would never want to get others into it. It was the Connelly version of the Golden Rule. My birthright, coming straight down my mother's branch of the family tree: I don't scratch your back, you don't scratch mine.

Don't visit me in the hospital, Carolyn used to say, stating her worldview, *because I sure won't visit you when it's your turn.* Allegorical, yes, but literal too. Mary Jo called the bluff on this alleged philosophy the time that Carolyn had a massive cardiac incident while on vacation. She was airlifted from Stone Harbor, New Jersey, to the acute care ward at Abbington Hospital outside Philadelphia.

Mary Jo was certain Carolyn's *don't visit* line was just shtick.

"I don't think so," I warned. But there was no question; we were getting into that car and visiting Carolyn.

An hour later we found my mother's room in the ICU. Weak, Carolyn looked us up and down. "What are you doing here?" Not softly, full of gratitude, but as mean as she could muster in her state. She was actually annoyed. I'd warned Mary Jo that this might be the reaction we'd receive. Carolyn had declared it in no uncertain terms.

It was barely eight months later that disease brought *me* down like a shot dog. My head pounding for two weeks before I finally went to the ER. One breezy spinal tap later, the situation had been made clear: I'd caught a seething case of viral meningitis and was staring down roughly a 50-50 chance of dying. I ended up in a hospital less than forty minutes from her retirement community, Carolyn had a car, no job, no other place to be.

She didn't visit.

I didn't hold that against her in the slightest. We come from a long enough line of people who make their own beds, dig their own graves. Carolyn never wanted to owe anyone anything. She never wanted to be on the receiving end of pity, but more importantly, when she had clear sailing, she certainly didn't want to be dragged down by someone else's misfortune. If we had a family crest, *Every Man For Himself* could be emblazoned on it.

"JUST LET ME do it alone, okay? It's easier that way."

There was another reason, a quieter one, that made me insist on solitude. A more selfish reason, I suppose, like most of the steps I take creatively – *Everything is copy!* – but one I didn't want to discuss. Even if my family wanted to meet me in Syracuse, I didn't want the audience. Not an audience for a "ceremony" that had no form. I didn't want the responsibility of it being special. I couldn't take my family being disappointed, looking on with expressions that said, *Is that it?* Not for their final memory of Carolyn. And I didn't know how to plan something that wouldn't disappoint.

But all that went unspoken.

And even so, we agreed that I'd light out for the territories on my own, each believing we were doing something for the other. The fate of my mother's ashes had finally been settled. Mark it on the calendar: a road trip with a banker's box of pictures, letters, documents, to begin on Carolyn's birthday, to end on mine, and in between, a winding journey to the places that shaped her, shaped me, shaped our relationship.

I wasn't sure exactly what I'd learn, but something deep inside told me this: events build us, brick by brick, and events that happen to us jointly fuse us together in some unknowable but profound way. I wanted to reach back into the events the way you plunge your hands into a river. To grab tight around whatever memories were alive and darting beneath the surface. I wouldn't use this with Mary Jo or anyone else in describing my plan – it seemed too triggering – but the word *autopsy* felt right. I'm not slicing anyone open to determine the cause of death, but I am retracing some steps here, trying to complete a picture. And the origin of the word, at least as far as its Greek roots are concerned, is not quite as invasive as we've been led to believe. It's simply a combination of *autos*, which means "self," and *opsis*, which means "sight." To see for oneself. Figure out what's what. In order to put Carolyn Black Connelly to rest, there was going to be a week-long autopsy of sorts, and Mary Jo had just grudgingly agreed to let me scrub in.

AUGUST 22ND, 2018: I saw a New York license plate on Concord Pike right ahead of me, which I took as a good sign. Though I was heading south for Delaware, this journey would eventually wind up to the north, right smack in the middle of the Empire State. Not one to look for guidance from the universe, I noted my enthusiasm over the Chiclet yellow plate with mild surprise.

As I drew toward my destination, I couldn't help feeling the neighborhood might be a little dicey. The main thoroughfare, Washington Street, seemed a boomtown of corner bodegas, and all manner of folks were crisscrossing in the midday sun with paper bag-sheathed bottles. But when I turned right onto 36th Street, things opened up. There was a big church with a parking lot and then several blocks of twins – a configuration similar to rowhouses or brownstones, but where rowhouses take up a whole block, twins are paired off, with each half owning one side yard along with the front and back yards. These houses were set farther back from the sidewalks, displaying a length of green lawns and blooming trees along the curbs that made the area seem more welcoming than the last half mile of Washington Street.

I parallel-parked the Audi and went to the trunk to retrieve my navy-blue Jack Spade computer bag and a single manila folder, which I slipped into the outside pocket. Though a bit scuffed and tattered, and probably older than any other car on the block, my German convertible stood out. It drew the curiosity of those few on the block at home in the middle of a work day. When I eyeballed the house across the street and halfway down the block from where I parked, number twenty-five, I noticed a man kneeling on the front porch. He had a slightly Middle-Eastern look – it was just after twelve noon, was it time for Dhuhr prayers? When I slammed the Audi's trunk lid down, the noise caught his attention. He locked eyes with me and the situation became clear: I registered the open boxes of tile and the wet saw. The man wasn't praying; he was working. And he wasn't the homeowner, he was a flooring contractor.

I stepped up onto the porch and, in my friendliest voice, told him that my mother had lived in this house as a child, and asked if it would be okay to look around. He hesitated, then let me know that I had to ask his boss, who was inside.

Great. I stepped through the open vestibule and made it part way into the house – I could see the stairs leading up, and maybe the dining room beyond, no cellar door in sight – before a slightly older contractor came up to me, stopping me decisively in the parlor area.

"You can't come in here."

I explained my situation in a bit more detail than I already had to the man on the porch and asked if I could just take a peek around the place. I actually thought it might work, since clearly there were no possessions in the whole house. It was an empty shell.

"Homeowner's not here," the builder told me in no uncertain terms. "I can't let you in."

Knowing it would come off pushy, I still asked if there was a way he could reach the owner, see if I could explain my situation over the phone. I was certain it would be fine.

The worker looked at me coldly. "She's supposed to be back soon."

"Okay, I'll just wait outside," I told the builder.

As if I had a choice in the matter.

The homeowner rolled up in a Subaru Outback within ten minutes. The driver's side window was rolled down and she didn't look happy. From her clothing I could tell she worked in a hospital, possibly the same one where my father had done his residency.

"Are you the man who wants to get inside my house?" she asked, her question edged with I-will-brook-no-crap disdain. She'd received a call from the workmen about me.

"Yes, I am," I offered, smiling into the car. I don't have a great smile, but I try.[5]

"That's not going to happen." Final. If she'd been on the other side of that front door behind me, it would've shut in my face. I realized that I was standing between the woman and her house. Literally. Bad *feng shui* of the human variety.

---

[5] Full disclosure on the record of my smile: in the summer between freshman and sophomore years of college I had a market research job, going door to door giving surveys. One homeowner turned out to be the columnist for the newspaper where I'd shortly work. He wrote about the encounter, saying, "With his smile I thought he might have been a mayoral candidate collecting signatures." On the other side of the argument, I'm now at age 54 on my second set of orthodontics, so I think the jury's out on my smile's quality.

But this woman in scrubs – a woman of science! – I knew I could reason with her.

"See, my mother used to live here."

Still stiff: "You're not getting in my house."

Tough cookie. Guard up. No wiggle room.

"I totally understand," I said, moving slightly to the right so that I was no longer blocking out her view of *Chez Subaru*. "Could I just show you some pictures?"

She shook her head, defiant. "No."

Oh, this was going to be a long trip. But I hadn't started it thinking yes would be the answer to my every question, that open doors meant open invitations. I had armed myself with a computer bag; it was slung over one shoulder and filled with answers to "no." I let it slide down and reached in for a single manila folder. Opening it against the soft late summer breeze, I quickly scanned through to find one that best showed what I was after; tying the teen version of my mother to this box of bricks.

"I'm not going to look at any pictures," the woman said, still practically bolted to her driver's seat. I noticed she had her ID card badge clipped on backwards, with whatever identifying information hidden against the folds of her scrubs. Not an accident. This was a woman used to staying vigilant.

"I know," I said as I picked out what I hoped would be just the right shot. It was a tiny one, true. But it was pretty high contrast, and the background, so crucial, had the best detail. The woman was young; I figured she was armed with better close-focus eyesight than me. Besides, if my quick triangulations were right, her car was sitting just about exactly where the camera had been placed when the shot was snapped. The effect should be worth something.

The House in Question

The woman in the Subaru melted. "Oh, my heavens! Is that your mom?" She was looking at it the way I had been at first. As an impossibility. But it was the truth.

"Nineteen forty-nine," I said.

Now pointing at the smiling young man in the photo next to her: "Is that your father?"

It most assuredly was not. "That's just one of her dates," I said. I pointed to the front door in the photo, a very recognizable grid of glass panes. "Look at the door."

Her eyes flew up the porch. Even though the door in 2018 had been propped open by the tile men, she could see. It was the same door. The woman offered her hand. "I'm Cachet," she said.

I could tell she was softening up. Maybe she took a shine to the pictures, or perhaps it was simply that the pictures proved that I was not some kind of grifter trying to case a joint that hadn't even been occupied yet. I pressed this slight advantage and pushed further, taking out a photograph of my mother and another child I assumed was her younger sister Lana. This turned out to be a tactical mistake.

The shot was closer, focused on the top step of the front porch. Cachet squinted at it. The house number was printed along the bottom of windows in the door, beneath the matrix of small panes. Her face dropped. "This says twenty-seven." She seemed to find this inconsistency upsetting, as if after she'd finally convinced herself she was being included in something special, the offer had been suddenly withdrawn.

I took a moment to think it through. "Then this was probably some next-door neighbor friend, not my aunt," I told Cachet. Now that I looked closer, it appeared to be a little boy, not a girl, next to Carolyn. "But I know twenty-five is the right address. I'm sure." I pulled out the piece of information I had that proved it. Despite all my efforts over the previous months talking to relatives both long-lost and far flung, no one seemed to have any idea of the street where Carolyn and her sister grew up. There were a couple of false leads, words scribbled on the backs of various photos that mimicked street names, but up until August 20th, perilously close to the go/no go decision on whether or not to move forward with this trip – this undertaking – I had no address. Two days before, I'd come across a telegram that Carolyn had saved.

Now, Cachet may or may not have ever held an actual developed black and white photograph that wasn't an x-ray, but at her age I was certain she'd never seen a telegram outside of a movie. I handed it to her. There was the address, with a street number of 25, printed out on a strip of newsprint and glued down. She took it through her car window two-handed, like it was an archeological find.

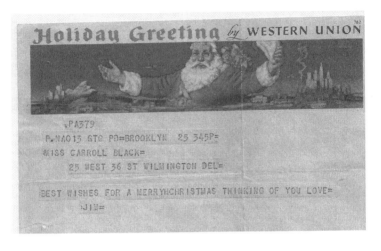

Jim from Brooklyn Points the Way

"So, Jim? Is that your father?"

I smiled, shaking my head. "Another one of her boyfriends." I let out a soft breath and, voice lower, suggested, "She had a lot of boyfriends."

"I'll bet." Cachet got out of the Subaru and moved closer. She'd changed since she'd arrived. Now she was standing next to me so we could both study the pictures in my folder from the same angle. "Come on in," she said. We walked up the distinctive path the photos showed so well, the handful of short steps up the grade, then the long chunk like a section of sidewalk, then the final two steps up to the porch. Cachet let me enter first. She showed me all around. Showed me the future bedroom of her one-year-old son, the master bedroom in the back with a view of the yard where my grandfather once kept a goat.

She showed me the dining area off the kitchen, and I was forced into reconciling my mental telemetry with the brick-and-mortar reality of number twenty-five. The place was far smaller than it lived in my imagination. To illustrate her father's convivial nature, Carolyn would often mention him allowing her to sit at the dinner table in her roller-skates (something her dour mother disapproved of, naturally) and I somehow pictured Carolyn skating all over the first floor of an enormous house. But it seemed there was barely room for a decent sized dining table. In the stories, this place housed all manner of exotic animals and various cars, motorcycles, boats. In reality it was probably all of 800 square feet.

Not counting the cellar.

"Is there a basement?" I asked. "I think I remember my mom talking about playing down there." That was a line; the best I could come up with at the time. A lie: *nobody* played in the basement of this house when my mother was growing up here.

We can't go down there, because of the floor.

Cachet pointed through the passthrough that separated the dining area from the kitchen. The work on the floor was blocking the swing of the cellar door. "Nothing much to see down there, anyway."

Maybe not for you, I thought.

Cachet walked me back out to the front porch. She looked at the photos and telegram again. Took a couple shots with her phone so she could share with her mother, who as described was almost as thrilled about her daughter's new house as the daughter was.

The new homeowner looked over at the steps and told me she'd had a dream just the previous night, of the happy family who had lived here before. All sitting together on this front porch. There were kids, and smiles, and she took it as a sign that this was a place that grew happy families.

I smiled the best I could.

Cachet took down my email address and promised to invite me to the housewarming, just a couple weeks away. I didn't know if I would go (or if she'd really follow through with the invitation after the novelty of our meeting wore off).

The party would be after my trip. After everything. The work would be behind me by then. The case would be closed.

On the other hand, it might be my only chance to see into that basement. That's really what I'd come to this house for.

But then I'd have to look Cachet in the eye again. Then I'd have to explain.

I hate to be the one to break the news, I'd have to say to her, but that dream about the happy family, this being a place of warmth and harmony? Well, my family, the one in these pictures here, it's a family borne of tragedy.

BEFORE MY MOTHER was conceived, before there were any other children, there was Colbert. The first and only son. The beautiful baby boy. Born to Elizabeth Black (née Melson) and Harry Clay Black sometime in 1921 or '22 – it's not entirely clear – young Colbert was destined to be adored by his parents, groomed to take over his father's jewelry store downtown, maybe play football for the University of Pennsylvania. The three of them together were a happy blossoming family, Harry's parents' money cushioning them like down, here in the front car of the rollercoaster that would become the Roaring Twenties. Poised for all the adventure you could muster.

There was, however, no family money to count on from my grandmother's side. Elizabeth Black had been raised a poor farmer girl from rural Delaware. She'd lived a hardscrabble life; her single mother took in boarders when they could, and it was little Elizabeth's room that they would occupy, with Elizabeth left to sleep on the kitchen table for the duration of their stay. About the only thing Elizabeth took with her from her childhood into adulthood was her love of chicken. Coastal Delaware is scrubland, flat as a top hat, with sandy soil and salty air. In the rural areas – 42% of the tiny state's land now and probably more than half back then – the farming just isn't all that great. But chicken farms do all right, and they were everywhere as the nineteenth century came to a close. Frank Perdue and his chicken empire in Salisbury, Maryland, was only about thirty miles to the southwest.

So poor and undereducated Elizabeth manages to marry a Philadelphia scion's boy, Harry Clay Black, and moves to the big city, Wilmington. In the 1920s, it had every convenience: street trolleys, telephones, and grocery stores. Now from Elizabeth's standpoint, the fresh chicken – the only good thing about her about childhood – had been taken away, replaced by the cellophane-wrapped quartered birds the butcher in the back of the local store put out in the display case every morning. It was an insult, this grocery chicken. It was untenable. Elizabeth needed her chicken fresh. This was the law, foundational and as unassailable as Thou Shalt Not Kill.

Harry was only too happy to comply. Kind of an overgrown kid, eager to please though quick to strike out hard if you hurt his feelings, he just wanted to be surrounded by people who were exuberant and appreciative. Oh sure, and worshipful too, that'd be a plus. He delighted in making others happy. If he could use his money to solve your problem, he was glad to do just that. So he managed to put together a system for his wife to have fresh chicken once a week. Very fresh. They would drive to the farmer's market, buy a live chicken, take it home and then behead it in the basement with an ax. The headless chicken was then thrown into a cauldron of boiling water to soften the skin so the feathers would loosen and could be easily plucked.

The vat of boiling water wasn't that big, but it wasn't small either. It wasn't a pot. The size of a low, wide bushel basket, it sat atop a heating element of some home workshop design. My best guess was that Harry pulled a new copper loop off the furnace that was right there and controlled it with a simple cut-off valve. Fresh chicken, that was Elizabeth's thing. Now, what Harry kept there in the basement was a small push lawnmower. Not the kind with the engine and the ripcord starter that never seems to work, just a simple two-wheeled roller with a few blades strung across the axle and a long handle. A confluence of events, one Saturday afternoon in 1925: a three-year-old, a lawnmower canted at a steep angle against the basement wall, a vat of boiling water for defeathering chicken. If the boy had tripped over the ax and fell in, that would've been one thing. That would've been all on my grandmother. The guilt most likely would've driven her to suicide. But what Colbert stumbled over wasn't the beheading device, it was my grandfather's lawnmower. Why the hell did it have to be there, anyway? This was what raced through my grandmother's mind. What careened through my grandfather's was: this is the price of fresh chicken? Too goddamn steep.

There was blood on that cellar floor, all right.

No more Colbert. He was scalded to death.

Because the chicken had to be fresh.

And that tragic event might just be the key to under-standing Carolyn as a human being, separate from her role as a mother – a role that for me filled the entire vista, but for her were just some of the smaller patches of a life that was made up of more than I could envision. The boy died, and the mother, my grandmother, just couldn't get over it. She couldn't shoulder her part of the blame, and because there were two intersecting mechanics, her boiling water and his push lawnmower, she seized on the latter and held her husband responsible. Her husband blamed her. Which came first, the chicken or the mower? A cold war started and churned away, hung in the very air of the twin house year after year.

And my grandmother marched into her future handcuffed to this dead boy, dragging him with her into everything that came after; resenting her husband quietly while he tried to cheer her up with his fun and games and new cars. All of which she despised. Which fueled his explosive rage. A nightmarish co-dependent wrestling match into which my mother was born.

These were the days when the doctors were all male chain-smokers and, as in the final season of *Mad Men*, it was usually the husbands who were given the details of a wife's health crisis and made the decisions. My grandparents' doctor had simple advice: have another child right away, a place to put all that dried-up love they both had for Colbert.

But there was no replacing Colbert. Certainly not with a girl. Carolyn grew up at 25 36th Street with a chilly mother and an amusing, easily manipulated big-kid father. Carolyn saw the writing on the wall and chose sides. She was daddy's girl, trying to control his temper by going along. Sometimes she loved the adventure, sometimes less so. But it was better than the reign of terror that would be the alternative. My mother's approach to men, myself and my brother included, had been set. Pacify. Maneuver. Stroke the ego, stay out of striking distance. Take what you need from them.

My grandmother didn't get the game. Or didn't want to play it. Nor did my Aunt Lana, the next attempt at a replacement for Colbert that failed. But at least my grandmother had a co-conspirator now. Those two baited the big man every chance they got. They knew how to needle and pout and get under Harry's skin. Unpleasantness always followed.

My grandmother went back to killing chickens in the basement. Nobody knows what happened to the lawnmower.

I SAID MY THANKS and good-byes to the eager young woman in scrubs and left the first stop of my tour in a hurry. I had a long trip ahead. The great gray American highway and the late summer breeze were calling. Out of the past, and deeper into the First State.

And I knew I would never be invited to that housewarming and would never speak to that proud new homeowner again.

But if she's reading this now, I can tell her one thing. I'm sorry a little boy died in your basement almost a century ago, but take consolation in this, Cachet: there are no such things as hauntings except those we bring upon ourselves. Carolyn's son, like yours will, grew up in a house where death took place. (In my case, what I'd always been told was a murder-suicide, though the truth would turn out to be a little more subtle than that). Your one-year-old and I started out in the same boat. I turned out more or less all right, I think, and so will he.

In fact, Cachet, if, many, *many* years from now he isn't driving around the country carting your ashes from town to town, trying to fit puzzle pieces into place, he may well be doing considerably better than I am.

CULS DE SAC

MY EXTENDED FAMILY did not extend very far. Connections to my father's side ended with my parents' marriage, but we didn't have much of a relationship with his two Ohio-based brothers' families even before that. My mother had the one sibling left, little sister Lana Taylor, and all family get-togethers were just working out whether the four of us went to Lana's place or she and her family came to ours. The schedule wasn't a complicated one. Thanksgiving and Easter tended to be at the Taylors, with Christmas more likely to be at our place. Syracuse had the real potential for snow – lots of it. The Taylors lived in suburban Wilmington, which had a more temperate climate. The dried brown grass of wintertime in their neighborhood just didn't stir the holiday spirit the way our white Christmas could.

Then there were the summers. School vacation provided lots of time for visits, often just Carolyn and I making the journey together down Route 81. We lived in an area where most of the neighbors didn't have kids my age. I was a loner, and though I didn't feel particularly lonely, my mother firmly seemed to believe that I needed at least one good friend.

Friendship wouldn't be found with my siblings.

At best, my sister, eight years my senior, put up with me. Some of those traditional "mother-to-be" traits Carolyn tried to instill in Lisa took root, making her a bit sympathetic toward her asthmatic little brother. She made spending money babysitting and could at least handle younger children. But some of the more sociopathic aspects of my father's personality coursed through Lisa, particularly the importance of the appearance of perfection. As a result, she focused on schoolwork to the exclusion of almost everything else. The primary image I hold of Lisa growing up is that of her closed bedroom door at the top of the stairs, with the soft rock strums of Joni Mitchell, Cat Stevens, Carole King and the like leaking out from beneath the crack along with the glow from her up-all-night study light.

My brother David and I had a more adversarial relationship. Five grades ahead of me, David was my opposite in every meaningful way. He was ski slopes, I was complaining about the cold. He pumped iron, I flipped pages. He roared, I wheezed. Only our gender connected us, which probably made matters worse: as a little kid, I wasn't behaving in a way that indicated I'd grow into the man he thought I should be. It was like living with a gym teacher. David definitely didn't want to deal with a baby, particularly one that didn't share his jock aesthetic and alpha fearlessness, but I was always underfoot. When I was lucky we steered clear of each other or he ignored me; when my luck changed I'd pay a price. If he became interested in changing me, showing me the errors of my ways, things would devolve quickly. A lot of tears, a lot of "I'm telling." A lot of novel punishments and tortures. I dreamt about David leaving for college.

So becoming pals with the siblings was not a realistic option. Early on, Carolyn set her sights on my cousin. Aunt Lana and her husband Aaron had two children. Their son Craig was just a year younger than me, and kind of in the same boat. His sister Hannah was older – between my age and my brother David's – and probably as a young teen was as annoyed by Craig as David was with me. So our mothers made it a point to get us together as often as possible. The bond with Craig, in those early years, was the closest thing I'd had to what people who really feel something for their siblings have.

After my visit to 36th Street I headed over to Brandywood and pulled up in front of the Taylors' old place. Brandywood was a development, and in my days in Syracuse that wasn't a word being thrown around. Yes, we did have neighborhoods that builders seemed to have developed, but they were from the 1940s, not the '60s. It made a difference. This was a real planned community, right down to the sidewalks threaded along the curb, even though the street went nowhere and a car might've drifted through once every twenty minutes or so. I knew this house almost as well as the one I grew up in; I'd done some growing up here as well. 2227 Glenstone Road. I could almost see, memory superimposed on the present like a Photoshop layer, the car I most associated with my uncle parked in front: the 1964 white Ford Galaxie 500.[6]

Craig and I loved to play together, and in the analog age of the 1970s, that mostly meant recreating our favorite television shows. Craig's hometown had no television stations of its own – because it was so close to Philadelphia, it simply adopted those stations from its big brother, the same way small towns around major markets always do. The news and weather out of Philadelphia extended to include Wilmington, and the sports didn't matter; Delaware has no professional teams. This was a bit of a problem for Wilmington, which always had a kind of minor league identity crisis. If it weren't for banking and DuPont, I'm not sure it would have anything at all. But for me Philadelphia TV was amazing,

---

[6] As a young single man, as well as an engineer, my uncle had treated himself to a Porsche (in those days something difficult to get, involving real importation and not just an import car dealership). The family legend had it that – even though he'd laugh along years later – he never really forgave my brother, two years old at the time, for digging into his full diaper and smearing the paint job with... well, everything he had loaded in that diaper.

because it offered a choice to which I never had access, an independent station. This was a station with no network affiliation that bigger cities often have, but Syracuse did not.[7] Instantly thirty-three percent more TV shows for a kid like me. The show I remember the best was called *Ultraman*, a painfully cheap Japanese superhero import with laughably bad dubbing and rubber suit monsters. Children of today would probably have a hard time imagining the low bar to entry for filling the needs of broadcasters, both during and, especially, outside of prime time. But it was something to behold.... *Mystery Science Theater 3000*-level cheese.

Craig was family, but he was also my friend. We looked forward to seeing each other those handful of times each year, and always got along really well. At some point we discussed how great it would be for the two of us to live in the same city when we got older, hang out like best friends. Planned a future where we became roommates or business partners.

Now he lives quite close to me, relatively speaking. But we don't ever see each other.

Were there some transgressions that affected our relationship? There were. Was I to blame? Well, I'd definitely let Craig down. I was like one of those bullied kids who thinks if they ever achieved a position of power, they're sure that they would treat people differently, and then, when given that opportunity, do all the same things. I remember visiting Brandywood one summer and Craig introducing me to a new boy who'd moved into the development, Andy. The two of us hit it off so well that I kept insisting we invite him to play with us the entire visit. Craig was fine with the dynamic at first, but as the visit went on, he started suggesting that

---

[7] I do remember a short period where I could tune into some independent station on the UHF dial that pulled in some snowy signals from – where? Buffalo? Toronto? Rochester? – that had a few shows I'd never seen before, but the memory is as hazy as the television picture.

maybe just the two of us might do something. But I kept wanting to include this Andy. At one point, Craig shot down some activity I'd suggested, and instead of working to come up with something we both felt like doing, I simply went off with Andy, leaving Craig – my *host* – all by himself. That strikes me now as a pretty uncool move, but there were more. And worse.

How about the time Craig was in Syracuse for a two-week summer visit and, as the trip was winding down, working secretly over the phone, pleading with my aunt and uncle, he made arrangements to extend his visit. Craig presented the offer: "If you want, my parents say it's okay for me to stay another week." He expected enthusiasm; he didn't get it. I declined. *Nah, we're good here.* What I didn't say but still managed to make clear was that I was ready to bail. I had friends on hold, my buddies Mike Royce and Bill Rapp, and they had the Super 8 camera all revved up and ready. Enough was enough.

I broke my cousin's heart that day. I know it now, and I probably knew it then. Not as the words were coming out of my mouth perhaps, but the moment they landed, when I saw his face fall, I knew. A better-raised boy, a better friend, would've turned it around then and there. Maybe a "Gotcha, you thought I was serious." Or even a white lie: "I figure you must be so homesick…" Nope. None of it. I had said what I wanted to say, put out by the fact that I had to deal with it at all. I saw it as more of an inconvenience for me than an affront to Craig: why did he have to put me on the spot?

But I've learned that the straw that broke the camel's back was my behavior at Craig's wedding. I'd been asked to be the best man, a request that resonated inside with a little dread, because I knew I wouldn't be able to reciprocate when the time came for me to marry (although Craig would have a spot in my groomsmen's lineup). I would have to make the best man toast, and I got it in my head that if I

didn't plan the thing out, if I just stood up and improvised, at least I couldn't feel like too much of a failure if it bombed.[8]
I had a premise, an idea. If I sat down and wrote it out, memorized and practiced it, then it would be A Speech That I Gave. However, if I phoned it in – if I Hail-Mary-ed it – then should it go belly up... well, what do you expect? I'd shot from the hip. This was par for the course with me throughout eleven-and-a-half grades of my school career... don't put in the effort, so you don't have to take any negative results personally. Where the hell did it come from? Why had it been so difficult for me to commit to a task and give it my best?

Regardless of this pathology's origins, it was the backdrop to me showing up at the reception as the best man with nothing more than a conceit. I've already mentioned the shows we loved and recreated in the backyard of Glenstone Road. Well, as the older cousin, I was able to demand the lead role in most of our pretend games. To take the classic example, I would be the Lone Ranger and Craig would have to play Tonto – though that was before our time; when we did the western, *Wild Wild West* was our world. I'd be James West, he'd be Artemis Gordon. He was the supporting player, by dint of the birth order.

But our most frequently mimicked show at playtime was *Batman*, the campy pop art masterpiece that was in syndication at the time. I not only insisted on playing Batman and forced Craig into the Robin the Boy Wonder role, I had my *au pair* – an excellent seamstress – make us color-coded capes. Dark blue for me and bright red for Craig, sealing his Robin fate permanently.

---

[8] In my defense, I used the exact same approach when I made the best man speech at the wedding of a stand-up comedian friend of mine, where people like Ray Romano and Dave Attell were among the guests. I adlibbed the whole thing, but it went over so well that one of the guests, a comedy club booker, told the groom she'd book me. So that was the baseline I was starting with regarding Craig's wedding: no prep, no problem – get laughs, be the hero. That was not how it worked out.

Batboy?

I brought all this up in my speech, to the delight of... well, who exactly? I only heard the laughter coming, and assumed it was coming from all quarters of the ballroom. I was standing behind Craig and his bride Amy and could not see their faces. It turned out they were not amused.

I'm certain a video exists of this speech, that Craig and Amy hired a videographer to capture the day and that they have a nice VHS or even DVD copy that they pop into the player on anniversaries. I could check the record, though there's a decent chance they asked the video editor to cut the speech, so they wouldn't have to fast forward every time they watched it. But even assuming it's committed to tape, I don't think I would be able to watch it. I might see it through their eyes, and that would be rough. For what it's worth, I meant well. At least, I meant to be entertaining and loving. How it landed is another story.

I remember hearing a lot of laughter that possibly may have just been coming from my immediate family, who enjoyed a good joke no matter at whose expense. I recall Lisa doubling over, David hitting the table with delight. It was just fuel to the fire for me.

We Connellys were known by our stories. The reality was usually just a starting point. I pictured a system similar to the proof in alcohol with respect to the stories' truth – its strength varied, but never quite reached one hundred percent. They ran the gamut from lightly exaggerated to riddled with inaccuracies to almost pure fiction. The goal was always the same: to tell a hysterical tale. Like the time I got into an argument with a Walmart employee over a tomato whose barcode was scanning as "Tomato Knife." It was sorted out in forty seconds of real time, yet I was able to turn it into a fifteen-minute yarn upon the retelling. And so it went with the toast, though that required no such padding. The metaphor was simple. The heart of the bit was that here, finally, was Craig: at the center of attention, in the spotlight, behind the wheel of the Batmobile. And I wasn't even the sidekick. He and his bride were Batman and Robin. Me? I was relegated to the role of Alfred, the butler. At least in my tuxedo I was dressed for the part.

This approach didn't work the way I'd hoped. The extended family failed to find the Batman speech endearing. The laughs I got were at the ends of the range: from the distant tables who weren't keyed into our history, and from the Connelly family, who seemed to judge humor separately from the harm it might cause. The speech may have set a standard in my nuclear family, though; a year later David would skewer me, Mary Jo, and both our families as my best man and it was a comic performance I truly cherished.

Is it that Craig and the other Taylors had no sense of humor? Absolutely not. But a wedding was a serious event. Gentle ribbing was one thing; mocking the man of the hour quite another. And here's the key: if you think you're getting belittled, then you are. Intention has no bearing. If Craig felt mocked by my words, that's how he felt. My intentions didn't really factor into the equation. A roast only works if the guest of honor has thick skin.

Not that I noticed. Read the room? Better advice for me could be "read the world." None of it seemed to operate according to rules that made sense. For that, the blame lands squarely at my mother's feet. We Connellys were known by our stories all right, and there was never any shortage of collateral damage in the telling. My mother cut her teeth on sparring with my father. I lived *Who's Afraid of Virginia Woolf?* before I ever saw it. Sometimes I wonder if Edward Albee took notes on David and Carolyn. I never knew a thing about sincerity. We love, so we tease... right? Or is it that we passive-aggressively tormented, and hid behind the love so we could keep on doing it? Were we trying to get some point across with the jokes? Get even?

I wouldn't find out until years later how much the incident had upset the entire Taylor family. In the last years of her life, Carolyn began taking perverse pleasure out of turning the screws, letting certain secrets leak as if to illustrate that she still had power. One such revelation – the Taylors' resentment over my best man's speech, how they couldn't let it go – was among the first. I thought about it when she told me this. Hadn't they been at my wedding a year or so later? Didn't they see how it all went, how my own brother had eviscerated me, my friends, my new in-laws, quite savagely? But with heart? Maybe. But perhaps they sat there during his speech with their arms folded across their chests, jaws set hard. Unsmiling. Unlaughing. Unwilling to reconsider their feelings.

What amazed me the most was how unaware I was of this fury. The key problem stemmed from the fact that the Taylors were all quiet and non-confrontational; they always have been. Demure and proper and buttoned-down. Hannah came off as dour, judgmental, Craig's demeaner read shy, with his voice seemingly aimed at the back of his mouth rather than the opening. Lana was like her mother, Carolyn like her father: big, brash, seeking the heat of the spotlight. The Connellys seemed a frequent source of embarrassment for the Taylors. Raucous laughter, too loud voices, outgoing to the point of sucking attention toward us like a Shop-Vac. I think my mother wanted to be Shirley Temple her whole life. My father, a respected professional, somehow still carved out time to star as Harold Hill in a production of *The Music Man*. We were show-boaters, behavior that didn't connect with the Taylors at all. So if, every time I saw my aunt and uncle after Craig's wedding, they were giving me the cold shoulder, it probably didn't look all that different from how they'd previously behaved around me.

So I found out years later that, in the eyes of the people I intended to honor, my best man's speech was viewed as more like a *Seinfeld*-style curse toast than anything else. Am I sorry about this kind of behavior? I am. If I were in a twelve-step program and got around to the making amends portion, I think I'd be tied up for quite some time. But I also understand that I am both a product of the two personalities whose DNA makes up my own and the ways in which I was raised. I am what you get.

I'm sure Craig still loves me, in that way one continues to love family despite everything. I think it's safe to say that. But he probably doesn't respect me very much, and to get over the wounds that I've caused he's had to place some distance between us.

Did I notice? Maybe a little. Or maybe I'd been a little too busy to notice until I decided to look a bit closer at myself. Or... maybe it's wrong. Bad intel. Perhaps Carolyn was only speaking for her sister, and not for the cousins at all. It's not too late for me to find out.

It is, of course, too late to change anything.

THERE ARE NO Taylors on Glenstone Road anymore. Craig and Hannah's parents died about six months apart last year, with both their funeral services and burials taking place less than five miles from this house. I went to both services, assumed the role of pall bearer for the first one, but I was the only representative of the Connelly side of the family. My mother expressed concerns near the very end of her life, fears that the remnants of her family would drift apart and scatter like so much dandelion fluff. I think that's exactly what might be happening. And I'm not sure that I can do anything about it.

Her concerns seem not only justified, but also predictable. At the drop of a dime, Mary Jo flew three thousand miles for the funeral of a childhood friend whom she hadn't seen in ten years. My brother and sister, each living less than five hundred miles from Wilmington, couldn't make the trek. And what about me, living a scant thirty from the cemetery; how is it that I could barely dredge up the energy to show my face? What is the difference between these two reactions, down at the root?

The difference, naturally, is parenting. Carolyn. How she raised us. What meant something to her and what didn't. And how she passed that down. Mary Jo's parents had a far different take on things – my brother only had to spend a few hours with them to get enough for the broad strokes of his best man toast. And he saw clearly how differently he – we – had been raised.

So when that's the map you lay out for your children, is it really fair to express concern about the family unit disintegrating? Maybe not.

IT WAS DAY ONE, and I didn't know yet precisely what this trip was going to be about. Lots of strands were destined to get woven together, I imagined. Memory and myth, connection and disconnection, exploration, understanding.

But idling in front of 2227 Glenstone Road, it was starting to feel like I might be primarily coming to terms with two intertwined feelings: regret and shame. That binary star of emotion. If my brother reads this (and knowing who his mother is that's certainly not a forgone conclusion) he'll likely focus on the part about him smearing feces on a beautiful classic car, a tiny footnote. Because a) it's about him; and b) he'll wish I hadn't trotted it out for the world to see. But there should be no shame in being a two-year-old and doing two-year-old stuff. And as far as regret is concerned, without a time machine to fix the past it's a pretty useless emotion for anything except self-improvement for the next time.

Or this trip might be about coming to terms with my own shortcomings, taking responsibility, and setting the record straight. If I'm to make amends, I figure I'll start with Craig. But in my defense, I wasn't used to anyone looking up to me, so I suppose I handled it all poorly. I would've made as terrible a big brother as David.

I DON'T BOTHER getting out of the car and knocking on the door. No one's home at the Taylors' old house. The Galaxie 500 hit the highway a long time ago, and I was going to follow its lead.

DEATH'S WAITING ROOM

THE WOMAN MANNING the lobby's reception desk looked me over suspiciously. As if I might turn out to be some kind of intruder. Yet she didn't seem to have enough skin in the game to do much to stop me. Almost as if it was beyond her pay grade to assess why this man wanted to poke around Naaman's Manor.

I had driven barely two miles from Glenstone Road, rediscovering the nursing home's name and location at the last minute via a quick text to Hannah. I hadn't been here in years, and if you'd asked me as a child, I would have told you I'd never show up at Naaman's Manor voluntarily. Among the best aspects of the Taylors coming to Syracuse rather than vice-versa – hand in hand with getting to sleep in my own bed instead of on a cot and the not spending six hours in the car – was avoiding the mandatory visit to Naaman's Manor. It was torture to me, and I couldn't imagine how Craig and Hannah must have felt, having to show up a couple of times a month, at a minimum. Maybe even every *week*, on the way home from church.

This was the only place where I could recall I'd had any interaction with my mother's mother. If she'd had a life outside of these beige walls, I hadn't been privy to it.[9] After

---

[9] I'd just come from the house where she'd ruled with a tiny iron fist, of course, but I wasn't able to elevate that part of my history the way I was trying with Carolyn. It was enough of an uphill battle with her, but at least

the stroke the old woman lived with the Connelly family in Syracuse for a while. It's hard for me to track; I have no memory of it in the house that I grew up in, purchased four months before my birth. She might not have been there; it doesn't seem wheelchair accessible. The previous house, the one on Wexford Road, was a single-floor rancher and a much more likely candidate. My sister would probably have memories of it. For me, Elizabeth Black never lived anyway or anywhere but on her back and in this place.

I haven't the slightest doubt it was a circle of Dante's Hell.

She had been decimated by a stroke in the early '60s, unable to move or communicate afterward. Doomed to lie in bed day after day. She was some kind of monster to me, someone with whom I had no connection, for whom no feelings. My mother, of course, saw her mother. Had memories and made connections. I would one day know the feeling, visiting Carolyn in her final years, though thankfully she didn't have to suffer the indignities of nursing home life. I could see now that Carolyn was trying to give her mother something valuable with these visits, and I didn't make it easy. I had very little generosity of spirit back then. I had no notion what life was like for her here. She was an obstacle to me. She appeared when we walked into that room once or twice a year and vanished when we left it. Some kids have object permanence problems longer than others.

Or maybe it was me that inherited the sociopath genes from our father.

"My grandmother used to be a resident here," I offered the woman behind the desk, trying to sound upbeat and leaving out the part about her dying there, too. "I wonder if I could..." but stopped midway through the sentence, suddenly realizing it might be better to change my plan of attack. It occurred to me that I wasn't realistically going to

---

I had detail and context to allow for reassessment; my experience with my grandmother was as one-dimensional as human interactions came.

get back to where the patients were; in our present war-on-terror and HIPAA regulations era, a request like that would raise too many red flags for even this hourly employee to shrug off. "Would you mind if I went out to the courtyard for a minute?" I'd seen the recreation area from the parking lot, fenced in around the front, with the blocky U-shaped two-story building filling in around the other three sides. I had vague memories of pushing the wheelchair outside, ever so often leaving the room where Grandmother Black lay in bed, so I added: "On nice days, my family used to visit with her out there."

The thing was, in that memory, outside wasn't any better than inside, and none of those days were nice. It had all been bad: the one milky eye rolling in my direction, the clawed left hand, the hairy chin, the guttural clicking in place of words.

The receptionist shrugged. "Sure," she said, and then back to the papers on her desk. End of eye contact. End of story. For her. I thanked the woman quietly and slipped over to the heavy glass door that opened to the outside.

MORE OF DEATH'S spindly shadow here. The body count was growing: Colbert first, now his mother. Tomorrow, it would be my mother.

I met eyes with three Mount Rushmore-looking women chain-smoking in their wheelchairs (as with babies, at this stage of life the delineations of gender begin to blur). But I didn't really smell the cigarette smoke. I smelled something else.

Even though we were outdoors, the scent still hit me, and I knew right away it was emanating from the nursing home. It hadn't been in the lobby; they must have had some filtering mechanism in the HVAC system for it. But it was out here all right. I hadn't known what the smell was when I'd been around in the '70s visiting Elizabeth – to me it was just the awful odor of old people. Now, having gone through parenthood, I recognized it, though I'd never connected the two: the air was thick with the deep, musty smell of full diapers. For me as a child, it had been the smell of death. In reality it was the smell of shit. It was the same thing skimmed on the side of his German sports car that had so disturbed Uncle Aaron. And it signified a loss of all control.

For a period of time my brother was obsessed with *The Denial of Death*, Ernest Becker's sociological tome that explores the psychological theory that every decision each of us makes is made through the lens of our subconscious trying to hide the reality of our own mortality from our conscious selves. Whatever statement I might make about my plans, or hopes, or chances for making it as a writer or filmmaker, David would shout back "Denial of Death!" like a battle cry.

I could see his point when it came to a places like this. At Naaman's Manor, I felt like I was confronting death for the first time on the trip, and I'd just visited a house where a toddler was boiled alive, while I carried my mother's ashes in my car during the tour. I wanted to tell myself it could never happen to me like this. The end of the road, somewhere down the line, looking like this?

Terrifying.

ELIZABETH DIED in 1975. I remember Carolyn getting the call from Lana. I remember watching her, that long twisted cord of the wall phone slouched, her free hand covering her eyes as she talked. And then after, her sitting me down and letting me know that she was gone, and went peacefully.

I didn't cry. Inside, I felt warm; we'd never have to go to that nursing home again. I didn't mourn my grandmother's passing, I privately celebrated it.

None of the three of the three children went to the funeral. Carolyn made some arrangements to head south to

Wilmington and that was that. There was no interest on her part in putting us through the service. It was hard to know at the time whether she was protecting us kids from pain or herself from the inconvenience.

That would become an easier call to make as the years went on.

Don't visit me in the hospital.

Is it any wonder Carolyn's ashes were just sitting around my house?

As I LEFT Naaman's Manor's parking lot, I wondered about the day my mother checked herself into her own retirement facility. I'd helped her move in, packing up her messy apartment and trying to jam everything into a room and a half. Not a nursing home, far from it. She'd done a lot of research, crunched the numbers, made the best call she could and pulled the trigger when she knew the time was right – which meant moving in while she was still healthy and relatively spry. When the actuarial tables told the decision-makers that she was a good bet.

The facility had a lot to offer, but still... she was moving to the *last place*. She would be surrounded by elderly people exclusively from that point onward. She'd make friends who would over time drop like flies around her.

Carolyn didn't want to be a burden on anyone. She and her sister Lana had to pay for Grandmother Black's nursing care for a decade or more, and the choices she made as an elderly person were colored by that quiet burden. As with the funeral expenses, she'd handled things herself.

Maybe she was stronger than I give her credit for.

BEACH BUNNY

I HAD CLOCKED quite a number of days in Delaware as a child. Most of those days had been during summertime, when I'd been sealed in a development house watching that magical fourth channel, air conditioning beating vainly against the sweltering humidity, sensing full panic rising in Aunt Lana and Uncle Aaron over the court-ordered desegregation bussing plan that riddled the news. While designed to help narrow the gap between rich and poor, the transferring of my cousins to inner city schools against the wishes of their parents seemed to be the burning political issue every summer I visited. Craig wound up in private Christian school.

The flatness of the state always got to me when I was younger. I was reminded of this on my drive out of the city. And I understood and acknowledged that the place was less than four hundred miles from where I grew up. But on the eastern seaboard, a lot could change in a four-hundred-mile stretch. Central New York's topography was carved by massive glaciers, giving it a splintered, rippled character that felt endlessly full of potential adventure. This part of the country – living here, it would be like living on a coin. The flat landscape made more sense as I drove toward the

Atlantic, though. It seemed to me to be how land and water should meet, slipping toward each other like pieces of paper. On the road from Wilmington to Rehoboth I passed a sign letting me know that there is an actual, real place called Slaughter Beach. If that isn't already a movie title, I said to myself, then I call it. Although now that I thought about it, any beach vacation with both my parents in attendance could have taken place at Slaughter Beach.

On the way to land's end, there was a mystery on my mind. I kept trying to reconcile the pre-, during-, and, post-married Carolyn, the line before and after becoming a mother. Trying to balance her out in three dimensions, to come up with some kind of unified field theory of her. The closest that I could come was an underlying image that revolved around water. That didn't make any sense if I were trying to categorize her by the traditional elemental areas of myth – Earth, Air, Fire, or Water. If I had to pick one of those I probably would *not* pick Water. But this was definitely a lower-case feeling, the idea that she loved to play in the water. The notion that she was a beach bum at heart, with all the trappings that went along with that.

I wouldn't pick Fire either, although my mother *had* been set on fire twice in her life, three times if one counted the cremation. Both of the earlier immolations happened in the 1950s. The first one took place at DuPont. The lab where Carolyn worked was developing Dacron and in use at the lab were some very flammable chemicals. She was wearing nylon stockings – also a Dupont invention, and as it turned out, as flammable as the chemicals. A few sparks flew off the lab bench and suddenly Carolyn's ankles were engulfed in flames. She took off as if her panicked brain hoped to outrun the danger, but a more experienced lab tech tripped her and helped her roll the flames out. The second time went down at the Drake Hotel in Chicago and happened the morning of her marriage.[10] The photographer arranged her train too close to the back light and the wedding dress caught fire. It was put out very quickly and she wasn't hurt, but there was a large burn mark on the dress' back; she walked down the aisle with it anyway. It didn't bother her much. She always said that she was hungry that day, that's what she found upsetting.

In-store packaging of lettuce can be done by hand or machine. The machine method shown above simplifies the wrapping process to a single operation. Du Pont Cellophane packaging offers *your* produce extra eye and buy appeal . . . greatly reduced waste costs.

DU PONT
PACKAGING AND INDUSTRIAL FILMS

CELLOPHANE · POLYETHYLENE
ACETATE · "MYLAR" POLYESTER FILM

DU PONT
REG. U.S. PAT. OFF.

BETTER THINGS FOR BETTER LIVING
. . . *THROUGH CHEMISTRY*

Carolyn, Before the Fire

I FOUND PARKING on the main street of Rehoboth, a wide boulevard with a generous village green-style median down the middle that slipped off a roundabout and dead-ended at land's end several blocks later. Nothing but little beach shops on either side: bakeries, bike rentals, wine bars, art galleries, bookstores, real estate offices.

I walked down past the bandstand and crossed the boardwalk. I stopped to pull off my shoes and socks, then stepped onto the beach. Reaching the waterline, I turned around and looked back up toward the sand, moving south

---

[10] For reasons unclear to anyone I'd talked to, David and Carolyn were married at the University of Chicago's chapel. An article about my parents from April 1960 that ran in North Carolina's *Durham Sun* mentions Carolyn's previous work at the Chicago Department of Health, which was the first and only time I'd ever heard of it. Illinois had never been on the radar in my mental list of where my family had lived before I showed up on the scene.

Carolyn and Friends at the Water's Edge

along the water until my view lined up with the photograph I held.

This was the process; as with 36th Street hours earlier that day, the sensation of positioning myself right where some Kodak Instamatic had snapped a picture half a century in the past or more produced a vertiginous effect in me.

If you'd ever visited the location where a favorite movie scene had been shot – the tiny pizza place that whips past in the opening of *The Sopranos* or the firehouse from *Ghostbusters* – you'd know the feeling. A kissing cousin to *déjà vu*. She was alive right here. With this photograph I could pick the very spot; that one time my mother was here with that particular guy, locked down. Maybe that was where the importance of graves and tombstones lay, in the idea of knowing where someone is forever, returning and even if you don't return, knowing inside… *this is the spot.*

I slipped the photo into my back pocket and took in the wider scene. This was Carolyn's beach, when she was a teenager, when she was carefree. When she was the kind of person I'd never known her to be. Part of a human pyramid? You couldn't prove it by me. I thought of all the ridiculous situations I'd gotten into as a kid, how none of them seemed like anything with which Carolyn would be associated. But then again, she pulled up to the dinner table in roller-skates, didn't she?

I stood there looking at all these footprints, just oval indentations in the sand really, but I felt a sense of awe. It wasn't that saccharine two-pairs-of-footprints-until-Jesus-starts-carrying-you thing, it was a different sensation entirely. One that came with the realization that the location may have remained constant, but the place was everchanging. This wasn't the same beach from these photos; it wasn't even the same beach it was the day before. Over the years an unfathomable number of pairs of footprints – some mine as a child, some Craig's or Hannah's, Lisa's or David's. Some my mother's or even *her* mother's. They came and they went with a billion others, disappearing with the motion, the wind and the surf. They were here one moment and the next… it all was washed away. The grains of sand meant nothing, to be sure; they were interchangeable, placeholders. Atoms. But the space where grains of sand aggregated under her feet, my feet now… that place remained. It's the alchemy that makes a place a place. It was Rehoboth Beach, even if every millimeter of it was different. It was sacred ground.

But not sacred enough for Carolyn's ashes.

I went back to the boardwalk to see what that felt like. Pretty pathetic when compared to its siblings to the north, Wildwood or Ocean City. Just a few blocks of tourist trappings here. My family was "down the shore"[11] in Rehoboth the week in 1977 that *Star Wars* was released; Carolyn bought me not one but two *Star Wars* t-shirts on the boardwalk, one orange and one navy blue – even though I'd yet to see the film. Something told us both that I was the

---

[11] The idiom "down the shore" was something I heard throughout my time in Wilmington and it always grated on my nerves. I just can't track it, no matter how many times I hear it. It's not like y'all, a word I don't personally use but can see its charm.

kind of boy who'd enjoy it. Further back still, I remembered the day walking the boardwalk with Carolyn and a friend I'd made there. We spotted a quarter pinched between the boards (this would've been a windfall back then for a couple of ten-year-olds). I got on my knees and fished it out. But how do you split a quarter?

I suggested to my new friend that I could take the coin and give him thirteen cents, careful to round in his favor so I wouldn't be perceived as taking advantage.

"But you'd have the quarter," he said, confused.

I told him, "If you want the quarter, then you could give me twelve cents." But he didn't have any money. So the only way to make it work involved math he didn't understand.

Carolyn reached into her pocketbook and found a quarter, which she gave to the boy. "Here, go have fun," she said and pointed us toward the arcade. This was a minor thing, of course. An adult and a quarter. But it made an impact. Because it involved solving other people's problems at some level of personal cost. Almost the behavior of a person who *would* visit someone in the hospital.

I turned off the boardwalk as the commercial outlets dissolved behind me. I crossed the dunes and landed on Surf Avenue, the residential street that ran more or less parallel to the beach. After wondering along for a few minutes, pretty sure I was in the right place, I came to the conclusion that the little pale blue A-frame bungalow I was looking for had probably been torn down. Why wouldn't it have been? A prime oceanfront parcel of land deserved a bit more than the wooden tent I remembered. We'd rented the house several times over the years, with 1970 standing out as the earliest in my memory. It was a two-week vacation and Carolyn had packed up the sage green station wagon. At the last minute my father let her know that some work problems were creating issues and that she should go, that he'd catch up with the family when he could. It was by then a standard sort of disappointment for her. Not so with me, however. I had my reasons to celebrate. For one, more room in the car; no middle seat and the hump with my brother or sister getting to ride shotgun.

He showed for a few days in the middle of the vacation, pulling up in his Mercedes convertible he'd travelled to Germany to hand select, the beloved plaything whose windshield my mother would take a hammer to before the year was out.

I had a photo of him with me from that particular Rehoboth vacation. Taken from the front porch of that A-frame I couldn't find. He looked like this back then:

No Shirt, Those Shoes, No Service

I can't explain the shoes, and there was a part of me that wanted to crop them out for publication. But I got over it; I'm not in the business of saving face for my father. That would be a full-time job.

∞ ∞ ∞

WHEN I OPENED the door to the Candy Kitchen on Rehoboth
Boulevard, not far from where I'd parked, I was hit by sense
memory. For the first time on the trip, I felt truly transported
in time. I was no Proust, but his Madeleine was going to get
a run for its money with the sensory flood inside that ice-box
cold candy store nestled in that seaside town. The shop felt
like a walk-in freezer; a brick wall of air-conditioning hit me
that was so cold it made my eyes sting. The cooled air wasn't
for the customers, not precisely; it was for the chocolates. To
keep them solid, perfect. No drips or employee fingerprints
to ruin the presentation. That mixture hanging in the air,
that heady richness of chocolate and sugar, not merely one
or the other but the combustible blending of the two, some
weird Frankenstein's monster made of both.

The particular candy store of my childhood was long
gone, but as a substitute, the Candy Kitchen was going to do
fine. In this case it wasn't about the specific location, but the
feeling of a candy shop at the shore. What I remember about
the candy store was the freedom; that's what it represented.
I lived on a suburban street near a golf course, Craig was a
development kid. There weren't too many places for us to
go. But Rehoboth was a *town*. Carolyn and Lana would let
us roam, the way city kids do. We were given money and set
free upon the summertime world.

First stop would usually be the candy shop, where Craig
and I discovered those indelible chocolate-covered pretzels.
These days sea salt-covered chocolates are everywhere, but
in the '70s the idea of a salty, savory pretzels encased in
chocolate sounded strange. Pretzels were a snack I didn't
even enjoy much, too dry. At the time I would've put them
below potato chips, tortilla chips, Fritos, even crackers. But
we took a chance and bought one to share one day. And
fortune favored the brave. For the rest of the vacation, Craig
and I bought chocolate-covered pretzels every day. For the

balance of my childhood, I don't remember ever seeing them outside of the beach.

I bought nothing there at the Candy Kitchen, though. The smell and the cold were plenty filling, more than enough.

THE AFTERNOON was winding down. On the way back to the car I came to a little bistro. The outdoor chalkboard boasted some happy hour specials. I grabbed my manila folder of Delaware information and headed inside for a drink.

I sat with my photos spread out on the bar and sorted through them. The number of pictures from this beach that Carolyn hung onto was startling.

Fun in the Sun

If I counted them up, I'd imagine shots of Rehoboth made up close to one third of the pictures the woman saved over her eighty-eight years. As far as the Delaware pictures went, the beach represented more than half. And then I began to notice something else. Even factoring for the general aura of sex that beach photos exude, the Delaware file alone made one fact clear: it was evident that my mother (before she held that title and crown) was a magnet for men. The photos, hand in hand with the saved telegrams and letters, painted a picture of a fun-loving and self-possessed young woman. *Joi de vive* mixed up with a powerful mystique. Carolyn liked a drink, she liked to be taken out, she liked to dance.[12]

Date Nights

And when I stared at the cover photograph of the two people who made me dancing together, what struck me was

---

[12] I found Carolyn to lack any calibrated sense of rhythm, but one of her earliest jobs as a teenager was as an instructor at the Arthur Murray Dance School. When pressed for details on the gig, however, she did seem to feel more of the job was helping nervous young men talk to women, and the emphasis wasn't really on the footwork.

the impression that, somehow – against logic and physics – their faces were both turned away from the camera and from each other. It's almost an impossible physiological feat: I couldn't see their features at all, and neither could they see each others'.

I've considered the idea my mother was on the verge of saying something to my father. There was a chance that, maybe a moment later, a millisecond, Carolyn was up on tip toes whispering some secret in his right ear. What would that have been, if it were the case? I love you? I admire you? We are living the dream, aren't we?

Or, as if caught up in a game of musical chairs she didn't have much confidence in winning, perhaps she was simply saying, "Don't stop dancing."

We are able to find everything in our memory,
which is like a dispensary or chemical laboratory
in which chance steers our hand sometimes to a
soothing drug and sometimes to a dangerous poison.

– Marcel Proust
"Remembrance of Things Past"

TWO

∞

MARYLAND IS DEFINITELY FOR CRABS

A LIFE IN FOOD SCIENCE

THERE WAS NO question about it, Delaware was a tiny state. On the map it looked like a rounding error, a land mass they could've thrown in for free when Ted Turner was buying up his huge tracts of Montana in the '80s. Delaware's diminutive size was the primary reason that I figured I could tackle a second state in one day, particularly since the second one wasn't that big, either.

In general, the mid-Atlantic states seem to have something of an identity crisis. They're small in a way that doesn't conform to the grand vision of America – the Rockies and Texas and the Great Plains – vistas the movies have been selling us and the rest of the world on for a century. The states of the mid-Atlantic region don't even have the colonial identity of New England. They don't easily categorize and no one who isn't from there can draw them from memory. They barely even count as flyover country. But I happen to be a fan of underdogs, even at the state level. I like the mid-Atlantic. Of course, they said "wooder" around here when they meant "water," but I'm able to forgive even that.

As I drove due west and into Maryland, I found myself marveling at the area. The Chesapeake Bay was an estuary whose water composition ran along a saline gradient, which meant there were areas of fresh water on one side, areas of salt water on the other, and a gradated mix of the two in between. This made its marine life unique; it was home of the Atlantic blue crab, the crown jewel of the economy that built the state. Life along the Eastern Shore of the Chesapeake revolved around the water in a very different way than it did in Rehoboth. It was more work, less play. The Bay didn't represent recreation, it represented a living.

Undoubtedly fun could be had on the water, but without the roaring surf it was hard to imagine Carolyn spending much time on the beaches around here. For her it was a place to make money.

ONE OF THE MOST startling pictures I had uncovered of Carolyn so far was wedged underneath the yellowing lamination of a security badge, from her time here in Maryland. In it, she was achingly young, and the shot exuded a sense of bitchy insouciance I had never experienced.

High Security

This Carolyn was vibrant and had a cherubic kind of face that didn't line up with the severe cheekbones she would sport as a young married woman. Baby fat, I supposed. The badge was from when she was nineteen, still a kid.

I studied her nose carefully; my eyes were pulled to it. It seemed surprisingly broad. Baby fat there, too? Does a nose have baby fat to lose? The badge's photo made me start to wonder if there was any chance that my father the plastic surgeon performed rhinoplasty on her sometime before my memories of her coalesced.[13] But a quick cross-reference to Carolyn's 1953 wedding pictures, from that photography session where the light burned a hole in her dress, told a different story. In these photos she has the sharp nose that I remembered growing up. In '53, David Connelly was still a surgical resident. There was no way he would've been cleared to perform an operation so early in his career. That was private practice stuff. Carolyn's nose looked slender on her wedding day, when she was twenty-six years old. In the end, I had to chalk it up to the flat lighting of the badge photography and the way a girl's face can change as she grows into a young woman. My father never cut my mother, not physically, at any rate.

Unlike my father, Carolyn's identity was never tied to her career. She was on record saying that she would've happily never worked a day in her life. But it was equally true that she had never been afraid of hard work when it was necessary.

Her first job came out of such necessity: according to Carolyn, she asked her father for a mink coat (all the rage in the '40s), but Harry told her no. That if she wanted the fur, she'd have to pay for it herself. This was completely out of character for him. It was also one of the few demonstrations of fiscal restraint as a parent Harry ever displayed, but Carolyn took it personally. *I'll show you*, she thought. She left the house and was back within an hour with her first job. This was the origin story for her short-lived gig as an Arthur

---

[13] He did do plenty of work on friends and family, including a nose job for Carolyn's sister Lana sometime in '69 or '70, the need for which was of course the hoary old line about the deviated septum.

Murray Dance School teacher. She taught every class she could get her hands on, racking up the hours, and quit teaching the day she'd earned enough money for the mink. This bit of business was harmless, but illuminates one of the pillars that anchored Carolyn's life. Her stubborn pride. It led her down many paths through the years; some ruinous, others to a kind of salvation.

A BUILDING STILL stood in Cambridge that used to be Philips Packing Plant F, but when I got to it, it was nothing but a lifeless husk. Just 60,000 square feet of rust and broken masonry sitting, slouching really, where a business that employed a quarter of the county's population once banged out can after can of tomato product.[14] The canning factory job was the second one Carolyn had ever had. She'd just come out of her first year at the University of Delaware, planning on becoming a biologist. Phillips had been going full bore during World War II supplying canned food for the armed forces. Her job: sampling tomatoes eight hours a day, checking them under a microscope. She was responsible for making sure the levels of mold in the fruit came in under the FDA-accepted levels. Some mold? Fine. Just not too much.

Her work in the industrial-grade produce business resonated with me for one critical reason: the summer with the tomatoes affected Carolyn's cooking, and not in a good way. Carolyn hated cooked tomatoes. The smell of the endless tomatoes stewing away in enormous vats in the swampy Chesapeake heat had turned her stomach and she never got over that. This is why there were carrots in her tomato sauce. Now I know that classical Bolognese does feature diced-up carrot but with onions and other vegetables, and that's not what she was doing here. No, this was a chemistry

---

[14] There are plans to turn Packing Plant F into an open-space, multi-use facility including retail shops and a beer garden, though it remains unclear how close the developers are to raising the twenty million dollars needed.

experiment. She was trying to use the base alkali found in carrots to obfuscate the acidity of the tomato. Clearly she was more Marie Currie than Marie Callender. The theory was sound, and perhaps with a better recipe or a cook with better instincts the results would've been fantastic. Instead, her sauce was thin, coated with a sheen of oil, with curled pieces of tomato skin and stalactites of carrot spearing up from the watery depths. As the fork moved to the mouth, the sauce ran off the spaghetti like sailors abandoning a burning ship.

Growing up in the '70s, a time when every kid was wild about Italian food, I remained steadfastly against red sauce. I refused to eat over at friends when they were excited their mom was serving noodles and meatballs, but I didn't actually know what I was missing.

Carolyn's spaghetti sauce was bad, but her chili was worse, with chunks of carrots floating among the skins of whole chopped tomatoes.

Food around our place in the wake of my parents' divorce was based on the idea that it was great to eat but an almost unbearable burden to prepare the meal. If it didn't appear as if by magic, it wasn't going to happen. Magic came one day in the early '70s, in the form of an unglazed terra cotta pot in the general rectangular shape of a drink cooler, but with the bulbus silhouette of a chicken on the lid where the cup holders should've been. This piece of Mayan or perhaps Crow People technology seemed to predate the actual oven, and possibly the evolution of the chicken itself. It looked like something you'd find on the cover of a Kansas greatest hits album.

It was some hippie version of a crock pot, and it was here from whence all our future meals would spring.

Just Heat... & Heat... & Heat... & Serve

The clay pot that would make the chicken or roast would take hours to do its thing. It would be prepared cold in the morning and my job would be to take it out of the refrigerator and put it in the oven at a certain time after school, which varied depending on the meal. The variance mattered little, as I consistently forgot to do my part of the job. Around 4:30 or so I would remember. Time to stuff the clay pot in the oven, crank the heat sky high and hope for the best. With food forever on her mind, my mother would come home an hour or so later, expecting the sultry scent of the roasting meat, only to be met with news that I'd remembered the kitchen duties two or three hours late; come home to find a quarter chicken (not a quarter of a chicken cooked, but chicken cooked a quarter of the way through). Looking back on it as an adult who now spends an inordinate amount of time thinking about meals, it is shocking to me that I never gave dinner a second thought. Carolyn would scramble around and come up with some concoction for us to eat and we'd try again the next day. New day, often same result. All she could think about was food, she would come home from work starving, and I'd be sitting there flipping through a comic book.

I genuinely felt bad when I realized I forgot. I had no interest in upsetting her or her dinner being late. The real truth of the matter is that, at that age, I was almost never hungry. At the time I probably weighed 110 pounds soaking wet. I bought the school lunches but didn't touch them, scraping off full plates of food when it was time to get up. I came home in the afternoon, wolfed down a bunch of potato chips, and I was good to go. The real problem was this: I never thought of food, and that may be all Carolyn ever thought of after the dissolution of her marriage. Her ability to sublimate her feelings, to push them down using food as the plunger, took center stage. I can only imagine her disappointment, time and time again, coming home and finding nothing ready to eat.

To be fair, my mother's ideas for dinner when it wasn't a workday were a little better. In those instances where we escaped the tyranny of the clay pot, she could prepare something edible. It was usually accidental, a kind of kitchen alchemy that was borne of desperation, but when it worked, she remembered the success and she'd always attempted to repeat the ones that went over well. She made me try pesto, a dish I fell in love with and have since introduced to my kids with great success.

It's also worth noting that her hatred of tomatoes didn't extend to fresh ones. Her salads were notorious for having huge wedges of tomato dropped into them. Chopping was not her strong suit, she had kitchen knives picked up from junk shops, rusty and dull. Her idea of slicing was more like blunt force trauma, and she didn't have the patience to make her food presentable.

Was it any wonder I was a skinny kid?

Carolyn, on the other hand, would find managing her weight a challenge most of her life. When I studied her in the photos, I could see the struggle. I could see the effort she put in to look the part of a perfect wife, since that didn't come to her naturally. I could see how the cigarettes helped her in the '50s and '60s – she smoked through all three pregnancies – and I could pinpoint when she concluded that their harm outweighed their value in the early '70s.

In her facial features in many of the pictures, I could see the pain. It was carved out of her inability to measure up to Dr. David's expectations.

In that *Durham Sun* article, the puff piece on the new couple in town, the lede tied to Carolyn describing a new hobby:

> *"I took a course in rug hooking at the YMCA in Wilmington, after I saw a demonstration," said Mrs. Connelly. She added that when she began her first rug, David became interested in the handicraft.*
>
> *"He did the background and I did the flowers. Now he likes to do the figures and I'm stuck with the background!"*

The fascinating thing about that line to me was how, while it seemed so specific and frothy nearly to the point of being weightless, it acted as a perfect metaphor, a tiny encapsulation of everything haywire in my parents' marriage. To wit: my father respected only perfection. My mother tried to find things at which she could be perfect in an effort to please him. But then my father's competitive side would blossom, and he would try (read: succeed) at besting her at the very thing she was trying to do for him.

The following exchange was shared by Carolyn on dozens of occasions, with anyone who would listen. It was almost as if she were going out of the way to point out that, even though she was the butt of the joke, she was still in on it:

"I asked David, 'Why can't you just love me?' An honest question. I really wanted an answer.

"And he said, '"You've never done anything well enough for me to love.'"

So here is a woman who wasn't interesting enough for her husband. And when she tried, time and time again, to become a more pleasing version of herself, he took whatever was the interesting part and ran off with it alone.

If I were to draw a graph of my mother's existence, charting her "quality of life" from an objective point of view, I would wind up with a trend line that looked like the Matterhorn: nearly straight up to a high point in approximately 1971, and nearly straight back down. This line would not equate to a graph of her happiness, which we could chart year-by-year as a sawtooth line resembling an EKG readout. There was a tenuous connection between her lifestyle and her joy at best, and any correlation would have to be negative correlation.

Money couldn't motivate Carolyn. Status couldn't do it, either. She had been the toast of the town. Arm candy with agency – desirable and desiring, lustful and lusted after. She had volunteered for all of that in her day and found it unfulfilling. She had it all, except for the love she desperately craved from her husband.

∞ ∞ ∞

THE SOUND OF CRICKETS pulsed the summer air. The smokestacks of the plant stood out against the deep blue of the Chesapeake night sky.

I stared for a moment at that monument to lost industry, then dropped the Audi into gear and pressed on.

PORTRAIT OF THE ARTIST AS A YOUNG SCOTSMAN

SOME YEARS AGO, I had written a novel that took place partially in Cambridge. This was nothing but a coincidence; I knew Carolyn's tomato cannery story but had no real sense of where the plant was located, and never knew that Carolyn had ever lived along the Chesapeake. Not while writing the book, nor after its publication. Not until after her death.

Here's the way I introduced Cambridge in that novel, *This Island, Made of Bone*:

> *McCready Memorial is the only health care facility in America with a dock for an emergency entrance. The number and severity of the crabbing-related injuries it treats annually make that emergency dock as integral to the hospital's functionality as its autoclaves and supplies of suture thread. There's the occasional fender bender at one of the town's four intersections, the rare split cheek from a fight in its one bar.*
>
> *On the whole, though, McCready's ambulance drive-ups are statistically insignificant; the real emergencies come off the water.*

My mother never mentioned the Cambridge connection after the book was released, probably because she didn't read it. The majority of the novel's action took place on my version of a real island in the middle of the Chesapeake, and in another odd coincidence, it turned out Carolyn's family had a hand in the history of the island that I'd fictionalized. I found this out during a road trip I took with Carolyn and my sister to Cambridge. This took place in the mid-90s, when Carolyn was visiting Washington, DC, during the brief few-month overlap when Lisa and I both happened to be living in the area. During the trip our mother got it in her head that we had to visit this cousin of hers – a lawyer named Ed Nabb – who she said lived nearby. Nearby was closer by boat than by car; it took three hours to drive around the Chesapeake Bay to the Eastern Shore. But we were game. We climbed into my car and went for one of the strangest get-togethers of my life.

By NOW, Ed was long dead. I had found his son's cell phone number online and called it on the drive over from Rehoboth to try and connect. I couldn't reach him, though; the outgoing message set up on the number presented it as only for emergencies. This definitely did not feel like one of those.

I drove to the address I had, my best guess for where I'd met Ed. One of the benefits of a handwritten address book like the one I'd dug up in my mother's desk was that it left a long shadow; you could trace people's moves through the crossed-out entries. It gave the sense that Carolyn was keeping tabs on those important to her. But it would've been troubling if there were multiple entries in this instance, since I would've had to try to figure out which one would've been the residence from 1995. Fortunately, my mother's book had only one address jotted under *Nabb, Ed*. The house squatted near the edge of a large pond, just like I remembered. That was a good sign. Without his son's help it was impossible to know if Ed lived in that one place forever or he and my mother had lost touch. But maybe it didn't matter if I was at the right house or not. Maybe what mattered was the effort made, and the memories the effort knocked loose.

At any rate, the house I drove to didn't have Ed inside, that was for sure. The lights were on, but I had my doubts that anyone living there now was a relative. So I parked a polite distance away and looked, simply trying to recall the details of that one indelible meeting.

THERE WAS SOMETHING feverish in Carolyn's excitement to introduce us to her cousin. He loomed almost as a legend in her mind – he'd fought in World War II and the Korean War – and it would be great to say he didn't disappoint... but he did.

Ed Nabb, on the Water

The phrase "gruff but loveable" sprang to mind. Half fitting. Ed sat in his living room, staring into the middle distance, and listened (maybe) to my mother prattle on to fill the quiet. He struck me as a guy comfortable with the silences, possibly preferring them. But nature abhors a vacuum and the Connellys have much the same feeling about a pause in the conversation. Carolyn did all the talking while he looked bored, opening his mouth only to sip iced tea or correct her on the name of some relative or another fact she'd muddled.

At some point Carolyn mentioned my work as a writer and that prompted me to mention the one thing Ed and I might have in common.

"I wrote a book about the Bay," I told him. "Smith and Tangier Island."

Suddenly his eyes lit up. "You know about the Holly Run, don't you?"

I did, it was one of the historic threads that had been an outcropping of my research.

Ed smiled with a hint of pride. "You know I started that, right?"

THERE ARE TWO ISLANDS in the middle of the Chesapeake, divided north and south by the state line that runs through the Bay. Smith Island belongs to the Maryland side, Tangier Island belongs to Virginia. The people who live on these two islands don't tend to get along well with each other, since each one's entire economy revolves around crabbing and there are a limited number of crabs. The differences between the Maryland and Virginia crabmen have long been played out on the water. But Ed Nabb could see beyond the man-made borders.

Sometime in the early '60s, Ed read an article that explained that, due to the erosion of Tangier Island, the pine trees and holly that should have been plentiful had been unable to get a toehold in the ground for years.

Because it was waterlocked, the residents were left without the traditional Christmastime foliage for decorating their homes. For reasons still unclear to me, cousin Ed felt as if this was an important problem for him to solve. He was an amateur pilot and owned a little plane at the time, and he organized a half-dozen of his other flying buddies into what they called the Holly Run, a soon-to-be annual tradition of bringing mainland greenery to the island. Amazingly, the island is on the Virginia side. More than fifty years later, the Holly Run is still happening, and still getting coverage in the local media.

I ASKED ED if the islanders were appreciative. Normally, this would sound like an innocuous question – if someone flies across with a bunch of Christmas decorations, what recipient would not be delighted? But I'd been to Smith Island for research, and I knew the brusque, no-nonsense attitude of the crabbing communities. I said that I'd found the Bay's crabmen to have some pretty thick skin.

Ed admitted the islanders were hardly effusive, but, he told me, "We understand each other." And then he said something the three of us didn't quite understand. "Our clan has some thick skin, too. We're cut from the same cloth. In his entire life, The MacNab never would've said thank you to anybody."

The MacNab? Was that supposed to be a person?

"You really don't know about The MacNab?" With a grandness of gesture that told me he'd done this more than once, Ed slowly lifted his hand and pointed straight up. I followed his finger to the space above the fireplace, where an enormous framed painting hung. It was almost life-size, this gigantic painting of a Scotsman sporting a kilt and looking angry as hell. The sky in the mountains behind him seemed stirred to chaos by his furious will.

I had no idea I was looking at a print of *The MacNab*, a fairly well-known Henry Raeburn painting. To me, it was just a family portrait. "The MacNab," I muttered.

Raeburn's "The MacNab"

Ed nodded. And then this man of few words suddenly set forth, telling us story after story about our Scottish ancestor, the ruler of a clan in the 1700s. According to Ed, The MacNab was quite the loose cannon; he had a first name but if anyone used it, he would shoot them. He apparently chewed through all the money and women of the Highlands he could get his hands on. In the end it sounded like anyone of European descent might've been related to The MacNab; he apparently fathered thirty-seven bastard children.

I couldn't help but wonder if perhaps The MacNab's genes were the source of Carolyn's iconoclastic approach to life. Hers and her three childrens'.

The rest of our visit consisted of a one-sided conversation about this long dead Scottish relation I didn't know I had. And though I thought the stories were interesting, at the time I didn't appreciate Ed's enthusiasm for a deceased relative. I didn't imagine that one day I would be writing a book like this. I never felt like the guy who'd be looking back, digging through the record, dragging the past into the present with an intensity akin to what The MacNab of the painting possessed, stirring the Highlands storm to life by sheer big-dick energy.

SEARCHING ONLINE through the *Baltimore Sun* archives later that night, I came upon Ed's 2002 obituary. The insights written about him there resonated, even though I'd only spent that one afternoon in his company:

> *Edward H. Nabb Sr., a colorful Cambridge lawyer, philanthropist and pilot who organized the annual Christmas Holly Run airlift that delivers loads of freshly cut boughs of holly to cheer residents of windswept Tangier Island, died in his sleep Sunday at his Cambridge home. He was 85.*
>
> *He neither smoked nor drank, and was outspoken and direct. In a 1964 interview in the* Sun Magazine, *he stated his philosophy: 'Maybe it's my background as an Eastern Shoreman. I operate on the principle of expecting something for something."*
>
> *He took great pride in his Shore heritage, said a 1999 article in Salisbury's* Daily Times. *"Every part of his life smacks of old-time Eastern Shore ways — he's a one-of-a-*

kind character even by Shore standards," it said. "And he loves being an individual in a cookie-cutter world."

Later the obituary mentions that Ed, too, once worked at the Phillips Packing Company. But then, so did one out of every four residents of the area at the time. And his stint there didn't seem to overlap with Carolyn's, so it was doubtful he'd gotten her the job.

Carolyn...

There was no obituary for my mother. If any of her friends back in Syracuse are still alive, they undoubtedly check the death notices and note the passing of people they know. In which case, they probably assume Carolyn is still alive. After all, she has three grown up children who clearly would be able to notify the local papers about her passing, right?

One would think.

I suppose this memoir will have to suffice; consider it a 90,000-word obit.

We all want focus
We crave company
But we're cross-eyed and punch drunk
From too much scenery
From our battles with geography

> – The Judybats
> "Geography"

THREE

∞

THE HOME FRONT

BOUGHT THE FARM

THIS WAS a road trip, yes, and technically it has started today: August 22nd, Carolyn's birthday. And yes, the plan had been to take a long and even slightly circuitous route from her place of birth to mine, and to connect those two points in a way that I never had before. And indeed, the plan was moving ahead, right on schedule. But the nature of the particular trail that represented the geographic history of my relationship with Carolyn looked like a top-heavy figure eight – a small southbound circle beneath a much larger northern loop.

The southern portion of my trip had been completed in one crackerjack day, so it made sense for me to spend the night at home. And so, whatever grand exit I'd pulled off that morning was watered down with my immediate return that night. It was like I'd gone to the office early and come home for dinner. But there were extenuating circumstances. Mary Jo and the kids gave me wide berth, as if understanding that talking about what I'd seen and done, the emotions that I'd been digging into so far, might drain some of the vibrancy from my eventual writing. No one wanted to be even in the neighborhood of blame if this project went belly up.

So my wife and I climbed silently into bed side-by-side even after I'd declared that I was lighting out on my own. This alone should have taught me something about making proclamations, about forcing my choices on other people.

But I still had a lot to learn.

∞ ∞ ∞

THE PLACE CAME with a name, in a way that relatively few properties in America do. At least, American properties that the average family can afford. It was called Modoc Spring. My sister was the type to hang on to that; whenever we would get a card or letter from her, that would be part of the address block. Lisa delighted in this type of specificity, and I get that. After all, I remembered our father's tics too, and which ones each of us inherited from him. That kind of thing, putting Modoc Spring in the address, would definitely be in Dr. David's wheelhouse.

This property was where Carolyn tried (and mostly failed) to help me with our ridiculous new lifestyle. We'd made the leap from San Francisco condominium to tending almost twelve acres. It was the stuff of tepid sitcoms. Those were actually pretty good times, me the young newly married man, her the still-somewhat competent mother/mother-in-law. She wanted to help the only way she was able, which was the exact way that ran counter to everything she was. Her best version of herself was *noblesse oblige*, living in luxury but giving the underprivileged a hand – probably for the sole reason of the endless thanks and praise. The reality turned out different. A five-figure retirement account meant the only thing she could afford to give was her time and effort.[15] She'd never done manual labor unless teaching dancing counted, but she gave it the old college try. She helped with the garden and the lawn. Cutting the grass on a John Deere riding mower worked for part of the first spring, until she rolled it directly into a tree, dislodging the drivetrain from the axle.

That about did it for farm chores.

---

[15] The twins were born, and Carolyn instantly proclaimed she wouldn't be doing any baby-sitting. It sounded selfish but upon reflection I've come to the conclusion that she truly was afraid of the responsibility.

∞ ∞ ∞

I'D ALREADY PACKED for the trip ahead of Day 1, so it was easy enough to grab my things and go. I kept Carolyn's photos of the house in Wilmington and Rehoboth and Ed Nabb with the others in my banker's box, with the idea that in the coming days I'd be shuffling through all the material and putting the pictures up against each other in new, insightful ways. I wanted to have absolute flexibility. I could see myself laying the documents out on anonymous hotel room beds as if it was an FBI murder board. If we'd had a ball of red yarn in the house, I probably would have tossed that into my suitcase, too.

I climbed into the car and looped around the paved oval next to the house, but I didn't even get a quarter of the way down our 600-foot driveway before I stopped. The building closest to the road was our bank barn. At nearly six thousand square feet, it probably could house a helicopter. But it was ancient and dark, a step down from a garage. The barn didn't exactly seal very tight; as barrier between inside and outside, it was unreliable at best. It leaked during rainstorms, and snow could often pile into the corners in the winter. In practical terms, this barn was where we kept anything that – at least subconsciously – we were willing to lose to the elements.

I wanted to check out Carolyn's belongings before I hit the road; I'd been communing with her in two dimensions – the photos, clippings, and letters – and I thought I might gain some insight by considering detritus of hers that was a bit more solid. I stepped inside and looked at the stacked pile of her belongings. They were tucked under old oak crossbeams and tented with a wide sheet of protective plastic that had started out taut but had settled, weighed down primarily with the very bat guano it had been put in place to protect against. It was a job about as well done as could be expected, considering the usefulness of most of the pieces. The collection looked less like possessions than dispossessions.

You certainly can't take it with you, I thought. You leave it for someone else to clean up. I supposed that every death leaves a mess behind, but Carolyn's in particular, because of the scattered life she lived, left a mess in a more literal sense. Her floor had been covered with books, office supplies and tools. Every drawer had been overstuffed with a random jumble of items.

As she'd moved to ever smaller quarters over the last thirty years, Carolyn had molted, casting off pieces of her past. And what remained by the end was the discord ringing between a handful of essential furnishings that she loved and the junky, practical bric-a-brac from Target and Ikea she'd made peace with owning. A shaker cabinet right alongside a plastic Sterilite storage tub. A carved wooden cat that looked like it was made of stone sitting atop a pile of vinyl folders. The brass footstool that had sat next to the fireplace in her old house that I'd stub my toe on at least three times a year. Antiquity and utility, cheek to jowl.

For a long moment, I contemplated her version of antiques, which were almost exclusively primitive northeast furnishings. I could see the aesthetic as a metaphor for Carolyn's life. Raw, not quite meeting at the seams, one of a kind, sort of a mess. And charming, at least to some. Her life hadn't turned out like she'd planned, and the degree to which the junky crud outweighed the rustic, artistic materials she'd always fetishized allowed for an easy gauge of success… or lack thereof. Outwardly, she'd become less and less the Carolyn that everyone thought they knew. Inside, all the more so. Opinionated, panicky, odd.

And looking around the rest of the barn, I could see my own detritus in exactly the same way: the '47 Ford tractor, the scythe, the rusted-out Montana license plate from 1952 with the bucking bronco on it. Even the wooden objects I'd gathered along my way were somehow rusty. The apple didn't fall far from the tree. What would my children make of whatever nonsense I'll leave behind?

The summer breeze whistled between the barnboards; the plastic tarp flapped like the twitch of a dying sparrow's wing, dropping bat shit onto the furniture with a sound like BBs poured out of a carton.

I'd seen enough. This was that moment where the cowboy hitches up his gun belt. The beat before the action. I grabbed the dolly we'd used to move all Carolyn's belongings on and off of the rental truck and carried it to the car. Time to hit the road.

ONE TICKET FOR PLATO'S CAVE, PLEASE

CAROLYN AND I ended up with matching cars, once upon a time. Pontiac Grand Ams; hers in a pale mossy green, mine light gray. As I traveled from my house in search of a tourist trap one county to the north, the memory of that car came flooding back. She had bought hers my senior year of college. When I started my first job outside Washington, DC, I needed reliable transportation. I'd liked Carolyn's Grand Am well enough, and a Pontiac certainly represented the path of least resistance – Bill Rapp, one of my best friends growing up, had started as a junior car salesman at his father's eponymous Pontiac dealership right out of college. One call and it was done.

As I passed through Pottsville, I experienced a kind of post-traumatic flashback. This was the closest town to where I broke down; the last place I ever laid eyes on my Grand Am. Of course, it wasn't mine. Not really. I'd leased it. Leasing was the only way I could afford Grand Am-level luxury on the meager earnings of my first job. That '89 DC-to-Syracuse trip had a dual purpose. The first was to celebrate Thanksgiving at home with Carolyn. The second was to return the leased Pontiac where I'd gotten it three years earlier.

Three days before the holiday, part one of the plan had fallen apart. Carolyn called. "I'm not going to be home for Thanksgiving after all," she told me. "I've been invited to the Virgin Islands."

The Virgin Islands? For Thanksgiving?

"What about our plans?" I asked.

"You should just have Thanksgiving in Washington."

I reminded her that I had to return the car.

She thought about that for a moment. "Okay," she said. "You can stay in your old room." Not a question about the holiday, and with whom I would spend it. She might've been mentally packing for the islands while we were talking.

So the trip had become a little more focused. Return the Grand Am and figure out what car I'd get to replace it for the drive back. But the Grand Am never made it back to Bill's father. Around five o'clock on Thanksgiving Eve, during a thin snow squall in the middle of nowhere, the Grand Am's engine sputtered and the steering wheel stopped responding. I was barely able to get it off to the shoulder, and when I tried to restart the engine, it wouldn't kick over. In a stroke of coincidence, my friend Bill, no longer a car salesman or living in Syracuse, was catching a ride back with me.

The two of us hitchhiked in the cold. A truck driver took pity and delivered us to the only mechanic's garage that was still open where we found two men arguing over the outcome of a particular high school football game from what sounded like decades earlier. One was the owner who, if he was interested in new business, didn't let on. The other man seemed to be a local who was excited to talk local sports history. Bill and I could only stand there and wait for them to finish a conversation they'd clearly had before. More than once before. It was like a performance of rustbelt kabuki. Finally, we were able to get the car towed. This sojourn was interminable. We had to go back on the divided highway northbound, in the opposite direction we'd been traveling, past where the car sat to the next exit, getting off and then back on again heading south to pick up the car. Then around another time south and then north for the drop-off at the Pontiac repair specialist.[16]

---

[16] There was no question in my mind that there had to be a more direct route, or that this tow truck driver billed insurance companies by the mile.

The tow truck driver unloaded the Grand Am and left us to our own devices. It was a time before cell phones, of course. The General Motors repair facility was closed, but there was a pay phone outside. We managed to reach Bill's stepfather, Bernie Gerthoffer. Bernie was crusty by nature but always reliable and he agreed to pick us up at the facility (the stepfathers among our group of friends liked us to refer to them by their first names).

Even if Carolyn had been at home, we both knew she wouldn't have come for us. Bill and I got our suitcases out of the trunk, tossed the keys on the driver's seat and waited outside the place as the smallest sprinkle of snow fell. Bernie arrived, three hours later.

I couldn't have imagined then that I'd ever choose to live in rural Pennsylvania.

On the drive back to Syracuse, a surprisingly chipper Bernie asked a few questions about the incident. He quickly rooted out the fact that I'd only bothered to change the oil once for the entire duration of the lease. With a laugh, Bernie said, "You seized up the engine, you varmint!"

At the time, I had a downtown job and commuted on the Metro, so it wasn't like I was driving the Grand Am all that much. But you're supposed to change the oil every 3,000 miles and, after three years, I'd certainly put a lot more miles than that on the Grand Am. The lease entitled me to 12,000 miles per year, the car was on a three-year lease, and I was past the mileage – part of the reason I wanted to return it to Bill's father was the hope that he'd waive the excess mileage penalty – so we were talking 40,000 miles with only one single oil change.

I made it back to my mother's house around two in the morning. The side door was unlocked, as it always was, whether she was home, out for the day, or out of the country. I slept as soundly as if I'd walked from Pottsville.

The Gerthoffers knew of my situation, so I ate Thanksgiving dinner with Bill, his mother Judy, and of course Bernie, who wouldn't let me forget what ignoring the oil light had cost us all. No Carolyn, no car. A long trip for nothing. Less than nothing, actually.

Worse than nothing.

IT TURNED OUT Bernie had been right. The engine had seized, a fancy term for when the moving parts run out of lubricant and start grinding into each other at 4,000 RPM. It's like I'd given it a sudden, severe case of arthritis at sixty miles an hour. And the car, which I didn't own but for which I was financially responsible? They declared it a total loss. I never set eyes on the Grand Am again. Before the new year, an agent of General Motors' finance division tracked me down by phone and informed me that I owed GM the resale cost of the vehicle I'd never returned, an amount surpassing ten percent of my annual salary at the time. What choice did I have? I charged $300 of what I owed GM on my credit card and told the man to send me a coupon book for the balance and I would start making the monthly payments.

Strangely, that payment book never arrived. I waited and waited, at first thankful for the temporary reprieve of the obligation. But eventually I called GM because I didn't want the problem – or any interest – to compound any further.

I was told there was no balance. My debt had been erased from the database as if in some kind of second-rate spy movie. Somehow it came up PAID IN FULL.

I asked Bill and he claimed to know nothing about it. I had the chance to spend a little time with his father in San Francisco many years later and asked him if he'd pulled the strings. He told me he had no idea what I was talking about.

Maybe. I had no way to get to the real answer on the Pontiac. People keep secrets.

∞ ∞ ∞

NORTH OF POTTSVILLE, just past Kutztown, a tourist trap had been carved by nature itself into the Pennsylvania mountainside. Tucked away in the shadow of the Poconos, with only a million roadside signs pointing to its existence, was Crystal Cave. Carolyn had taken me there one time, and it hadn't ended well. I'd gotten scared, which should've surprised no one. I scared easily.

But there was something else. I had always told the story of taking the cave tour as a five-year-old and getting traumatized when the lights went out. Afraid of that hideous inky dark, that was how I'd positioned the events in the telling. But one day when I was in my thirties, Carolyn told a different version. She remembered a part of the cave tour when I suddenly clung to her side and whispered that I was afraid of falling. If true, I had to overwrite my memory with this new data. It was counterintuitive: the idea that my very real, very strong fear of heights, was ignited underground.

My acrophobia had always made sense to me. Your body shot off alarms to warn you of danger, right? Tried to get you to stop doing the dangerous thing. Sure. But swimming was dangerous, driving was dangerous. Starting a fire in the fireplace. I was aware of the need for concentration in all these areas, but only going up on a ladder created a sense of panic in my reptile brain. No, it wasn't reasonable caution, it was panic. And it wouldn't help you if you were actually in danger. Sweat made one's hands slippery and fear clouded judgement. So... if it was an illogical disease, could it have been contracted in an unusual way? For all these years, I couldn't parse the idea of being underground and yet feeling as if I was high above something. I wanted to revisit Crystal Cave to try and unearth the truth.

Around one o'clock on August 23rd, I bought my ticket and waited outside the gift shop for the next cave tour to begin. First, my group was filed in to what Crystal Cave called a theater but was more like someplace they show movies to the incarcerated. We screened the pathetically produced time-filler on the history of the cave, which chewed up at least ten minutes of the promised 50-minute cave experience. Finally, they opened the big wooden door and we started in on the tour proper.

Inside, it started to come back to me. The claustrophobic first chambers didn't create much interference in my central nervous system, but there were sections deeper in that opened up, with damp cement steps climbing up and up under cathedral-high vaults. I followed our tour guide to the top, the fear starting to make more and more sense with every step. We may have been underground, but with vistas this large, it might as well have been an atrium of a W Hotel. Under the dripping stalactites at the top of Crystal Cave's farthest chamber, I felt like I was standing on a balcony above a dry waterfall bed... a balcony with very poorly welded railings. As the climax to the tour, the guide illustrated what it was like when old-timey explorers' candles and lamps went out. I saw her reach behind a rocky outcropping and had just a split second to brace myself before the cave plunged into the deepest darkness I'd experienced since I was five. This was as dark as the grave. As the guide described how long the rescue would have taken for the early cave explorers who often dropped their candles into the muddy streams that ran throughout (multiple days), something in me snapped. It suddenly felt like my feet were no longer beneath me. Without vision, I felt untethered. Like I was falling. The past and present superimposed and twisted like a mobius strip. It wouldn't have surprised me if when the lights mercifully came back on, I found myself holding hands with my mother, the way she looked in 1971.

The lights reignited with an echoing snap. Nervous laughter rippled through the tourists. I found my nails digging into my palms. This was where that fear of heights got its hooks into me, all right. Carolyn had nailed it.

I followed the single file toward the exit, doing my best to resist the urge to stampede and trample to get out faster. And yet, I did better this time than I had as a five-year-old. For that matter, I've actually gotten better with my fear of heights. The occasional ladder work around the house gets less disturbing every time. But I'd had it with Crystal Cave, that was certain. Twice was my limit. If the kids ever wanted to take this tour, Mary Jo would have to bring them without me.

DEATH'S WAITING ROOM, THE NEXT GENERATION

I PULLED UP to Foulkeways around four in the afternoon. Parking near the main reception center was easy; there were endless open spaces. I popped the trunk and took out the dolly I'd brought along, then thought better of it. Why walk in with something clunky like that before the conversation? It might have come across less unseemly once the people there knew the backstory. I returned it to the convertible and headed toward the main entrance.

The woman at the enormous reception desk/switchboard smiled. She was giving me the quizzical look that seemed to say: Do you need a brochure? I didn't think I came across at this point as someone old enough to be looking into retirement options for himself. But did I look too old to have a living parent here?

"Hi, how can I help you?"

"Can I speak to someone on the maintenance staff?" I asked.

The woman at the desk started to look a little concerned.

"Or the Physical Plant?"

She sighed. "Those departments start early in the morning. I'm afraid they're already closed for the day." That damn Crystal Cave had chewed into my timetable. Why did they have to show that awful movie? "Is there something I can help you with?" she asked.

"I have a dolly I need to return." I could see the words weren't resonating with her. It was kind of an odd sentence, if you weren't holding an image of the object in question in your mind as it's being discussed. I came at it from another angle. "My mother used to live here, and when she died, we had to empty her apartment."

The receptionist immediately moved into sympathy mode. "I'm so sorry."

I told her it was fine, that the death was three years ago now. "But we borrowed a dolly from maintenance, and I haven't been back this way since to return it."

In fact, Mary Jo's father Paul, along with my mother-in-law Kathleen, had spent a weekend helping me clean out the apartment here, and my father-in-law had seen the dolly at my house. "Aren't you bringing that back to Foulkeways?" he wanted to know.

I'd told myself that they wouldn't miss it, that it didn't matter, it was homemade and they had dozens of them. We took the thing because we needed to unload the truck back at the farm. And once we'd done that, there was really no reason to ever return to Foulkeways. Except for the crappy dolly. But my father-in-law's point was dead on: regardless of the inconvenience, the thing wasn't mine.

"The dolly's in my car," I told the receptionist.

Now that the situation had become clearer, the receptionist pointed past me. "You can leave it on that." Beyond the automatic sliding glass doors I'd come through, where the covered walkways diverged and spread out across the campus like fingers, a little vehicle was parked. It resembled nothing so much as a toy train engine a child might straddle. Army green and electric-powered, these things were the main mode of transportation around the campus for the physical plant.

I told the receptionist I'd do just that and went back to my car, parked maybe twenty-five yards from the front entrance. I took the dolly out of the back seat and looked at it closely.

It was made of a pair of 2x4s and a pair of 2x10s with their ends draped with old knotty carpet strips. Four caster wheels allowed it to roll; a simple enough tool, but it had been exceptionally handy in loading up the rental truck. I slipped the dolly over my shoulder and brought it over to the train engine. I looked through the glass doors at the receptionist as I placed it on the driver's seat, jamming it between the dash and the upholstery so it wouldn't slide if someone touched it. The receptionist didn't see me, she'd moved on to other problems.

And so had I. Moved on to problems like wondering how I was going to get to see inside my mother's former apartment.

CAROLYN'S RETIREMENT COMMUNITY always struck me as the best possible version of the concept; as far from Naaman's Manor as it was possible to get in terms of the type of housing one only moved out of draped in a coroner's sheet. Maybe I'd just drunk enough of the Quaker's Kool-Aid to believe their pitch, but there was a lot to do on Foulkeways' sprawling campus and they demanded participation, which seemed to keep people younger longer. There was more outside than inside here, too. That seemed to make a difference. Another key difference between the two: Elizabeth had been put into the nursing home by her daughters; Carolyn found Foulkeways all on her own. But then, ever since the divorce, she'd behaved as if she couldn't count on anyone but herself.

Carolyn had lived in three different locations on campus over the years, but the one I wanted to visit was the last one. She'd been moved to Assisted Living Center in 2011 because she'd been having some difficulty getting around. Assisted Living was brand new at the time, designed like a hotel (whereas the rest of Foulkeways was made up of individual houses or garden apartments that opened out into the world). At Assisted Living, Carolyn could charge the electric wheelchair Foulkeways provided in the hallway outside her door. She didn't have to go outside to get to dinner, if she didn't want to. There was an auxiliary dining room just down the hall from the light-drenched two-story library. There was a gift shop. And of course, there were huge freight-sized elevators.

I didn't run into any security; visitors came and went as they pleased at Assisted Living. I took the library stairs up a flight and came out near the second floor's central meeting area. It featured a television, a piano, and a full kitchen, but in all my visits, I'd never seen a single resident spending any time there. It was still empty, though someone had set up some kind of mass bridge-like card game with score pads and matching hands-free card holders.

Leaning against one wall I noticed, of all things, a set of brand-new steel dollies with gleaming aluminum casters. Three of them, nestled together. They looked like the wheels hadn't even touched the ground. So much better than the wood and carpet thing I'd just left by Reception.

Nevertheless, the dolly had to be returned. I needed to be able to tell my father-in-law I'd done the right thing, even if it took three years, even if I was now certain that they were going to toss it into one of their backstage dumpsters. Come to think of it, that was the same thing I needed to be able to tell his daughter.

MARY JO, THE KIDS AND I had all been at home the Saturday that the call came in on my cell phone: it was someone from Assisted Living's healthcare staff, telling us that right now would be a good time to get over there.

Is she dying? I'd asked. I could feel my mouth going dry.

We think it's best that you come out, came the diplomatic reply.

Okay, I'll try, I said, and I was thinking… so help me, I was thinking, This had better not be a false alarm. An early fall Saturday meant there was a lot to do around the house. Warning shots of this nature had been fired a couple of times before, and Carolyn had always ended up on her feet. But I couldn't think of a concrete example of Foulkeways telling me to prepare for the worst, so this felt different.

But was it really?

The reason for my tepid reaction, at least partially, was this: Carolyn hadn't been sick. Not really. Yes, overweight, yes, high blood pressure. Trouble walking without a cane, battling diabetes. And yes, in her eighties. But still… this wasn't expected. We'd been together for her birthday less than two weeks prior. Lots of food and laughter, the Connelly way.[17] It didn't feel like the day my mother was going to die.

But I found Mary Jo downstairs and told her about the phone call. She was ready to roll in a heartbeat. I asked her about the kids. Do they stay or come along? Get dropped off at her parents' house?

"They have to say goodbye to their grandmother," she told me, as if she were instructing a toddler on basic human concepts. I didn't even know where any of my grandparents were buried.

"Right," I said. I figured she was.

OUTSIDE OF CAROLYN'S BUILDING, I had noticed that the signage had been changed. I could still make out the ghostly outlines of the original lettering that used to read: ASSISTED LIVING. Now it read: PERSONAL CARE.

This felt like a sign of the times. Was one better than the other? Did one mean more than the other, contractually speaking? One thing was for sure: they don't just change the names of things, and the signs, for the hell of it. Foulkeways had always been analyzing the risks and rewards of their services, their promises to their residents. Like a private school, the admissions process here was particular and not exclusively transactional in nature, but when you agree to take care of a person for the rest of their life *no matter what*, you're certainly going to keep fine tuning your system. That is, if you want to

---

[17] By which I mean the food was prepared by someone else and most of the jokes contained a sliver of cruelty.

stay in business.

Well, the deal worked out for Foulkeways on Carolyn. True, in her last few years as the prices of room and board went up, they offered her some financial relief. But she'd put a large amount of money up to buy her way in, and she didn't end up bleeding the place dry with chemotherapy treatments, brand name medicines, ambulance trips, physical therapy, eldercare, or hospice days. She lived mostly within her means and then died easy.

A win for both parties, I'd say.

Most of the apartment doors in the Assisted Living Center were decorated, and all had name plates. But number 89, Carolyn's place, it was blank. Not even a name plate, and I instantly knew it was unoccupied. Which likely meant the door was locked.

I tried the handle. It turned; the door opened. The doorway revealed a pristine apartment. The place where she'd been born and the place where she'd died... both empty, both unlocked. Getting inside either one would've been a win. But both? Unreal.

So I was two for two in gaining egress and I took full advantage.

I stepped inside. Carolyn's room was empty. It seemed exactly as Mary Jo, the twins and I had left it three years ago. That couldn't possibly be true – it must have been used for someone in the interim. There was something haunting about the way the room was so clean and so empty. What were the chances that this room had remained unoccupied for three years? Infinitesimal, the way the Quakers manage things. No, I was here between occupants. Some other family's loss had happened in the intervening time, maybe several families'. It was a strange fluke of timing, coincidence and nothing more.

There was nothing to see in the living room-kitchenette area. I peeked in the bathroom and saw, in pristine condition, how large it really was. With Carolyn, there had been boxes and bottles everywhere. Barely enough room to turn around. The arm supports on the toilet caught my attention. They had been there. Or maybe they'd been replaced, and these were new ones for the next person in line for the apartment. I was filled with a certain cold appreciation about life's basics. At some point in time, these things on the toilet became as crucial to Carolyn as any technology. Her wheel, lever, pulley. Simple machines doing critical work.

In the bedroom there was nothing but the putty-colored hardwired phone, like an old hotel room unit. It was sitting on the floor, its cord pulled taut. Undoubtedly the same phone on which I had been called three years earlier.

WHEN WE ARRIVED at Carolyn's apartment that last day, we found her on her back in bed, unconscious, but not alone. There was no medical equipment, not even an oxygen tank. Just a quiet breathing coming from the woman. It was no imitation of sleep, however. It seemed more like a coma, just looking at her stillness. I'd spent many nights in bed with my mother growing up, scared little child that I was. I knew what she looked like sleeping, and that wasn't it.

Seeing Carolyn in that in-between state, it sunk in that coming here when Foulkeways called had been the right move. This was no false alarm.

A woman who volunteered at Foulkeways' palliative care group was sitting next to her bed. She greeted us with kindness and sympathy but was quick to remind us that Carolyn wanted no kind of resuscitative measures. She'd been clear on that, we were told. It sounded right.

It was off-putting, standing around with this woman we didn't know and the unconscious woman we did. After a while the volunteer left us alone and it was a bit better. We took turns talking softly to Carolyn, saying precisely the things you say in such situations. *It's okay, it's alright.* The kids lay next to her on the bed. Mary Jo stroked her hair. The three of them recited the Rosary together. I had a hard time sitting down, I wanted to keep on the move for some reason. I paced whenever I spoke on the phone, no matter how long the call, and I was pacing here.

We hadn't had a chance to prepare; Wesley and Callie, our twins, were being troopers, but after a couple of hours passed, it became clear there was no deadline. We were on a vigil now, it was going to go on as long as it was going to go on. They didn't need to go through that. Mary Jo's brother Paul had come in from DC to work on a film of ours that was going into production the following week, so we called him. He happily agreed to pick up the kids, get them home and fed and keep an eye on them.

When he called an hour later from the parking lot, Mary Jo whispered to Carolyn we were bringing the kids down for Paul to take home and we would come right back. The children kissed their grandmother and told her that they loved her and we all headed downstairs.

Not even five minutes had passed by the time we returned. Carolyn's breathing had stopped. I touched my mother's cheek and thought her skin was slightly cooler than it had been; Mary Jo thought the rosy glow was fading. There was no way to know, but Mary Jo and I had the same instinct: that Carolyn had known we were there somehow, and she'd been holding onto life while twelve-year-old children were present so as not to traumatize them. It seemed she died the moment we left her side – based on the heat of her skin, she'd been gone almost the whole time we'd been gone.

Her face lined with tears, Mary Jo hugged me tight, asking if I was all right. My feelings were out of reach at that moment. I knew I was looking at what was left of a person who, through a series of decisions made or abdicated, had entirely shaped me. I knew that person was gone. I glanced at Mary Jo to see what it was like for her. Veteran of dozens of Irish Catholic funerals. She was doing all right. She believed in God.

"I should call David and Lisa," I told her, not really wanting to do it.

"You should."

IT WASN'T CAROLYN'S hotel phone I'd reached for to call her other children, of course. I had my cell phone with their numbers in my contacts. I'd left voice mails for both of them before driving to Foulkeways, so if they'd listened to my messages, they would've been at least braced for the worst. I tried my sister first, but didn't get her this time, either. I managed to get hold of David.

Mary Jo, meanwhile, was talking to the front desk to report the death and set the funeral machinery in motion.

David took the news like I thought I was taking it. Calmly, stoically. I tried to walk him through the experience. I'd assumed I would see him in the next few days, maybe a week at the most, but as far as I know David hasn't stepped foot in Pennsylvania from that day to this. This wasn't really surprising: *if you don't visit me when I'm in the hospital* was her mantra, *don't come when I'm dead* must be gospel. The Gospel According to Carolyn.

Still, someone had to clean this place out. Without my brother and sister, the job fell to me, Mary Jo, my in-laws and my twelve-year-old kids.

At least we had the dolly to make things a little easier.

RUNNING DEEP

As EVENING CAME ON, I was driving north along the double-lane roads that followed the contours of the Delaware River. From time to time I'd get glimpses of the calm waters peeking between the trees or fenced-in properties to my right. Like Carolyn, I'd spent a lot of my youth by the water, but now I was searching for a place I'd only heard about, and not experienced. I had never been to Stillwater.

The country retreat had been built on riverfront land purchased by Carolyn's father's father sometime in the mid-1800s. Simply noting that date made me consider our family's place in the fabric of American history. It had always been true that it took a certain level of wealth to afford a house in the city and a weekend estate. But as true as it was today, it was that much more so a century and a half ago. That kind of property ownership in the northeast was the province of robber barons and blue bloods.

We weren't quite blue bloods on that side of the family. My great-grandfather had the foresight or good fortune to own a printing press in Philadelphia at just the right time, and he made a lot of money. It may have been my legacy, the way Bill's grandfather's car dealership still keeps most of an extended family afloat, living past even the Pontiac brand itself. But there was no Black Printing Works legacy for us. This fortune wasn't lost in the traditional three generations of family business, but

Stillwater, Bucks County, PA

it was lost nonetheless. At least, my grandfather's share was. Though Carolyn's father was one of eight children, there had still been plenty of money to go around. Harry had inherited a sizable sum, but the man absolutely burned money. He bought trinkets, bought whatever it was that made him feel good at the time. New cars, animals, boats. He was a grown-up kid in a candy store, and he lived for the pleasure of the moment, head in the sand about the future. By the time I was born, money on that side of the family had been squandered; perhaps the last of it paying Naaman's Manor's monthly fees. Whatever money the Connellys had when I was growing up was strictly the proceeds of a plastic surgeon's private practice. And that only hung around as long as the surgeon did.

There was a scene late in *Citizen Kane* that I've connected to my mental picture of Grandfather Black. In the film Thatcher, the banker and voice of reason, was saddled with the thankless task of trying to keep Kane from self-destruction. He had a deep well of patience but couldn't help scolding his charge when financial mismanagement forced Kane into selling his beloved newspaper. Thatcher said, "You never made a single investment, you always used money —"

Kane cut him off: "— to buy things... to buy things..."

That summed up my grandfather's view of finances nicely. Come to think of it, Charles Foster Kane spent his money trying to fill that hole inside from his lost youth, and perhaps Harry Black, in the exact same way, was filling the void left by his lost son.

THERE WAS ANOTHER vacation home somewhere in the region. I had found one photo, only one, of that place. On the back, in her inimitable handwriting,[18] Carolyn had scrawled *Our cottage on the Delaware Bay*. This was not the home where I was currently parked. Stillwater sat along the river proper, nowhere near the bay. I hadn't known of the existence of this other place until I started to go through Carolyn's papers and discovered the picture.

The more I thought about it, the more I realized water had been a way of life for my mother. In this box of pictures that I'd been dragging around, there were probably more shots of my mother in a bathing suit than any other cut of clothing. Yet she wasn't a strong swimmer, never longed for a swimming pool in the yard. But something about the open water spoke to her, and it was clearly in her genes. Mine too, I suppose. When I'd first moved to San Francisco I'd looked for apartments in the Richmond and Sunset areas, because I wanted to live by the ocean. Cooler heads eventually prevailed. People generally don't live there if they can help it, because of the fog and the cold. Where the Pacific met the San Francisco shore, I soon discovered, felt like that permanent red eye storm on Jupiter. It was not beach house living.

THE COTTAGE ON the river had been out of the family for many years by the time I appeared on the scene. It had been beloved but dispensable.[19] Possibly Harry had convinced his siblings to sell it,

---

[18] Well… not quite inimitable, as I'd been known to forge her signature on report cards and school notes from time to time.

[19] I had found a color photograph of Stillwater among Carolyn's belongings, indicating that she'd visited the place in 1994. That picture didn't look too different from the photographs from the '30s, when Carolyn had splashed in the river. I wondered if she'd brought these old pictures to show

Charles Foster Kane-style, because he needed a quick infusion of cash. For me, memories of Stillwater were the memories of hearing stories, the memories of Carolyn's face lighting up, voice filled with reverie as she talked about her barefoot and grass-stained time here as a child.

Looking at the photos of the interior of the cottage, I began to understand the origin of the spell on my mother that drew her to what could most charitably be described as rustic antiques. Stillwater had been ragged back in the day, even by 1920s standards. It had a certain scale that bolstered its image, but the furniture, the floors, the walls were really rough. All hand-hewn and not by expert artisans.

What had always struck me as a child were her descriptions of the cottage's great room, the idea that there was heraldry in the place. Suits of armor, crossed swords above the mantel. As a little boy, this mental image meant the world to me. I'd often wondered with real irritation why the family didn't save the swords and armor for me when the property was sold. My imagination had never been challenged by an actual glimpse until I found this photograph:

Gun, Shield, and Crossed Swords at Stillwater

the current owners, the way I'd brought pictures of 36th Street to Cachet.

Now, at age fifty-four, I'd found myself taking fencing lessons with Mary Jo and the twins. Fencing was the only sport in which I'd ever taken any real interest, and I had no doubt that it tied back to Carolyn's description of the Stillwater interior.

Then again, there was a chance swordplay came on my radar a different way. One of the few activities in which my brother allowed me to participate were trips with him to the movie theater, and in particular cool revivals at the Lowe's on South Salina Street in Syracuse. Just ahead of the premiere of the latest James Bond film at the time (1971's *Diamonds Are Forever*), Lowe's played a series of double features: *Dr. No* and *From Russia, With Love*, *Goldfinger* and *Thunderball*, *On Her Majesty's Secret Service* and *You Only Live Twice*. David took me to them all; my tiny seven-year-old brain downloaded the entire swinging '60s spy genre gold standard in one week. Big screen, thirty-five millimeter. It was a seminal experience, and a kind of James Bond checklist of manhood sprang up – begotten, not made, as the saying went. This checklist adhered to my psyche and had been acting as a kind of subconscious steering star for me over the ages. Could you do the following (because anyone who's anyone should be able to proficiently):

Scuba dive	Ride a motorcycle
Fight with a sword	Ski
Ride horseback	Pilot an aircraft
Parachute	Mix a cocktail perfectly

I'd checked off, if not mastered, many of these activities. They held a lot of the promise the films depicted, although I did have a sense for my preferred frequency with each one. Not all of them were created equal. And I doubt I'll ever skydive.

Now that I had seen what Stillwater looked like these days, I figured that was a wrap on Pennsylvania. Any other memories of Carolyn and the Keystone State revolved exclusively around breaking down on Interstate 81. Our wheels must've dug grooves into its asphalt with the number of trips we took back and forth between Wilmington and Syracuse over the years. And even when the car wasn't broken down, the drive still might've been; my mother used to tell the story of how good I was at being quiet for the six-hour drive when she needed time to think. Whether pre-, during, or post-divorce, I can't recall my father behind the wheel of those drives, but I can recall my mother using those miles to try to sort things out.

I remember my legs dangling, not reaching the passenger seat floor. I remember staring out at the landscape humming by, my mother always speeding. And I remember believing that every hill that had been cut through to keep the road level, leaving a short stretch of raw brown rock on either side of the car, meant that we were moving through another state. No one had told me this in an effort to have a little fun with a gullible child. No, I'd told myself. Kid logic. I thought I was seeing the cross sections of the map lines. If true, Delaware would've been a hundred states or more away from New York, quite a feat in a country with only fifty.

About halfway between Syracuse and Wilmington was a restaurant called Cork N' Fork, off on a bluff overlooking 81. Nowhere near an exit ramp. No matter what time of day or day of the week or of the year, no matter when we passed Cork N' Fork, that place was closed. You could see the set tables within. Always looking a moment away from opening its doors. But we never saw the place open for business. It was a chimera of a restaurant; Central Pennsylvania's Brigadoon.

That evening I veered west of the Delaware River and went a half hour out of my way to drive through the town of Emmaus. Here was where I had my first job out of college, where I first wondered what the hell I was doing in Pennsylvania. It was a magazine publishing company and although the vast majority of American magazines are published in New York, there existed a small empire in this hamlet near Allentown. Rodale, whose offices were in a retrofitted mill, published *Bicycling, Men's Health* and *Prevention*. A family friend had given me a canary yellow '78 Plymouth Volaré my senior year, and that first summer out of college, I'd packed it up with every record and CD I owned and moved to Emmaus. My college friend Joe and I both had writing gigs at Rodale, and we moved in together, subletting an apartment from another Rodale employee who'd gone off to write a book about Elvis Presley's secret daughter. We were not writing for *Bicycling, Men's Health*, or *Prevention*, but for everyone's other favorite magazine: *Good Toys*. Well, you had to start somewhere.

Driving through the husk of Emmaus' town center, I quickly remembered why those were days when the weekend was the unfortunate part of the week, when Monday was to be looked forward to more than Friday. I'd spent a lot of weekends in New Jersey that summer; between the two of us, I had the car and Joe had the parents' house in Bergen County with the Italian mother, the upstairs and downstairs kitchens, the marinara sauce *sans* carrots. In other words: perfect synergy.

I CONSIDERED NEW JERSEY again as I made my way toward New York City, and somewhere out in the night, across the Delaware River and into the Garden State, my sister was living at my brother's house in Bayonne. Both had hit a couple of rough patches, with failed marriages in the rearview mirror. David was raising a son who, the last time I'd checked, had a mother who was under the impression that the two of them lived in California. It had to be a high-wire act, keeping up that transcontinental illusion.

Earlier in the year I'd texted them both, saying that I wanted to discuss Carolyn's remains. I didn't hear anything back.

I suggested a quick call a few weeks later in a follow-up text. Again, I received no replies. A part of me was happy with this lack of communication. After all, the writer in me knew this was a journey best taken alone. It was a story of balance; of one dead person and one living. My siblings only muddied the storytelling waters.

What I didn't realize at the time was that I didn't have my sister's current cell phone number, so her lack of response made sense in retrospect. For my brother's part, I could chalk up his radio silence to a lack of understanding of precisely what I wanted to discuss. He had been dealing with a number of work distractions, and since dead was dead, he couldn't see the urgency of the situation. After three years, he may have had a point. The urgency was complete artifice, manufactured by me, around the conceit of this book. The timetable of a dead woman's funeral was artificially goosed by her son with his own story to tell. And for his own reasons.

And yet, precisely because I had the conceit, I pushed the issue. I finally connected with David over the phone and explained my plan as simply as I could. His first reaction was to suggest that the ceremony be postponed until sometime in the fall, when he thought he might have more bandwidth at work. He was focusing on the ashes, not my book.

He was *not* a writer.

"Look, the idea is for Mom to be buried on my birthday in Syracuse," I told him. "That's not changing. It can't change." I told him what I was planning on doing with Carolyn's remains and the exploration I intended to do. It took a few runs at it for me to make the case for the book, and then I added, "Now it's fine with me if you don't want to – or can't – join me." I could sense David's relief over the phone. That freeing feeling of getting let off the hook; I'd known and relished the same feeling over the years. It was like the sensation of waking up to learn a snow day had been called and you didn't have to go to school. "In fact," I said, "it's probably better if I do this thing alone." I offered a compromise: "If it's important to you or Lisa, I could drop off your two-thirds of the ashes on the way, and you could…" I searched for the right words… "dispose of them as you see fit. You could have your own ceremony."

That led to a discussion of me spending the night there. Perhaps Lisa, David, and I having a little get-together on the way, do something with some of the ashes as a family. Maybe. But the more I thought about it, the less like a good idea it seemed. For one thing, I had no important memories of Carolyn that took place in New Jersey. And as the conversation went along, it became clear that David was trying to do something for me while I was simultaneously trying to do something for him. He didn't want the ceremony or ashes in his yard. I didn't want to open the box and divvy up the remains like leftovers at a dinner party. It was that O. Henry story of the watch chain and the combs in reverse. Since when did the Connellys do things for each other?

If David didn't have to do anything for this burial, the plan worked for him nicely. By the time the conversation wrapped, we were in agreement; no stopping in Bayonne.

EACH OF THE THREE Connelly children had a different problem with Carolyn. If one were to try to superimpose the issues upon each other, it would result in very little commonality on the complaints. The Venn Diagram forever and always consisted of three separated circles.

Lisa felt a heavy burden being the only other female in the family. There was no question that Carolyn lived with, suffered with, an internalized sexism as only a (semi) southern woman born in the Jazz Age could. She brought her double standards up along with her into parenthood and force-fed her first born on a strange stew of gender role expectations. Both of us boys had her maiden name as our middle name, but Lisa did not (she was going to lose it when she got married anyway, right?) Over the years Lisa had never read that as anything but an insult. If I could give her my middle name to soothe that injury I would… but only Carolyn could have given that gift. And she chose another direction. Our mother put chores and responsibilities on Lisa not because she was the oldest, but because she was the girl. And Lisa didn't complain, but the resentment was harbored, stored away, stoked from time to time and fanned from a glowing little ember into something smoldering and angry.

For David, it was Carolyn's lack of faith in his abilities that cut deepest. It said something about his lack of faith in himself that he took it so personally. David wanted to be a creative force in the world, but Carolyn was too afraid of the disaster that would certainly follow in the wake of that. She needed David to play it safe, and that struggle was at the heart of their relationship. Even though Carolyn had laid it all on the line when she demanded a divorce from Dr. David, security was a primal concern with her, and there was no doubt she projected outward... and onto my brother. She undermined David's confidence in himself by urging him to take the safe, responsible route. This was how a young man who wanted to be a musician eventually became a Harvard MBA. A Certified Public Accountant.

It also may have been at the heart of David's issues with women. David was great at getting girlfriends, and Carolyn was every bit his equal in chasing them away. Or attempting to, at any rate. At the first chance alone with them, she would warn David's dates that they should do themselves a favor and run, not walk, away from the relationship. (She did this to my girlfriends too, though I wasn't the Casanova my brother was.) This drove David berserk. This meddling, the stirring of the pot and the sabotaging. Messing around in someone else's business. What was the point? And it wasn't like she wasn't going to get called on it. Later that night, alone, the girlfriend would turn to whichever one of the Connelly boys she'd hitched that weekend's wagon to and repeat the horrible things Carolyn had whispered to them.

Next day would come the confrontation. Her impish little "who, me?" smirk. Carolyn wasn't sorry, merely caught. Her take had a feminist flavor; that she was looking out for her gender by warning them what a heartbreaker her son was. Carolyn claimed to be protecting them from her boys, as if, simply by dint of being our father's sons, David and I were villains. The mark of Cain and all that.

The truth seemed somewhat less altruistic. It became clear to David that Carolyn somehow both a) had come to resent men; and b) wanted to keep her sons for herself. It was some serious Mrs. Bates behavior.[20]

David felt she wasn't on his side. Maybe he was right. Of the two of us, I sported a personality more like my father – hell, I even looked more like him. My mother considered my father handsome, which I do not. Inside or out. By extension, I don't consider myself handsome, though that might be something I could work on. It's not that I don't care about my looks, it's that I have no idea what steps to take. I wonder what she was really attracted to in him? It was a package deal. In any event, I could see why I might remind her of him, and why she might react accordingly.

The question must be asked: was she trying to somehow keep ahold of us? Did she harbor a fear that we'd be secreted away by the harpies and never spend time with her again? Was it the opposite of what she wished for her daughter – i.e.; that someone would take Lisa off her hands. Or was she just so anti-man after the psychic hits she'd taken at the hands of our father that she really had developed an us-against-them mentality?

My issue with Carolyn was different. She barely prepared me to be a human being in this world. She barely raised me at all. She was completely hands-off, perhaps because I reminded her so much of my father that I repelled her. When I looked at the photos closely, I could see it. I was beginning to wonder if she wrestled with some built-in hatred of me because of whom I reminded her. It may have simply been less painful to keep the distance. Suppose Adolf Hitler had a twin brother. Even if the man had nothing at all to do with the Third Reich, how well would things go for him wandering around post-war Europe?

---

[20] Although I mentioned that there was no overlap in our complaints with Carolyn's behavior, as an adult I did see my own brushes with Carolyn's "girlfriend scare tactics" mirrored exactly what David had experienced. I was just a late bloomer, so it didn't have the formative impact on me that it did on my brother.

Nobody wants to be constantly reminded of pain and disaster.

Carolyn would've kept those feelings secret and fought an internal battle against them. And she may have even felt more fondly toward me than her other two kids on some level – after all, there were certain aspects of Dr. David that she'd been attracted to…

Perhaps Carolyn didn't believe in her kids because she didn't believe in herself. All these years later, for me to keep on making a living as a freelancer, without the stability of a paycheck to depend upon, was surprising to her. It made my mother sick with concern. When my brother graduated Harvard Business School, he was offered a job at Johnson & Johnson, and though he desperately wanted to be in the music business, Carolyn urged him to take the bird in the hand.

I didn't know it during my formative years, but I was conceived as a kind of marital Band-Aid. A bargaining chip or… better yet, a game piece. Already ten years into my parents' marriage, in the early '60s Carolyn had been struggling with the connections between her and her husband. She saw a split on the horizon and desperately wanted to avoid that fate. A kind reading of the situation would be that Carolyn had fond memories of Dr. David's behaviors when there were infants in the house. A less kind assessment: that she would try to use the guilt of another mouth to feed as leverage; I was pressure applied. If she thought guilt would truly work, she didn't know her husband as well as she thought.

So it can be pinned roughly to the shadowy weeks between President Kennedy's assassination and the booze-fueled doctors' Christmas parties around town that Carolyn set the trap. Two people who deeply resented each other fucked, maybe for the last time ever. And in 1964, I was born not into a loving household but a cold war. Little Baby Stuart's homecoming was designed by Carolyn as a kind of détente. I was to be the poster child for a recommitted marriage. It didn't work out that way. And Carolyn could throw away the poster, but what about the *child?*

Knowing that everything comes to an end is a gift of experience, a consolation gift for knowing that we ourselves are coming to an end.

         – Tobias Wolff
           "This Boy's Life"

FOUR

∞

I'LL TAKE
MANHATTAN

OPEN HOUSE

IT WAS LATE at night when I emerged from the Holland Tunnel, and my iPhone's GPS had decided – apparently because of the time of night – that the fastest way to Brooklyn was directly through Manhattan. It wouldn't have been my call, but I was following by this point, not leading. So my first glimpse of Manhattan, which I'd planned for the next morning, came twelve hours early.

When you say you're from New York to just about anyone, that person will make the assumption that you're referring to New York City. You can't blame them. Numbers wise, it's a pretty safe bet; New York City has sixteen times the population of the state's second largest city. But there was a vast difference between life in one of the biggest, busiest cities on the planet and living upstate. Central New York has as much in common with Manhattan as it does with Vienna. So even though this trip was organized on a state-by-state basis, I'd imagine all would be forgiven if I handled the New York City part of my mother's story on my way from Pennsylvania to Maine.

Carolyn had lived in Manhattan during the fleeting time in her life when she thought she was happy in her marriage. My father labored under no such delusion, but I don't think happiness was necessarily on his radar anyway. Perfection was its own reward, and it existed on a higher plane than basic joy. As newlyweds, Dr. and Mrs. Connelly lived on 72nd and York Avenue. Young, unencumbered by children, 1950s New York as a doctor's wife may well have been the high-water mark for Carolyn living out the sophisticated dream she'd picked up like a contagion watching those MGM white telephone comedies of the '30s. At least, as far as she could on their finances; my father was doing his residency, so money was tight. The apartment was part of the package, provided by New York Memorial Hospital. Carolyn was playing house. There were the stories about hanging a Thanksgiving turkey out the window on a rope because their icebox wasn't big enough, about navigating Lisa in her stroller and their standard poodle Nikki through Manhattan's endless revolving doors, about sitting in on night court for entertainment instead of a Broadway play because they were broke.

My memories didn't start here, of course, but growing up in the cultural wasteland of suburban Syracuse, I found myself flown to New York City fairly often, mostly for shopping trips. Carolyn's conundrum was that just as she'd accrued the resources to live a stylish life, they'd arrived in a city without style. The irony was that they'd been broke in Manhattan but rich in Syracuse, where there wasn't a designer label in sight.

Nearly the only real friend Carolyn made in Syracuse was a woman named Joan Apple, and it was no coincidence that Joan came from New York City. She had flair, urbane wit, and the two of them bonded at least partially over their distain of the hayseed nature they felt suffused Syracuse. Joan's husband Alan seemed to come out of Central Casting. He was what writer Richard Cohen would call a "tough Jew" and would end up doing time in a federal prison for a white-collar crime he committed… with some assistance from my father. Joan managed to extricate herself from the marriage while Alan was serving time in a Georgia federal prison, but with her husband's misbehavior, her local reputation had been burned to the ground. Nothing was going to grow there again for her. She headed back to New York in the early '80s – Joan Apple and the Big Apple, reunited.

Since I was in Manhattan anyway, I drove north past the Weill Cornell Medical Center, which had been New York Memorial Hospital back in the '50s. Looking at the vast complex, I felt toward it the same way I've felt toward every other hospital on the planet; I hated everything about it. I didn't care that this place had ever housed or fed my family, or that they helped sick and injured people. If it were up to me, I'd never set foot in a hospital again.

I WAS STAYING in Mary Jo's sister Kate's townhouse in Prospect Heights. She, her husband and their daughter had already made plans to go camping when I'd asked if I could stay, but she hadn't hesitated. Without suggesting it was any effort, she made arrangements for me to get in the place and stay by myself. In the kitchen a lovely note, a drawing by their two-year-old welcoming me, and a cold bottle of Chardonnay were all waiting. The Bucks were gracious hosts *in absentia*. Clearly they had been raised right.

Shuffling around the impeccably restored brownstone, aware of my place as a man in need of shelter, I thought of Carolyn's comfort with taking in strays. Perhaps through some coincidence, or perhaps something else was at play, each of the three children had a shadow version, a reflection from a cracked mirror. For each of us, there was one friend that needed to be saved, that came to us with no other options. We each pleaded their cases before Carolyn. We had become fishers of men, somehow.

It started with the eldest; one of Lisa's friends had a bad home life. Her name was Maureen Gordon, Mo, and there came a breaking point senior year of high school when she decided to run away. Some combination of an evil step-father and a boyfriend named Greg became explosive. When my sister got wind of this and asked Carolyn if Mo could stay with us, Carolyn found it easy to say yes. She did have a strong empathetic streak running through her, as long as she perceived the recipient to be desperate.

Not long after, perhaps the next summer, my brother's friend Mike Lawler was kicked out of his house for some infraction (related to marijuana, if memory serves) and David made the request. Carolyn let him stay, too.

I was next in line, though my reeling in of the desperate and downtrodden would come years later, the summer between high school and college. That delineation was important. It was a time of transition. And it was embarrassment more than empathy that caused me to ask if one of my friend's could live in our house.

Though I'd had a tight group of buddies for a long time – from middle school on through until now – I had made a new friend senior year; Paul Doherty was a transfer student who, due simply to alphabetical order, had been assigned to my homeroom. He stood out right away with his taste in punk rock T-shirts – The Ramones, Blondie, The Buzzcocks. I soon realized that Paul had no class last period, because driving home from school I'd see him on the road, maybe a mile away, hoofing it home rather than waiting forty minutes to get on his bus.

One day when I caught sight of Paul walking along East Genesee Street, I asked my friend who was driving to pull over. Assuming he lived near the school, I rolled down the window, shouting, "Hey, you want a ride?" The walk wouldn't have made sense otherwise; it would've meant that his bus would've passed him every day on the walk. But that turned out to be a misguided assumption. Paul lived farther from the school than I did. His bus passed him every single day. If I had known that before, I would've asked him in homeroom why he would ever make the hike. *His bus passed him every day* – that should have been my first clue. He walked, not because he was in a hurry to get home, but because he just couldn't stand to stay in school a minute longer than the state made him. Every time I spotted him from a car, I picked him up and dropped him at his house, and through all this we got to know each other. He was in a band, The Trend, which I naturally found exciting, and by the time I'd taken Bill and Mike to see the first of what would become many of the band's shows, we'd all become close.

At the time I worked an afterschool job cooking in a mall steakhouse, and when Paul told me later that senior year that he was looking for a job, I told him I'd check in at my place. I thought it'd be great to have a friend as a co-worker, and since I got along well with the restaurant's managers, I felt like there was a decent chance I could get Paul hired.

I presented my case to the general manager, a skeptical rotund man we were forced to call Mr. Cleveland. "Is this guy Paul heading to college next year?" he asked.

I told him that yes, he was, not understanding the intention behind the question until Mr. Cleveland shook his head. "Sorry. I don't want to train somebody new just to have him take off a few months later."

That made perfect sense to me from a business standpoint, and I told Paul the story the next day in a kind of shrugged, "Well, I tried" way.

Paul looked at me like I was insane. "Why would you say I was going to college?" he asked me.

"I don't want to lie to my manager."

"But you wouldn't be lying," Paul said. "I'm not going to college."

"You're not?"

Paul shook his head. Not angry, and not offended either. Just confused. "No."

He had not claimed anything different during the time

we'd known each other. It was nothing but assumption on my part. It became a *check-your-privilege* moment for me a generation before the phrase was invented. *People I'm friends with go to college.* Beginning and end of the story. Flawed logic; not that I seek out college-bound kids to become friends with, but the ineffective corollary: if you and I are friends, then you must be going to college.

I'd felt this exact sense of shame once before, when I was eight, and I hadn't been in a hurry to reexperience it. Back then, what was at issue was a musical instrument. It wasn't until I was in second grade that I'd stepped foot into a house that did not contain a piano. We had one, our neighbors all had one, the Taylors had one. But when my new friend Ben invited me over to his house for the first time, I immediately noticed the instrument's absence.

"Where's your piano?" I asked Ben.

He told me his family didn't have one.

"Really?" This just didn't add up to a kid like me; I figured they were just part of the basic appliances, like the refrigerator. I double checked with Carolyn when I got home and she explained that, indeed, some people didn't own pianos. She told me they were expensive. It never crossed my mind, and I felt terrible about that fact.

Right up there with the "Where's your piano?" question was this clarion clear moment: when Paul told me that he wouldn't be attending college, that his mother had no intention, interest or ability to pay for it. Or anything else, in fact; she'd moved out of the house, which had only been rented (rented!) through June. Paul told me the day he graduated high school, he would be on his own. His twin brother had seen the writing on the wall and enlisted in the Army the year before, but Paul had nowhere to go. And so I pitched Carolyn the idea of Paul moving in with us. I'd known him less than eight months at that point, but I'd always had good instincts when it came to people, and I trusted those instincts. Despite his short attention span, grungy clothing, and hatred of high school, I knew Paul was a person with integrity. What he needed was a chance to get on his feet. Carolyn gave that to him, as she had with Mike before him and Maureen before that.

And it was strange to think that, as bad a guide into the world as Carolyn had been for me and my siblings, for other children, this shadow brood, she was a savior.

RIGHT THEN, at my age, I couldn't think of a single peer who believed their mother to be anything short of a saint with the possible exception of those three runaways, my siblings, and me. To explain this phenomenon, I'd figured it all could be boiled down to two options: either becoming a mother triggered a biological reaction that made 99.999 percent of women click the genes that drive selfishness into the off position, or most children couldn't see their mothers as they really were. Either way, what muddied this theory was the fact that those three runaways thought so highly of Carolyn. They knew bad parenting, and they didn't see it in her.

She was lucky enough to have known how she stood in their esteem; among my mother's belongings were three letters, one from each of those kids. I don't suppose I ever wrote a letter to my mother in my life. I was too practical. I saw her every day growing up; why send her a letter? If I had something to say, I should just say it. Again, look at who raised me.[21]

The thing was, the messed-up teens mostly had better

---

[21] I did write one thing that she held onto: this horrific arts-and-crafts project that was trying to be a plaque but was in reality a piece of cardboard around which a dress-shirt company might wrap their product. The two sides were serrated to mimic broken wood and I attached a couple of pinecones to the bottom left corner. It read, "God Bless This Happy Home," in glued-down glitter lettering, though between my actual beliefs on religion and my experiences within the walls of the place, it could have more accurately been edited down to "This Home." The pinecones were a nice touch, though.

manners than I did. Or at least, appreciated my mother more. Her "open door" policy helped these kids and others through some tough times. Yeah, Carolyn did have a way of taking in strays. Maybe she got the gene from her maternal grandmother, though I think primarily that woman rented her Depression-era rooms out based on a need for the money. That had a real *The Postman Always Rings Twice* veneer to it, but Carolyn was motivated by that warm feeling she got from playing the savior.

All the letters were stripped down and simplistic, consisting of a handful of lines with an average of fewer than ten words per sentence. Maureen wrote, "If it weren't for you I would really have been totally lost." Paul wrote, "Thank you so much for helping me and teaching me so much about responsibility." Mike Lawler wrote this: "Thank you again for this summer. You gave me the chance to do a lot of thinking and live without any pressures."[22]

These were kids who, to varying degrees, were treated poorly by their own mothers, and Carolyn became a lifeline. They adored her for this, and I believed they still keep that vision of her in their hearts. I knew Paul did, since the two of us have stayed in touch. Carolyn came up often when we'd talk. Just five days out from my visit to Manhattan, over burgers and beer in a pub in Syracuse's Brooklyn-lite Amory Square, Paul will say to me, "If I were going to write a book about your mother, I'd call it *Carol Connelly Saved My Life.*" A title I think she would've appreciated.[23]

Of course, I didn't carry around that version of Saint

---

[22] Mysteriously in that same letter, Mike wrote, "If you can, keep Stuart interested in football because as a junior he could definitely be starting as split end." I had no memory of playing football with my brother or any of his friends. It certainly didn't sound like me.

[23] Paul would also inform me that he's now referred to as Professor Doherty during the scuba classes he teaches at Syracuse University and Ithaca College, even though "I've never stepped foot in a college classroom."

Carolyn. And personally, I welcomed the acuity of my vision. People say that they keep their elders in their heart, as part of them, when they pass on. But if my honoring Carolyn was to mean anything, in my opinion, it almost had to be the opposite. The pedestal was reserved for a version of the person we wanted to believe in. I didn't have that luxury, true, but I was also able to avoid the curse of having to conform to it. Let's love her and celebrate her for who she actually was, not a sanitized social construct of the woman. Let's do her that courtesy, at the very least. Not perfect, but perfectly unique, and perfectly herself.

This was freedom; it meant I could embrace her in her best moments – braying laughter, arms outstretched for a hug – or at her worst when, as she'd no doubt put it, she was "mean as cat dirt." I'd seen her brandish hammers and sawed-off baseball bats, not afraid to use them. Something I doubt Paul or Mo had ever seen.

My vision of her was balanced. But that didn't mean complete. Seeing someone's dark side along with their light side was only part of understanding. The job at hand, the point of this journey, was finding out where that light and dark came from. In the effort to understand Carolyn as a complete person, I would have to go deeper.

TOY STORY

THE NIGHT IN BROOKLYN was a rough one. On my way up to New York I'd stopped in New Hope and had sushi for dinner. I had chosen a very respectable-looking – and busy – restaurant, but when I woke up around one o'clock, sweating and with a searing cramp in my side, I was pretty sure I'd come down with a case of food poisoning. Waves of nausea washed over me, punctuated with a physical pain that no amount of doubling over could offset. I only used the toilet for vomiting; nothing else in my system seemed to be working. It had mostly passed by 2:30, but then flared up again at four.

By sunrise I was doing all right, and I managed to get a few hours of sleep while the rest of Brooklyn was starting the day. By ten I was on my feet, but still completely constipated and dehydrated. The sheets were soaked through with sweat and I had to figure out Kate's washing machine to put my room back in order.

I went out into the late morning to try and clear my head. Should I call the trip off? I wondered. I rang Mary Jo and let her know that I was thinking about ending the adventure and heading home so I could see my doctor. And while she knew that hypochondria wasn't one of my myriad neuroses, she cautioned me against it.

"You're not going to the ER, are you?" she asked.

"No."

"Then it's probably not too bad."

"I'm in the laxative aisle of the Flatbush Avenue Duane Reade," I told her. "That's almost as bad as the ER."

"You'll be okay," Mary Jo reassured me. "If you don't keep going, your whole plan is going to fall apart. You know that, right? And it won't come back together again."

On this issue, my wife was a hundred percent right.

I picked some medicine that looked like it might do some good and jumped on the Q train, headed back into Manhattan.

So, FAO SCHWARTZ on the corner of Central Park South and Fifth Avenue, a kind of Mecca to the six-year-old me, was no more.

I stood in front of Apple's giant cube-shaped entrance on the plaza of Fifth Avenue that led to its bunker of a retail store underneath, but where the eight-foot-tall wooden soldiers should have stood flanking the street level door, there was just more Apple.

I could've searched for it online, of course. I could have double-checked. Research, after all, was about the fine detail. But I was taking a journey through the past, feeling my way like a blind man. I had a path in mind as well as a destination, and I had memories that intersected in precise locations. Why would I bother to check if something was still there when I was destined to go there either way?

Still, I had to admit that the absence of this iconic store took me by surprise. I could've imagined many places from my childhood plowed under, but FAO Schwartz wouldn't have been high on that list. Besides, it wasn't even simply an idolized totem from my past; I'd spent a lot of time in Manhattan throughout the 2000s and I'd taken Wesley and Callie to FAO Schwartz frequently. It felt like I had *just been there.*

Perhaps there was really no way for me to wrap my brain around the actual impermanence of the things in my world.

I had my mother, all three pounds of her, in a sealed plastic box so you'd think the transient nature of matter would've struck me by this point, but this was FAO Schwartz. Are you kidding me?

The best gift that was ever bestowed upon me as a child came from FAO Schwartz, and I'd be willing to bet that I'd been in possession of the only one in the entire City of Syracuse. This was back when I was still a doctor's kid. That's not to say my father stopped practicing medicine. Rather, "doctor's kid" was a designation, one that only had any weight behind it when the family unit was securely in place. It wasn't just doctors' wives that had a position of esteem in society; that reflected glow bathed the children, too. Everyone at school knew my father was a plastic surgeon, and assumed I wanted for nothing. At a time when the space beneath the Christmas tree held record albums, board games, hockey sticks, and coloring books for my friends, I received a real live, climb-aboard-and-drive electric battery powered Ferrari. Orange, no less.

I'd told people over the years about the Ferrari, and the story was often met with some doubt. A ridable battery-powered toy? In 1971 it sounded made up. There were times when I wondered if I had actually invented it, creating some lost talisman for my idealized version of childhood before the whole thing went belly up. A perfect, rare, and joyous thing I'd had ahold of but which somehow simply vanished one day.

I'd gone through all my mother's photographs several times hoping to find a shot of me skittering around our family room on it, but I couldn't find one. It's odd how you can look at a picture a thousand times and never register some tiny part of it. Here's this Christmas photo, I'd seen it before dozens of times I guess, and what always pulled the focus was the magnetic board desk. That Christmas morning wasn't about what was in that photo, it was about the full-sized battery-powered Ferrari I could straddle and drive around. There was no evidence of it ever existing. Until, like that scene in *Blade Runner* where Harrison Ford keeps telling the computer give him more information on the photo and eventually it shifts the objects' parallax enough to reveal a clue, I noticed something new.[24]

There it was, hiding in plain sight. Sort of. The nose of the thing was sticking in there down in the left corner. The reason I hadn't seen it while sifting through the photographs could probably best be chalked up to a magician's technique: misdirection. Accidental misdirection, but misdirection nonetheless. Clearly, there was a desk with a magnetic board front and center in the photograph, sporting little plastic letters that some Santa's elf had spelled out **FOR STUART**. It seemed

Christmas Car

---

[24] In 1982 when I first saw the film, I found myself taken out of the story during that scene. It was frustrating because I knew photography simply didn't work that way. Things have definitely changed a lot since those days.

to be the focus of the picture. Or, if it was meant to be a picture of a tree, at least this desk and board created a certain negative space. My eyes were just automatically drawn to it. Helping this process along might have been the fact that it was, you know, for Stuart. And... I'm Stuart! But down in the corner, there it was: the front driver's side of the Ferrari.

I remember it had been charged overnight and was ready to go. It was small enough that a rider didn't climb inside but rather sat on top. The feet would be positioned on the orange hood, which had two black doorstop-shaped turn signals on either side. One was permanently glued into place, but the other, the one on the right side, was actually a button, the secret accelerator pedal for the car. It was binary, just stop or go, but it moved. This kind of technology exists pretty widely these days; there are ride-on, battery-operated Jeeps and Hummers and Lightning McQueens from the Pixar film *Cars*. But in the '70s, something like that was as rare as rose gold. It was the coolest present you could ever get a little boy.

Maybe I *was* the kid who had everything, after all.

I'D TAKE ROAD TRIPS to New York City often with my high school friends. One time in particular stuck out in my memory; my trip was planned, but at the last minute, Carolyn asked me not to go. Some out of town weekend opportunity had developed for her, and someone needed to stay home to take care of the dog, a toy poodle named Blackberry.

I took the path of least resistance, as I always did then, and agreed to cancel my plans. I'm not sure at the moment of agreement that I knew it was a lie, but certainly by the time Carolyn's bags were packed I'd hatched my very simple plan. Let her drive off, dump a shitload of dog chow into the bowl so the guy won't starve, and jump in my friend

Gerry's Torino.[25] I piled up Blackberry's bowl with food and headed for Manhattan. We stayed in the Carter right off Times Square, a welfare hotel at the time. We wandered the streets. Dug through The Strand's eight miles of books. Hit up Jerry Ohlinger's Movie Material Store, the only place before the Internet that you could buy movie one-sheets and lobby cards (which were and still are a kind of contraband).

The problem was timing our return relative to Carolyn's. Naturally I had intended to beat her back to the house, clean up whatever dog food had gushed out of the bowl. Live the lie. It didn't work out that way.

I had to admit the move I'd made was, to say the least, uncool. I can't recall if the reason was that Gerry didn't have quite the same urgency to get home that I did (it was his car, after all) or whether Carolyn's timing shifted, but when the Torino pulled into my driveway late Sunday afternoon, my mother's car was already there. She would know everything or nothing, I supposed, depending on what kind of work the dog had done on his two days' worth of dinner. Unfortunately for me, I'd grossly overestimated how much dog food would get eaten. She knew. I'd been caught.

Inside, tears and apologies burst forth, but the contrition was a put on. My selfish nonsense would continue on a bit longer. Carolyn demanded that I find some discipline inside, but course-correcting felt like too much. I liked getting what I wanted, I was all id.

The thing was, I listened. I wasn't persuaded, but neither was I combative. I was like an inmate on death row ordering his last meal – lobster, filet mignon, French fries, a cheeseburger, three different flavor milkshakes – and she

---

[25] In my defense against animal cruelty, I'll restate here that my mother left the back door open at all times when no one was in the house so the dog could come and go. Blackberry wasn't penned in. Still, admittedly, it was a bad call.

was trying to tell me vegetables were good for me. Deaf ears. But I nodded, I was contrite. I may've been a sociopath. No, I wasn't. Because I cared about my friends, I cared about the less fortunate. I cared about the animals. So I don't know what I was. Selfish and short-sighted, for sure, but maybe nothing more malignant than that. I wanted what I wanted.

I ASKED AROUND there on the corner of Central Park South and learned that the street level Apple situation was supposedly temporary. That the flagship store for the athletic wear company Under Armour was on its way to occupy the FAO Schwartz location.

That may have been a step in the wrong direction. If forced, I could make an argument that the Apple Store mostly seemed like it was a toy seller for the twenty-first century. But the toys certainly did a lot more these days.

The stomach pain suddenly returned, swooping in as quickly as an ice storm. So, limping along with a kind of mind-obliterating pain in my abdomen, I headed down Sixth Avenue, trying to walk it off. I was thinking about the trips to the Macy's Thanksgiving Parade I'd taken when I was so tiny and helpless, using the memory like a pacifier to work through the pain in my gut.

If it meant anything, New York City meant Carolyn and David to me. Big David, that is. Dr. Connelly. My father. I think it was only natural to conflate the parents with the town; the money to fly into the City That Never Sleeps from the sleepy Central New York wasteland came from his wallet, not hers, and after he was gone, those trips dried up fast.[26]

---

[26] I did recall the trip we made to New York in 1980 when Carolyn scored some tickets to see the King Tut Exhibit. She brought Lisa and me along, but after landing I somehow came to the conclusion that I would rather visit comic book shops by myself than see the exhibit. Carolyn let me. No guilt, no questions asked. Meet back here at the Times Square subway. It was another version of roller-skates at the dinner table, another generation down the line.

It was a strange disconnect: you could ask any of my friends, any of my family, what my opinion of my father was, and you would get a common answer. The data points would all align. This is what I would say: mechanically he was talented, clever, educated, hardworking, concise... emotionally he was cruel, disengaged, selfish, sociopathic. Good machine, bad father. This story, my story of him had never changed over the years. Not once. But... but...

Even though I couldn't picture the details on how I got there, I could remember the trip to New York City for the Macy's Thanksgiving Day Parade. I had a sense memory of my parents each holding a hand of mine and swinging me up onto the curb. And in my memory, it almost feels like a normal family. It almost feels like their hands are jumper cables passing a warm, alternating current of love through me.

But I had to be misremembering that, didn't I?

TALK ABOUT a sense of wonder: I suppose I'd seen the balloons on television, but nothing could have prepared me for staring up at those massive things in person. To a little boy, it seemed as if the balloons took up the entire width of sky between the two sides of the street. It was like the Hindenburg explosion had never happened and the world was full of dirigibles, currently dressed for Halloween. My only regret was that the trip to the Macy's Parade was long before the Spiderman balloon came into being. The five-year-old me would've done anything to stand in the shadow of a gigantic Spiderman drifting between the skyscrapers. At the time, comic books were fringe, they were kids' stuff. Of course, so were balloons and parades, but this was different. Macy's was mainstream, so there were no superheroes to be found and there wouldn't be for years. The character I remembered most clearly was Snoopy. Carolyn loved *Peanuts*.

She empathized (identified?) with Charlie Brown's life and took every opportunity to share his struggles with me. The balloon looked only vaguely like Snoopy, and I remember being disappointed that his head, the most distinctive part of him, was covered with the "World War I 'Flying Ace'" leather helmet. But I was nevertheless delighted.

Reading Peanuts Together

MY TIME WAS nearly up. If I wanted to avoid a Brooklyn parking ticket, very soon the Audi would have to either be moved or gone. I needed to jump on the train. I saluted the sliver of empty Manhattan sky between the glass and steel. And I made a silent promise that I would make a real effort to catch the King Tut exhibit the next time it went on tour.

Dodge: *I never went back to my parents.*
Never. Never even had the urge.
I was always independent. Always
found a way.

Tilden: *I didn't know what to do. I couldn't*
figure anything out.

Dodge: *There's nothing to figure out. You*
just forge ahead. What's there to
figure out?

– Sam Shepard
"Buried Child"

FIVE

∞

YANKEE
TERRITORY

TRASH VS. TREASURE

I FOUND MY WAY to a supermarket, a borderline-rural outpost of a chain I'd never heard of, trying to get something else for the abdominal pain. The Flatbush Avenue laxative hadn't moved the needle a whit. And since I was considering any and all options to get "regular" again, I asked the young woman at the checkout if there were any good places nearby to get coffee.

Her answer was immediate, chopped out in a thick New England accent: Dunkin' Donuts, right down the street. The response immediately put me in mind of the *Saturday Night Live* commercial parody with Casey Affleck as the rowdy Southie "Mayor of Dunkin'." Ah, Massachusetts… keep on being you.

Dunkin' Donuts was not my idea of the world's best cappuccino. But beggars couldn't be choosers.

I HAD BEEN DRIVING the back roads of New England in search of an effigy, a stand-in antique store that could represent all those that Carolyn dragged me into over the years. It didn't have to be Massachusetts, it could've been Vermont, Rhode Island, New Hampshire. Or even back in Pennsylvania or Maryland, come to think of it. There were a lot of them all over the eastern seaboard. Anyplace people were making things before the invention of power tools was fair game.

These were not Upper East Side antique dealers; they were junk stores, barns, tents, and flea markets. But they held some of the oldest contraptions in America: butter churns, hand-printed road signs, carriage wheels, wooden tools, and milk cans.

Carolyn had never been in much of a hurry to get to wherever she was going. If there was an interesting looking stop along the way, it would be indulged. She tended to avoid the interstates to up the chances of finding a store. And if she found a treasure she had to have, it would get thrown in the back of the station wagon and brought along for the ride. The twist was, I wasn't an unwilling participant. I liked the places, too. I saw what she saw inside those barns, the wood, tin, and rusted steel. There were a million "Rosebuds" out there, but without Orson Welles to give them context, we had to find our own meaning in them. The imperfections and grubbiness spoke to us both. For one, they were originals, not mass produced. Hand hewn and not machined. Made out of necessity. Those rugged products gave both of us, people who didn't have the finesse or competence of my father, something to hang our hats on. We could be of value, of service, even if our seams didn't match up. Though it went unsaid between the two of us, there was no question: we both saw ourselves in those sloppily-made pieces of Americana.

No STORY COULD bring Carolyn's rustic aesthetics into better focus than that of our kitchen facelift. The context was simple if a little hazy. Back in the '60s and '70s, the grateful patient (and for the plastic surgeon there were many) would often give their doctor a gift for performing good work. After the bandages came off, Dr. David would often be sent thank-you clocks, paintings, figurines, and of course endless bottles of booze. One present, however was a unique. Someone gifted my father with a farm to thank him for his surgical artistry. This made absolutely no sense to me as a six-year-old, and the intervening years haven't made things any clearer. I was unaware of what happened to the property itself, but by the time the family went to see this new farm, the barn had been bulldozed.

Rarely one to let lemons get in the way of lemonade, my mother came up with a plan. They had whatever was left of the structure, silvery foot-wide planks, delivered to the house and my father used them essentially as wallpaper in our kitchen. This made almost no sense, because the wood was at least a half an inch thick and everything in the kitchen was already set to its current wall thickness. All the sockets and switches and window sashes theoretically would have had to be reset to the new depth. Furthermore, many people would be concerned about how sanitary it was to have two-hundred-year-old wood hanging over the food preparation area. Carolyn ignored both issues.

This was how the result looked:

Carolyn's Idea of Wooden Paneling

And that hayfork there, screwed to our kitchen wall? That was exactly the kind of raggedy find that Carolyn would fall in love with out on the backroads of New England. And keeping the garlic tied there, hanging off it within easy reach? Taken together, Carolyn in a nutshell.

STURBRIDGE WAS THE TOWN where we would meet up with my sister once in a while. It sat more or less halfway between Syracuse and Northampton, Massachusetts, where at one time Lisa was employed by a boarding school. The middle ground was two hours from each place. Carolyn and I would drive to Sturbridge and meet Lisa for lunch. To me at the time, she was not merely in the next state over but a million miles away, because she was out in the world. Surviving and working. Being an adult. But it was always nice to see her and remember that, with the proper escape velocity, there was life outside of Syracuse.

I drove around winding roads in the hills of Sturbridge until I found one of Carolyn's barn-style antique shops. Walking through the dusty rows, I had a sudden memory flash. It was in a place just like this that my mother bought me a particular toy. An image of it had just been sent to the consciousness from the recesses of my brain, vivid and tangible. It wasn't antique, but I'd never seen anything like it. The lobster toy was no rideable Ferrari, but it did move. I loved magic as a kid, and mysterious objects from Chinese finger traps to puzzle boxes captivated my imagination. So did this lobster. It wasn't the world's best stuffed animal by a long shot, but I loved it for its mystery. It had two red felt claws and little plastic eyes, but it was the lobster's body where the real magic happened. The body was a ten-inch long strip made of two different materials glued together. The top was a fluffy red fur while the bottom was of some kind of artificial leather. When you ran your hands along the lobster's furry back, it arched up and seemed to rise to meet your fingertips, like a cat. Something about the physics, the differentials of the two materials, made it bend when stroked front to back. If you rubbed it hard enough the lobster would flip its front end over spastically.

Remembering the lobster instantly made me wonder what happened to it. Thrown away? No... Given to the Salvation Army? More likely. I didn't notice at the time. I must have stopped finding the magical spark in it. It must've just been sitting on my bureau or the floor of my room until Carolyn decided it was time. Yeah, that made sense. But I can't attest to it. Nor could I do the same for the beloved Ferrari, which I would've certainly outgrown. Wasn't that the fate of all the unique details of each of our childhoods; they must dissolve into the ether. I know practically that someone along the line must've been making cleaning-out decisions, but that never actually registered. Instead it felt like this: one day you had all that stuff around you, and the next day, or the day after, it's all been purged... first from your immediate reach, your world... and eventually even from your memory.

My sister and her husband at the time, Cyrus, worked at the Williston-Northampton School. Growing up I'd had no exposure to boarding school, so it blew my mind a bit to learn that the faculty there – like jungle explorers – lived among the high school savages. I was a kid who dreaded running into a school employee beyond its walls (i.e.; in real life), so I couldn't imagine hanging out with teachers, their little kids, their pets. Other kids had lived it, though. Plenty of others. Lisa and Cyrus were given a place to live their first year of teaching, and because it was boarding school, the home had a name, and because this was Lisa, I would learn that name. The place was called *Swann Cottage*. Lisa and Cyrus hosted us for Thanksgiving. Being a sullen teenager by that point, I had very little interest in leaving my friends at the holidays, but I went anyway.

The thing was, when I arrived at Swann Cottage something unexpected happened: it turned out I loved the whole atmosphere of the place. It was a tiny hobbit hole of a one-floor house, but the back door, instead of going out onto the lawn, opened to a three-floor dormitory building filled with bedrooms and teenagers that were missing their families. From then on, I looked forward to trips there.

I even visited on my own once, which given my relationship with my sister, wasn't an easy ask. But it felt important to me. My sister was welcoming, even though I'm not sure she understood why I'd want to spend that thin sliver of time between college graduation and my first job at Swann Cottage. Part of my attraction had to have been the connection to the New England writing life; a life of letters. Hawthorne, Emerson, Dickinson, Thoreau, even the horridly-racist-but-undeniably-talented H.P. Lovecraft – all of these giants, bound and inspired by New England heritage. Though my plan was to make films, I'd always understood that fundamentally filmmaking was art by committee, while writing had the benefit of being a singular pursuit. A poem didn't need a budget or tractor-trailers, a cinematographer or a production designer.[27] A book's ingredients were minimal. Maybe that was the way to go. Cyrus served as an example. He was an English teacher who smoked his pipe and read books by the fire in the evenings. Summers off. It seemed to me there were worse ways to spend one's life.

MY CONNECTION TO my sister feels tenuous these days. Our age difference had always played against us, but she was a reader (unlike our brother) and there was a bond there between the two people who found answers in the printed word. That doesn't mean we're friends, though. She may look at it differently, I can't speak for her, but to me our

---

[27] I actually did write a poem about Swann Cottage, though I'm sure I considered them lyrics to an as-yet-unwritten song – I couldn't have been so pretentious as to write poems during my high school to college summer break, could I have? I was in a band at the time, with the usual suspects Bill Rapp and Mike Royce. The claim to fame of that endeavor was that the band's name, Free Money, would eventually pop up in an episode of the TNT dramedy series *Men of a Certain Age* – along with the certified backstory.

relationship has always seemed civil but not particularly warm. And I think that was because her personality is civil but not particularly warm. She of course inherited that trait the way we all inherited some, directly from Dr. David.

At the end of the day, I suppose I viewed Lisa essentially as a stranger. Like my mother, but without the bank box of photos and documents. Of course, Lisa was also currently alive, which was the preferable state if one was interested in asking questions.

Getting them answered, on the other hand... that all depended upon whom you were asking.

THE NOT-SO-GREAT BEYOND

I ARRIVED IN Brunswick, Maine, as darkness fell. I had made it pretty far north by that point, and the geography, combined with how late in the summer it had become, meant that night was coming on ever earlier. I parked on the main street, which was naturally named Maine Street. I got the quip, all right, but was so tired that I couldn't decide whether it was clever or stupid. I was certain, however, that my sister, she who always wrote Modoc Spring on the address block, liked it. I imagined my father approving of it as well. Once I had a firm hold on both of those opinions, I knew where I came down on the Maine Street question.

I'd come a long way for a place where I've spent very little time. My friend Mike Royce visited somewhere along the jagged coast of Maine nearly every summer for family time on rocky beaches, but for me mostly it was restricted to trips dropping Lisa off at college. And thinking harder about it, maybe we only dropped her off the one time, freshman year. Once she went off to school, she never really came back. At least, not with all her belongings. She'd moved out.

My brother was different. David would be home every summer from UMass. The phone in the house would start ringing a day or two before he was back in town, his buddies eager to hang out with him again as soon as possible.

Before the days of mobile phones, caller ID, or answering machines, this is what we had: the surprise of not knowing who was on the other end of a phone call until it was answered; then the responsibility of dealing with that call and passing the messages along. It was the clay cookpot of telecommunications.

Lisa seemed happier to be away from it all, out and on her own. It could've been because Carolyn's inclinations ran along gender lines, and she had a lot more to say about Lisa's choices than either of her boys'.

Maine felt like another world; in addition to the early twilight, the August night air was starting to hold a chill. I walked the little college town for a few blocks on either side of Maine Street, partly to stretch my legs after the long drive, and partly to get the lay of the land and bird dog where I might want to eat dinner later. There was a combination record and bookstore that was doing the kind of business I would've expected if it were 1993, there were some decent looking restaurants and a bar or two that looked all right. But after a few minutes of this, I'd chewed up enough of the clock. The twilight had faded; night was in full force now. I got back into the car and headed over to Pine Street. It was a place I knew I needed to find in the dark.

IN 1980, LISA MARRIED her college sweetheart in the chapel of the Bowdoin campus. The ceremony was exactly one week before my sixteenth birthday, which meant it was the day after Carolyn turned fifty-three. My age right now. I found this math, like a lot of the alignment of dates and ages on this journey, somewhat troubling. I wasn't told about any of the finances, but in addition to getting the time off from work, it seemed that Carolyn had somehow managed to pay for the wedding and still have enough left over to rent a townhouse for our family for the week.

I drove to the complex where we'd stayed, across a wide thoroughfare and down a side street, less than a half mile from the main campus quad. The sign read Pine Street Apartments, and indeed it did look like it had been carved out of a towering pine forest.

Three days earlier I'd parked at Ed Nabb's house at night purely as a result of the idiosyncrasies of my travel schedule. But this evening was a different story: I only wanted to be at the Pine Street Apartments in the dark. I had driven to Brunswick because the place had long held a pressure point on my memory, one far disproportionate to the time spent here. Back then, it was like there had been a pair of vice grips squeezing my amygdala. Now, even while most of my memory had the haziness of scenes captured through a Vaseline-smeared lens, I could still recall the incident at Bowdoin in pin-point focus. Pine Street Apartments brought it entirely back to life.

The dim illumination from the sodium arc lights in the gravel parking area threw the buildings' '70s architecture into sharp relief against the inky trees. Three stories tall including the attic, each townhouse had a long roof sloping down to the first floor. The buildings were all roof, it had seemed to me then. And now as well. These were keeping in a certain style with the vaulted ceilings and the open stairs, as if a ski chalet for suburbia. I had been terrified inside one of these townhouses. I couldn't say which one, though it felt very much to me like it had been an end unit. I thought that because the master bedroom had a side window as well as one to the back, and the townhouses sandwiched in the middle had no side windows. I knew the master bedroom, because as an almost-sixteen-year-old, I'd crawled into my mother's bed in the middle of the night.

∞ ∞ ∞

To TAKE THE POSITION that I had been a generally frightened child would be drastically understating my condition, minimizing my neurotic patterns of behavior. I may have been cursed with an overactive imagination, if such a condition exists. Fears of abduction, of strangers and monsters roaming the house, of the dark, small spaces, heights, torture, getting lost, maimed, beaten up, getting murdered, witnessing the murders of others – those were all constant concerns for me growing up. An unstoppable background buzzing, like a tinnitus plugged not into my ears but instead my brain, filled me with a sense of impending peril.

I had always been susceptible to horror films. It would stand to reason that I rarely glimpsed much as a very small child in the pre-cable TV era, but my tolerance for terror was extremely low, and there were some made-for-TV movies that left an indelible impression upon me. Two in particular; I've never been able to track them down, I don't know their names, but they would've been from the early '70s. I've never been able to find any trace of either one on IMDb or anywhere else on the Internet, but the experiences of watching them has been engraved into my prefrontal lobes.

One was a ridiculous knock-off of *Diabolique* (though naturally I didn't realize that at the time). The images from that piece of junk tormented me for months after it ran. In particular the scene wherein a woman drowns her husband in the tub. For the weight she needed to keep him underwater, the woman used a large stone garden gnome that had been prominently placed in the frame several times during the first act. When the husband came back to life, his eyes had gone completely white; no pupil, no iris. One glimpse of the white-eyed drowning victim rising from the tub unscrewed something in my mind. It hit me particularly hard because it was the everyday surroundings – the yard, the bathroom, the closet – that was the world in which I lived. It bit deep because home was assumed to be a place of safety. We didn't even lock our doors. There could've been a reanimated dead man in my tub every time I stepped into my own hall bathroom.[28]

The other movie of the week was an amazingly trumped-up thriller where a woman is robbed and knocked unconscious in a department store bathroom and when she comes to, she finds she's locked inside the place. The kicker is that she's been locked in with bloodthirsty security dogs (German Shepherds, of course) who relentlessly pursue her all night long. I've never been afraid of dogs, it didn't seem to be in my DNA, but that horror of the trapped woman trying to outwit the monsters leached into my bones and wouldn't go away.

The last of the trifecta of unshakable and scarring is discoverable online, because this trauma happened to me at the hands of an episode of *Night Gallery*, Rod Serling's less-than-stellar but still well-known follow-up to *The Twilight Zone*. The time line had been in some question. I had always assumed that the show was in late night syndication when I stumbled across it, but looking into the production, it tracked that I was six years old during *Night Gallery*'s first season. It was a safe bet that this was December of 1970 and I'd stumbled into the original broadcast of "Certain Shadows on the Wall." I believe I was supposed to be in bed asleep but shuffled into the family room from upstairs and caught the show close to the end. The centerpiece of the episode was simple but chilling: a woman dies at home but somehow leaves behind a shadow on the wall – her own silhouette sitting up in bed – that cannot be eradicated. Moving the lights doesn't help, painting over doesn't help. It's some kind of haunting, and the people remaining in the house have to

---

[28] Years later I'd shoot a low budget horror feature in my own house, exactly the kind of thing that would have terrified me as a child. It's starting to occur to me that maybe all of life is some kind of on-going confrontation of our own weaknesses. Or maybe that's just for those of us who choose to examine ourselves closer.

live with it. I walked into the room while my brother and sister were watching, and seeing that disconnected unmoving shadow with the gnarled outstretched hand filled me with a rush of terror I couldn't tamp down.

Those were the big three, all black and white TV interactions probably experienced before I was eight. Taken together, though surely not particularly clean-burning, they have fueled my work as an artist. And though in retrospect I probably wouldn't have traded the experiences for anything, at the time it was something akin to torture.

As a child I could close my eyes and see these things, conjure them back up, the way afterimages of a camera's flash burned its way into one's retinas. As a kid, every night for me was a fever dream. Bad dream? Into my mother's bed. The bed was enormous. It had been purchased long before they invented the California king, but if felt like a vast life raft to me.

When David would find me in bed with Carolyn in the morning, it infuriated him. My brother despised my weakness. Physical, mental, all of it. I don't know if it was love disguised, his wanting to make me tougher for a tough world. Or whether it was really simply just a matter of the oldest boy trying to impose some sort of order on a fatherless household.[29]

But all this background, this discussion of my fear and sense of helplessness? It has been laid out in service of one story. Something about the nature of evil. Something about my sister. Something strong enough in the memory that it brought me back to Brunswick after almost forty years.

∞ ∞ ∞

---

[29] A little later, when I'd become just a bit tougher, David would take me downtown for the exploitation splatterfests like *Scream, Blacula, Scream* and *Dr. Phibes Rises Again*. These were better times, and among the best times I ever had with my brother.

On the way to Maine for Lisa's wedding, the talk had not been typical for a mother of the bride. Not a word about the flowers, the place settings, the music or who would be participating in the readings. Not that I could remember, anyway. The drive up had all been chatter about something miraculous. The sense of delight had nothing to do with my mother getting a son-in-law. Lisa had been talking to Carolyn about it on their long-distance phone calls, and now Carolyn was sharing what little she understood with David and me, but soon we were going to get more details. Soon Lisa could tell us in person.

That was in 1980. Lisa isn't talking these days. I ask her about the incident over the phone a few days before my trip, but my sister refused to go over it with me. She said that she was told never to speak of it again. She took that advice to heart, and she wanted me to do the same. And she certainly felt writing about it would fall under the same category. But I'd always been terrible at taking advice.

It being the '70s and Bowdoin being a very *liberal* liberal arts school, my sister was a member of a fraternity – there were no sororities on campus and all the fraternities were coed. Apparently, over that summer when my sister hadn't returned to Syracuse, some of her fraternal sisters and brothers had cracked open the old Ouija board and begun messing around with it. This was exactly the type of thing that bored and possibly high college students might be inclined to do in the pre-Internet age. But what apparently happened was that the planchette started spelling out answers to the group's questions on the Ouija board quickly. *Very* quickly – too swiftly and accurately, everyone agreed, for what was happening to be chalked up to the ideomotor phenomenon. Soon the board was explaining that the messages were coming from the afterlife. From heaven.

The questions from the students came fast and furious, and apparently the answers were satisfactory. The issue of angels came up, and through the board the great beyond explained that everyone had his or her own personal guardian angel. How I got pulled into it, I didn't know. Perhaps because Lisa had recently asked me to be in the wedding party I was on her mind. My sister just threw my name out: "Does my brother Stuart have a guardian angel?"

She received an answer.

Of course, I wasn't there for this discussion of guardian angels, but my sister had told Carolyn that word came back from the ether concerning me: yes, the heavens knew all about Lisa's little brother. In fact, I had a guardian angel named Amiel whose singular task was to look after me. Hallelujah. And *this* was why my mother had been so giddy on the long drive to Maine. Lisa and her fraternity friends had talked with my guardian angel, this Amiel. And when we arrived in Maine, we were going to talk to him, too. I might be the first human ever to be able to directly interact with his guardian angel.

According to Carolyn, who had no reason to doubt her daughter.

But I did. As far back as I could remember, I'd believed only in the things I could see, touch, smell, hear, feel, taste, or comprehend through fundamental scientific principles. I could understand the fault lines riddling my religion, Christianity, as soon as I was old enough to think clearly. Yeah, I was a scared kid, and I knew first-hand how scared people cope. They made wishes.

But I was also willing to bet that this sense of the realities of the world, which feels so concrete to me, could be ephemeral. If ever my back were really against the wall, I could easily imagine deep, primordial genetic memory might drop me to my knees in prayer. But it doesn't feel that way. I can't say I believe that the absolute limit of our perceptions terminates at our five senses, but there's an enormous gulf between acknowledging intuition and embracing ghosts, spirits, demons, or the astral plane.

Years later a series of what could only be described as ridiculous horror movies about the Ouija board arrived (including a few knock-offs produced by the company that distributes some of my films). Most people still don't know that the Ouija is a patented board game that, according to the entry in Wikipedia, "The Catholic Church and other Christian Denominations have warned against using… holding that they can lead to demonic possession. Occultists, on the other hand, are divided on the issue, with some saying that it can be a positive transformation; others reiterate the warnings of many Christians and caution 'inexperienced users' against it."

I figured I'd find out with my own two eyes what all this paranormal nonsense was about. A prank, or mass hysteria, or just maybe something truly inexplicable. But it didn't work out that way. Things had changed by the time we arrived in Brunswick. Something had gone horribly wrong. The only way out was to never touch that goddamn Ouija board ever again, and that seemed to have been a promise for which my sister found the resolve to keep.

As the story was explained to us when we caught up with Lisa, whatever was on the other side of the board wasn't one connection to another world. It was many. And it wasn't necessarily heaven, no matter what letters were spelled out. The fraternity showed one of the clergymen who worked at the college and after witnessing several exchanges on the board he put a stop to it. Lisa could never be certain who was doing the talking, but one thing became clear: there were bad spirits on the other side, those who would lie and trick you and try to turn your soul toward darkness and destroy your sense of self. They were monsters, manipulators, and they might tell you what you want to hear. Maybe this thing calling itself Amiel was really named that, or maybe that was a lie. But he was no guardian angel. He wanted to speak with me badly. He needed me. No one knew for what purpose.

That was our welcome to Lisa's wedding.

Now I understand that this comes across like a campfire tale. For those accustomed to reading horror stories, the tropes that are trying to be frightening on the page usually come across more like, "Hmmm, I get it. Yep, it's supposed to be scary." That isn't this. I saw nothing, not even the Ouija board (that thing was packed up tight). I had and have no proof of anything paranormal. But that isn't the point. To make the point, I need to explain the mechanics in the clearest possible way. The veracity of the events was unimportant. This demon wasn't the point, the point was my reaction to the story. I was an easily frightened kid with a highly active imagination. First I'd been told that a group of people had opened a portal to another realm and learned that I had a named guardian angel assigned by heaven exclusively to me. Later the other shoe dropped and it was revealed that the group was not talking to heaven and angels after all, but in fact communicating directly with hell and that one or more demons had been toying with them the entire time. And trying to get me to sit down for a talk.

This tale affected me. It was like something Shirley Jackson would've slapped together on an overlooked deadline. While I didn't believe in the supernatural on an intellectual level, my mind ran away with me at the slightest scary inclination. This was beyond any *Night Gallery* episode I could imagine. Ice chips rattled through my veins.

My fear was so urgent I was trembling. I could remember just what it was like to close my eyes in that rental townhouse on Pine Street, try to fall asleep after hearing my sister's story. Images of Dante's Circles of Hell danced on the backs of my eyelids. It was terrifying.

That's how I remember the master bedroom had that side window. I was almost old enough to drive at that point in my life, yet there I was climbing into bed with my mother because my sister had a ghost story waiting for me upon arrival. Cardboard and plastic and the possession narrative was all it took for me to look to Carolyn for protection.

I don't know if what Lisa experienced was real or not, but I could say with some certainty that the Bowdoin campus seemed ripe for haunting. Before the wedding was over, I would see a ghost. My father.

VOWS WE MAKE, VOWS WE BREAK

IT WAS BACK TO SCHOOL WEEK at Bowdoin, and due to the influx of people in town all the hotels around Brunswick were booked solid. Had been for months. I was lucky enough to find a motel twenty miles away in Lewiston that, for reasons unknown, had a vaguely Polynesian theme. This suited me just fine; a touch of the Lynchian at this stage in the journey seemed on point.

I woke up feeling somewhat better than I had the day before and decided to go for a run to help jumpstart my digestive system, which remained shaky in the shadow of that long Brooklyn night. Out behind the motel there was something that looked like an abandoned soccer field, but I figured I could get a better ambience with a little digging. After all, I was in New England. An online search turned up a nearby bird sanctuary, which sounded perfect. And turned out to be too good to be true. This alleged "bird sanctuary" was nothing more than a tangle of undeveloped land behind a grocery store. I stuck to the pavement. I would've been better off on that motel soccer field.

As I ran, I thought about my sister. In my family, you couldn't be in Maine and not think about my sister. The clearest memory I had of growing up with her was the time she found a baby squirrel that had fallen out of a tree. The poor thing had been injured in the fall, so Lisa, maybe thirteen at the time, brought him home. Over the next few weeks she managed to nurse the little guy back to health. When he was a hundred percent, she tried to return him to his tree. But the colloquial wisdom proved true; the missing time and scent of humans was too much for the other squirrels to handle. Lisa watched the others reject our guy. The squirrel was *persona non grata* in the nest.

So we adopted him. He lived in Lisa's room. But after a while, the noise he made at night began to grate on her, so she would put him in the bathroom when she went to sleep. One particular night, the latch on the cage door must not have been closed properly. The squirrel escaped, climbed or fell into the toilet bowl and ended up drowning.

That this was the most lucid memory I have of my sister has always been puzzling, but I've come to embrace it. Moreover, I've begun to get the sense that the squirrel story is the perfect metaphor for my life, though I'm still struggling to decode exactly how.

STEPHEN KING MAY be onto something: I came to Maine exclusively to reconnect to ghosts – one sent by the Ouija board and the two flesh and blood men that evaporated from my life.

Of the latter category, in an epitome of accidental symmetry, I had one photograph featuring both of them. Carolyn's single picture had frozen two marriages in time. It was a continuum, the yin and yang of the entire marriage bond... at least, the western concept of it.

Mixed Singles, Mixed Doubles

This picture behaved like a pair of bookends for history. It captured the first moments of my sister as a married woman. Simultaneously, it was the last opportunity anyone ever had to photograph my divorced mother and father occupying the same space. And I had no way of knowing, but it would also be the last time I saw my father in the twentieth century, and the second to last time I would ever see him at all.

So here we had a before-and-after portrait. Two marriages; one almost thirty years old and desiccated, the other fresh out of the proofing oven, raring to go, but destined for an off-the-road crash. What could I see in their faces about my sister's future, my parents' past? Nothing. Like the Kuleshov editing experiment in the early days of

Russian cinema, I'm destined to read into the images what I bring along from before. No, the photograph only shows the information – I can't even see Cyrus' whale belt from this vantage point.

The reunion of my parents was over in a millisecond. This came as no surprise, there was no end of animosity between the two. Standing next to each other for the first time since the divorce – they certainly didn't sit by each other during the ceremony – I remember feeling their mutual hatred pulse like a barometric pressure drop.[30]

Even though this book is about my mother, one of the things that pains me the most is that picture of my father with the receding hairline perm. It's remarkable how much I look like him, and seeing that made me want to leave it on the cutting room floor. He was younger in that picture than I am right now.

There was a part of me that blames my mother for falling for my father in the first place. And yet despite the fact that I'm stuck looking like him, I had to admit I've spent my life thinking that the kind of intelligence I possess comes directly from him. I hated that feeling, but I couldn't shake it. I saw even more of that intelligence in my sister, but also a lot of his tone deafness. That correcting people, quibbling over vocabulary, nitpicking because correct is correct. But also, taking some pleasure in the superiority. It was like a syndrome in need of a cure.

I figure that if this whole hair thing has this kind of effect on me, I might be a bit more forgiving when it comes to the fears, vocalized or not, that my siblings might harbor about this project. Yes, it could be that I need their blessing on everything that pertains to them. And who knows, maybe by the time you're reading this I've received that blessing,

---

[30] I can't remember the specifics, but it seems to me my mother made a point of losing weight going into my sister's wedding (not a rarity for mothers of the bride or the groom), but specifically to get the attention of her ex-husband. As if to send the clear message: look at what you threw away.

and anything you read about them has been processed, approved, and sanitized. But I doubt it. More likely, I've left some things out. Even *more* likely, I just said "Damn the torpedoes."

I WASN'T QUITE SIXTEEN the summer my sister got married, almost precisely the age my twins are right this moment, but I don't believe I comported myself as well as they do. Again, in my family there were not a lot of marriages, bar mitzvahs, funerals, or debutante balls to act as guideposts. I never understood my sister's reasons for marrying, in part because at the time I didn't have the proper angle of approach. At eight and a half years older than me, she seemed like an adult. But the other side of the coin, the ground level assessment, was different. I'd never known her to date during high school. She was in her room studying.

Cyrus was more like me than my brother; that was clear from the first time I met him. He was an avid reader and would become an English teacher and eventually the head of the English department of a famous New England prep school. He loved Hemingway, and though he had to coach as part of his prep-school teaching work, he was less a jock than a man of letters. He had the ultra-dry sense of humor you'd expect of a New Englander. He became an older brother, and he disappeared into the mist.

THE BOWDOIN COLLEGE QUAD seemed annealed against the passage of time; it was the only campus I've stepped foot on in the past decade that didn't seem to labor beneath a lock-down mentality, a keeping up of the guard – against active shooters, or really anyone who didn't belong. I'd have an easier time rolling onto the Paramount Pictures lot than I would trying to park at the University of Pennsylvania. But at Bowdoin, Longfellow's long shadow held the zeitgeist in a firmer grip than a Segway-riding security guard patrolling the grounds could ever hope for. I'd parked in a lot steps away from the quad and was genuinely surprised to find the car still there when I returned two hours later. And its windshield ticket-free, to boot.

It took me a little time to find the exact spot where the wedding picture had been taken. Mostly because I was working with trees that had grown, changed, or in some cases been cut down with just the stumps to guide me. Finally, I was able to use the background masonry to anchor things. In the picture it looked like statuary, but after some sorting out, I was able to make sense of what I had been looking at: it turned out to be the masonry base of a flagpole monument.

So I knew where the wedding took place, where the reception was held, and the direct route between the two. What had stayed with me through all the intervening years was the fact that the entire group – wedding party and all the guests – all crossed the quad together, heading from the chapel to the Alumni House where the reception was about to kick off. I tried to retrace the steps, but I couldn't make it efficiently line up with my memory. The Alumni House stood across a fairly busy street from the main quad, but in my memories, that road wasn't there. In my memory, it was almost a wide-open field between the Alumni House and the chapel where the ceremony had just been held, but from the looks of things here, that was not possible. A street had to be crossed, and it was lined with very old trees that weren't just put there last week. It was almost as if there was a field of battle that we had to cross to get to the *hors d'oeuvres*.

And the bar, of course.

This is how I remember it: a large group of people were moving across the quad, spread out like a team of volunteers combing a wheat field for a missing child. The people would shift about. We were walking, all headed to the same place, and I found myself separated from my mother. It was then that my father drifted over, sidled up next to me. I hadn't seen him in four years until that day, and even then it was from across the chapel. This was the first we'd spoken.

Dr. David had moved to Montgomery, Alabama, in the mid-70s – something about that state being one of the few that didn't mandate that doctors had to carry malpractice insurance. He'd developed a folksy southern manner in the intervening years and referred to himself as "a fugitive from Northern climes." When I'd last spent time in his company, it was because he'd flown me to Alabama so I could sit in the audience and see him play Harold Hill in *The Music Man*.[31]

MONTGOMERY LITTLE THEATRE
Presents
DAVID CONNELLY
In
Meredith Willson's
THE MUSIC MAN

Book, Music & Lyrics
by Meredith Willson

Story by
Meredith Willson
& Franklin Lacey

Produced & Directed by
ELIZABETH CRUMP
& BILL STRAIT

JUNIUS SMITH
THEATRE

July 15-17, 20-24, 27 & 28, 1976

*My Father,
Playing a Con
Man*

---

[31] I have to admit, the performance impressed me. We happened to have the Broadway cast album at home and when I returned from the trip, I began playing the record incessantly. This was the record I spun in sixth grade; not The Beatles, Creedance, The Monkees, or even the *Grease* soundtrack. I wanted to see if I too could memorize Robert Preston's con man patter like my father.

As we walked along, my father peppered me with questions. This was a classic technique; feigning interest would get me talking, thereby avoiding his having to answer any questions I might have of him. Anticipating my upcoming sixteenth birthday, my father seemed very interested in what kind of gift I wanted from him. Whatever I'd like; "blue-sky" it, dream big. Never mind that he hadn't sent me a present since the divorce. By that time, my best friends and I had set our sights on becoming filmmakers and had been working hard on shooting and editing our own movies for more than a year. The technology of the time was limited: Super 8 cameras were all we had to work with, but work with them we did.

Money, naturally, was always an issue. The Kodak Super 8 cartridges only held about two and a half minutes of film and cost real money both to purchase and develop. The cartridges and processing were the limiting factors in our film productions, and I told him I'd love an assortment of Super 8 cartridges. He mentioned what he knew about motion picture film, which, like most subjects, was some level of detail. ISO, speed, grain. Silent or sound, these kinds of things. He was a jack of all trades, and master of quite a few to boot.

As we closed in on the Alumni House, Dr. David shuffled off to the side, away from me, saying we'd talk more about the gift over dinner. "I'm going to send you a big box of film," were his parting words.

I headed inside. Waves of people were already in, more followed behind me. Everyone eventually made it to the Alumni House, and as the older, slower guests straggled their way across the finish line, it began to dawn on me that Dr. David wasn't going to make it. He never stepped foot in the Greek Revival-style building. He vanished from the wedding without a trace.

Dr. David hadn't had any intention of joining the family for a wedding feast. It became apparent in the post-mortem on our way home that he'd only shown up because his parents were coming and according to Carolyn, he'd always lived in fear of upsetting them. My father had his private pilot license, which was as clichéd a move as a surgeon could make in the '70s. And still today, I'd guess. He had his own Piper Cub and he'd flown it from Alabama to Maine – more than 1,300 miles as the crow flies – to spend roughly forty-five minutes at his daughter's wedding. I doubt he even had a hotel room. I believe he left the campus and flew straight back to Montgomery on an empty stomach.

My father and I would only see each other one more time. The next, and last time I would ever stand face to face with him, I would be the age he was the moment he disappeared from the Bowdoin campus.

I GOT DRUNK for the first time at Lisa and Cyrus' reception. I was unsupervised. I began the drinking because I knew no one would notice. I didn't realize it at the time; I stayed glued to an outdoor seat that overlooked a stream and drank, my lack of movement kept me from noticing the effects of intoxication earlier. It was rum and Cokes that did me in, a kid's drink. First run-ins with alcohol are notoriously rough, but add to that the fact that, like my father, I probably had next to nothing in my stomach – I was a picky eater and Maine was known for seafood, so there was probably precious little there to my liking – and I was a goner. I filled up on the drinks, the sharp alcohol taste I'd expected drowned by the soda's sweetness. There was a friend of my sister's from Syracuse in attendance, Militta Modesti, whose father was a neurosurgeon at the same hospitals where my father operated (doctor's children move in the same circles). I was friendly with her little brother, so I spent most of my time chatting with Militta as I downed one rum and Coke after another. Somewhere deep inside, I pondered my father's vanishing act, prodding it like a tongue exploring a bad tooth. If memory serves, it was Militta who scraped me off the floor at the end of the night.

   On the plus side, I was able to get to my own bed. Yes, it was a bed that immediately began spinning. But at least it wasn't my mother's.

NEEDLESS TO SAY, that box brimming with Super 8 film stock never arrived.

   Did I anxiously await my birthday, counting on that huge shipment with the Alabama postmark? Did I spend the end of that summer watching every UPS truck that went along our road, expecting it to stop at our place? No. The guy had vanished mid-walk. He wasn't about follow-through, he wasn't going to deliver. On that promise; on anything. That I nailed down in Brunswick in 1980. Like a guardian angel from beyond our world, he couldn't be trusted.

Your father and I won't tell the whole truth
Your father and I won't tell the truth

           – The Beautiful South
             "Your Father And I"

SIX

∞

INTERNATIONAL
AFFAIRS

POINTS NORTH

THE FIRST CAR Mary Jo and I ever purchased as a married couple, our wedding present to ourselves in 1996, was the forest green Audi Cabriolet convertible. We'd bought it in California, moved it to Pennsylvania, and held onto it for twenty years. At a certain point its value-to-repair-costs inverted, and it really made no sense to keep the thing on the road. And yet, we couldn't let it go. It held too many memories. So we kept it in storage, unregistered and uninsured. It was the kind of automotive cryogenics program that people who owned barns could pull off with little forethought. Finally, in a summer that saw construction of a horse ring and a down-to-the-studs kitchen remodel,[32] we added the Audi to the list of projects. Its restoration coincided with this late summer trip.

Everything had been working great with the car since it had been fixed up, except for this one outstanding, slightly unsettling issue: the **CHECK ENGINE** light had a tendency to blink on and stay illuminated after the Audi had been driven twenty miles or so. If I turned the car off and then back on, the warning would be gone... until another twenty miles passed. Based on a reading of the owner's manual,

---

[32] A misnomer; the house had been built of fieldstone, so every wall was two feet of solid stone and has no studs.

it was the oxygen sensor triggering the warning light. And I didn't know much about automotive engineering, but I was clear on two things: 1) the warning light pointed either to a crippling problem (faulty O^2 mix in the combustion chamber) or an insignificant issue (a faulty O^2 sensor), and; 2) it cost just as much to repair the sensor as the engine. The warning wasn't going to go away on its own, but that didn't mean it was accurate. Which one of those it was would make itself apparent one way or the other. Knowing this didn't make the travel any easier, though. The situation reminded me of the discovery of a heart murmur; it may well have been nothing, but once it was called to your attention, the natural by-product was stress. And if you weren't going to do anything about it except wait, you might be better off if you hadn't been made aware of it at all.

The uncertainty one has in a system's total reliability – mechanical or circulatory – was a feeling one could either grow to live with comfortably or not. It was hard to ignore, though. As I wound up the mountains of the Granite State, I was not expecting the Audi to give out, but I had mentally prepared for the possibility. The eventuality, really. I had come to terms with my car's mortality.

There was always an end to every road.

I SAW NO PERFECT angle of attack for my telling the story of Carolyn. The journey was an ascent, a climb no one had made before. Yes, there was an itinerary, a plan to the trip, and an assumed – or possibly the better word was *presumed* – shape of the narrative on the one hand. On the other hand, there was simply going to be what happened on the way, my reactions to it, my reportage. Time frame and place were locked in, but the route was murky. As in rock-climbing, one hand hold begot the next.

So while it made sense in the abstract to visit those places where I've always felt some event happened that galvanized my and Carolyn's relationship, I was also open, as I drove, to the possibilities of seeing other places. As a result, I delayed my arrival at an entry point at the Canadian border by a day, after driving west through most of Maine, New Hampshire (not far from the boarding school where my sister had her first job after college) and, finally, into Vermont. I decided to take a slight detour. On another project, I'd been working to obtain the life story rights of Warren Zevon, a brilliant musician, now deceased, who'd had a complicated relationship with fame. He was an idol of mine because of his ability to tell unique, pitch-perfect stories. Facility with story is the base unit of measure in my life.

Warren Zevon was one of the best; in a business overflowing with pabulum, his songwriting specificity virtually guaranteed career problems. But he couldn't change. Not a bit. Not if his life depended upon it (it did). So except for one accidental novelty hit he couldn't live down, Zevon was a relative unknown whose work was so transcendent that his songs were covered by people like Bob Dylan and Hank Williams, Jr. I thought there could be a movie in that. I'd been in touch with the songwriter's daughter Ariel, who led a complicated life herself there in Vermont. She had owned a restaurant and bakery but had recently packed that in for a catering truck. I'd called her when I reached the Vermont border because I figured there was very little chance that I'd be that way again anytime soon and thought a face-to-face-meeting might be valuable. Ariel told me she was working a music festival going on up on something called Dog Mountain in Saint Johnsbury and I was welcome to drop by there to say hello.

I found Ariel's food truck – the sky-blue trailer with roosters painted all over it was hard to miss – and she extricated herself from the grill long enough to chat with me. She introduced her teenage son, one of the twins that I'd known from my research were born the same year mine were, shortly before Zevon died. He'd been determined to stay alive long enough to meet the twins and succeeded. He was by all accounts a doting grandfather in those final months. The irony wasn't lost on Ariel, who had been treated mostly as an inconvenient afterthought by the same man. As a rock star, the title of father didn't factor into the mix. He had no rearview mirror.

We had that much in common, at least; fathers with agendas that didn't include us.

Looking around Dog Mountain, I spotted an older woman on a folding chair by a Ford F150. She was pretty far away from the food truck, but further away from the music and not even looking in the direction of the stage. It slowly dawned upon me that the food truck wasn't self-powered. It was a trailer, and the Ford parked there was the tow vehicle. Which meant the old woman sitting there was Ariel's mother. Which also means the ex-wife of Warren Zevon. That was Crystal Zevon over there. Why hadn't Ariel mentioned she'd come along? This was the woman who had first put me in touch with her daughter, the one who'd published *I'll Sleep When I'm Dead*, an oral history about her former husband.

I walked back to the car and opened the trunk. The bank box contained only one piece of non-Carolyn related material; my dogeared copy of Crystal Zevon's book. I had pursued Crystal relentlessly via email and text trying to secure the life-story rights and the film rights to that book. I grabbed it and headed back toward the pickup. Crystal saw her book from a distance, and sheepishly gestured for me to come over.

I introduced myself. "I'm the writer who's been bothering you about the dramatic rights to this thing," I told her as I handed over the book she'd written along with my pen.

Crystal knew. She remembered my name from my text. "How long has it taken you so far?" she asked.

"A decade," I said. I'd had to wait out Billy Bob Thorton, who'd acquired an option on the rights to *I'll Sleep When I'm Dead* before its publication. "But who's counting?"

Crystal told me that she admired my tenacity. I thought to tell her I couldn't help myself, because of the power of her ex-husband's music, but I caught myself. She knew him as a person, a troubled one at that.

When she asked why I was in the middle of Vermont, I told her that it was research for a book. I dreaded the follow-up question, bracing for her to ask me what the project was about. I didn't really want to tell a sixty-eight-year-old woman within spitting distance of her child that I was writing about driving around the northeast with a box of my mother's three-year-old ashes in the backseat, figuring out how to dispose of them.

But she didn't ask the follow-up. In truth, she didn't seem all that surprised that anyone would show up in rural Vermont. For a concert, for a gluten-free veggie wrap, or to look at the parade of canines on Dog Mountain. Crystal had already moved on. She inscribed the book for me, writing:

> *For Stuart,*
> *A fellow writer & traveler.*
> *Let the music show us the way!*
> *– Crystal*

BEFORE I LEFT, I stopped by the food truck and called out goodbye to Ariel, who was back at the grill.

"I met Crystal," I told Warren Zevon's daughter.

"Yeah, I saw." We both agreed she was quite something. Ariel told me she was taking her mother to Dartmouth Hospital the next day. Crystal been having some memory troubles and they were going to perform a battery of brain imaging tests in hope of determining the cause.

Here was this single mother of twins, self-employed in the food service business and a farmer besides, taking the time to advocate for her mother.

And it was then I realized that I harbored a secret. The situation was asymmetrical. We were both taking care of our mothers on some level that day, but I knew all about what she was doing, and she knew nothing of the boxes in my car. The box of pictures, the box of ashes. I tried to make sense of this person, this daughter of my idol, but Ariel contained multitudes. This was a woman who had been on the live Grammy Awards telecast *and* was serving cappuccino smoothies at a concert *and* was milking goats before sun up *and* was trying to keep her mother alive. I didn't know it at the time, but within three weeks she would be onstage with Jackson Browne, duetting with him on one of her own songs. Everyone was more complicated than they appeared. I had been learning that with Carolyn over the days, and meeting Ariel in person just underscored it.

I headed back to the Audi without filling in Ariel on the ashes or the journey. What would be the point? On the day before Crystal's brain exam, forcing a person into a discussion about the loss of a mother seemed cruel. Even by my standards.

I sat behind the wheel up on Dog Mountain and took in the American summer evening from up high. Vermont seemed as good a place as any to set up camp for the night. After a moment, I started the car and wound down the mountain, on the hunt for a place to stay for the night in Montpelier.

The **CHECK ENGINE** warning light did not come on.

THE NEXT MORNING, I reached the Canadian border, which had all the security of a turnpike toll booth. We had lived close enough to Canada that many of the local stores in Syracuse treated Canadian coins as American, although they never worked in any vending machines (an issue that caused a surprising amount of frustration throughout my formative years). But I have limited memories of Canada. One might think it would hardly seem like it was worth the stop, going in this huge triangle. But the truth of the matter is that even one memory, if it's clear, is worth the trip. If you think about your own life in relation to your parents, you may begin to realize, unless you're completely different than I am, that it is a smear of general feelings, but the specifics are few and far between. Mostly, like automobile accidents, the ones that are memorable are thus because some level of trauma slowed time down for us then and there, etched the details into the cerebral cortex. It doesn't have to be bad, of course (though that sure helps) but there must be some additional sensory data points, some electrical current that your average day-to-day activities didn't run. I had fewer than two dozen pieces of information, so chasing every one of them down felt important.

The woman inside the booth leaned out through the sliding window and asked me a couple of nonchalant questions without even asking to see my passport. Finally, just as it seemed as if she was ready to let me go, she asked, "Do you have any weapons?"

This was a tough question, because I'd realized moments before I pulled up to the tollbooth that I was in fact carrying one. In my messenger bag I kept a French folding farmer's knife. It had been a housewarming gift from my wife when we bought the farm, something with which to cut bailing twine or peel apples. I always remembered to take it out of the bag when going on a trip, but that's because I'm getting on an airplane. This road trip didn't fire the same synapses in my brain.

I told the border agent about the knife. She seemed cool with it.

"Is the blade longer than six inches?"

Not even close. A good sign, I thought. I didn't want to surrender the thing, it had a lot of sentimental value to me.

"Is it spring loaded?" she asked.

It was not. Another promising sign. I wanted her to understand just how harmless it was, so I asked if she wanted me to dig it out so she could inspect it?

Nope, she had no need to see it. Have a nice visit.

It was that simple. And nice to know our neighbors to the north felt comfortable with me slicing an apple on their green and pleasant land without fear of a terrorist attack. I would take their confidence in me seriously.

I asked her how far a drive it was to Montréal.

She had a number of brochures inside the booth and handed me one with some information about the province in French and English, as well as some basic directions. Underneath was the motto of Quebec: *Je me souviens*.

I never could understand much French and asked for a translation.

"I remember," the border guard proclaimed.

Perfect, I thought, and drove across the border. The farther I got away from home, the more this project ratcheted up in urgency somehow. I had just left the country with Carolyn's ashes in tow, and the clarifying strangeness of it all – life and death, childhood and parenthood, ceremonies and farewells, it all boiled down to Quebec's short, declarative sentence.

I remember.

GEODESIC DOOM

EXPO '67 TOOK PLACE in Montréal and it was apparently some kind of a big deal at the time. It holds the record as my earliest memory. It didn't have a lot on its heels, either, memory-wise. No close second place; I actually only remember one other thing that happened to me in the entire decade of the 1960s. I don't remember the moon landing, and that Earth-shattering event came along a good year and a half after Expo '67. But the fact was, for me Buckminster Fuller's dome became more of a mind sear than Neil Armstrong planting that flag on the moon. This told me something about the power of perceived scale, anyway. The moon may have been a massive celestial body, but standing before that two-hundred-foot tall geodesic dome in person made a different kind of impression.

The most heavily populated part of Canada was within easy driving distance of Central New York. In fact, Montréal was the closest A-level metropolitan city to Syracuse, nearer than New York City, which I'd always found a little strange to contemplate. One of the biggest cities in the world was in my home state, but there was one in another country that was closer. That didn't mean we visited there very often when I was growing up, however. Expo '67 was a unique circumstance.

In my memory I could picture the hotel suite – a corner room with two windows coming together at ninety degrees – and outside in the snow, like some disturbing ministry out of a science fiction film, loomed the massive silver Biosphere. It was all very David Cronenberg; still and stilted, antiseptic and silent, and quite Canadian. The only splash of color, sadly, was my own toddler vomitus. I was sick. Again.

I was a liability. It wasn't a pretty position, and I'm not proud of it, but it was the truth. I think even at that tender age, I'd gotten used to it. Throughout childhood, the image I carried of "self" had always been shot through with weakness, frailty, coming up short. Especially physically. I had a certain "can't do" attitude growing up, I suppose. As a kid I was sick all the time; trouble breathing, trouble seeing, just overall in trouble. My body sometimes felt like my arch enemy.

This was even worse than usual, though. Some kind of flu. Fever, vomiting, nausea, confusion. It had probably been cooking away inside me for days, but it caught up with me on the drive to Montréal, and by the time we'd checked into the hotel I was in the throes of real curl-up-in-the-fetal-position sickness.

My mother was insistent; the vacation had to be cancelled. My father couldn't believe this nonsense. Couldn't abide it. We had *just gotten there!* Besides, he was a doctor. Not the kind who could write a prescription that a Canadian pharmacy could fill, true, but a doctor nevertheless. He wanted me to stay in bed while the rest of the family went Expo-ing.

They argued, and as usual when it came to the children, Carolyn's relentlessness carried the day. The next morning my mother checked out while my father packed the station wagon back up in frustration. We left Montréal with Expo '67 entirely unexplored.

Now, standing at the base of what was left of the Biosphere – its exoskeleton – reliving that argument, I was beginning to realize that we three children were probably the wedge that cleaved my parents' marriage apart. Conflicting ideologies on how to raise us. Without us in the mix, my mother may just have soldiered on in a loveless marriage, but she was too tied to her own childhood. She deeply believed that kids should be kids, undoubtedly remembering her father going to bat for her on the roller-skates, motorcycles, dresses, goats and all the rest. She may not have wished for my grandfather's temper, but his way with kids left its impression on her parenting strategies. She remembered what it was like to be a child. How helpless the young are, how eager to please and most importantly how scarring the sharp tones and punishments of adults could be. Not my father. He had been brought up by a rigid German mother, so order and process and schedules were sacrosanct to him. For my mother, a child's right to run free was bedrock. Non-negotiable. Hell, she wouldn't even put a leash on a dog; there was no way she was going to let her kids be raised by a drill sergeant. How our father treated my brother, my sister, and me so tortured Carolyn that it gave her the strength to fight her way out of their marriage.

There is a sliver of a Bob Dylan lyric that's had its hooks in me over the years: *Staring into the vacuum of his eyes.* If this book were about my father, that could be the title. There was a clinical quality to everything about him, a dispassionate observer, amused at the pain of others.

There seemed to be no pictures of this charming man during our aborted visit here in the winter of '67-'68. That made sense, as truncated as it turned out. But among my mother's keepsakes, there was a photo of the Biosphere site after all. This one was taken less than eight years after the World's Fair visit,[33] and it should serve nicely as the introduction to a new character in the Carolyn Connelly drama: meet Tapan Sarkar.

---

[33] I could date bracket the picture because in May of 1976 the Biosphere caught fire and its Plexiglas shell melted away, leaving only the naked metal superstructure. It has remained uncovered to this day.

Fuller? I Hardly Even Know Her

At the time this photograph was snapped, the man in question was a Syracuse University electrical engineering student. It seemed that there were more surviving photos of Tapan with my mother than me with her. Certainly more than my father with her. There was a slew of other pictures of the man from India in Carolyn's possession when she died, shots of him throughout the years, but no matter when the shot was taken, the age difference between the two was always apparent. He may have actually been closer to my age than my mother's.

Tapan had been a fixture of my childhood. He was a gentleman friend of Carolyn's who, I'd slowly begun to realize, had a much larger footprint in Carolyn's life than I ever realized.

I'D KNOWN FROM THE START that this work, this thing I was planning on writing, was a feathered fish: half memoir, half investigation. Those can be very different pursuits, but what I knew they had in common was the fact that they both were narratives that had to be wrestled into shape. They both were bits and pieces that needed assembly. Both puzzles.

Tapan Sarkar was a puzzle piece that I hadn't placed on the board yet. I'd never even been able to gauge the general location. He wasn't a corner, an edge, part of the sky or bit of the horizon. No, Tapan was one of those off-putting puzzle pieces with the splashes of strange colors shot through so incongruous that you don't believe it forms any part of the picture and you suspect it might belong to a different puzzle altogether.

Until something clicks it into place and you can suddenly see the bigger picture.

CAROLYN MET TAPAN at the World Affairs Council, the perfectly mid-70s name for what would now surely be called something like the International Students Office. But like the clothing, make-up, discos and singles bars of the era, even the naming of college departments had a certain swing to them. The mission of the World Affairs Council was to offer a haven to Syracuse University's international students and help them with culture shock, with American social customs, with American educational system processes.

My mother was their director. I would have sworn that was where she flourished after the divorce, but upon checking the record against my porous memory, it turned out she'd started there before D-Day. Carolyn wasn't a working mother while she was married, and so I had simply assumed the World Affairs Council job happened after the 1972 split. But in going over the timeline with some detail and corroborating evidence, it appeared that Carolyn's work at the World Affairs Council wasn't a paid gig, so it must've played out more like volunteer work while she was getting her master's degree. This meant, and it was not a small detail, that Carolyn met Tapan while she was married, and not after as I'd always assumed. I had found pictures of Tapan in our kitchen with the barn wood walls and could scarcely believe it. He'd been around since before the beginning, it seemed. Coming to this fact was a little disquieting. It forced a shifting of perception that until now had been very tidily penned up. Perhaps Tapan was one of the causes of the divorce, rather than a simple beneficiary.

I've laid out all the information I could get my hands on. The order of events unfolded this way: in the early '70s, in an effort to be more stimulating to my father, Carolyn went back to school to get her master's in education. During that time, she volunteered to run the international student's program, which was so far off the radar that it didn't even have a paid position for its director. They were lucky to have her. She began hosting parties, first mixers to let the students get to know one another, then gatherings during holidays like Thanksgiving when campus would close down but most of the international students couldn't go home.

It felt like the United Nations Security Council to me. What I remember primarily from those get-togethers was dark skin with pops of color from saris, kurtis and head scarves. The aromas of food from far off lands – curry and Thai basil and garam masala. I heard of soccer being referred to as football back then, perhaps the first of my American peers to have that insight. Everyone was young and smart and polite and mysterious, and Carolyn seemed genuinely happy. Of course, she was the center of attention. And attention was a commodity that never accrued to her from Dr. David.

Early on, she met Tapan. At six-foot-six, twenty-five years old, with thick jet-black hair and a jaw so square you could crease aluminum siding on it, he may have been of some interest to Carolyn, married or not.

If she wasn't happy with her situation, she was going to get that way somehow or other. Water seeks its own level intrinsically. That's how Carolyn could be counted on to make herself happy. If the chosen man couldn't do it, maybe this man could.

My two children undoubtedly see me in certain light; they process their understanding of me through a very specific lens. They hold beliefs about my character that, sadly, will not be propped up by this book. I'm sorry, kids, but there was a real person who grew up to be your father, and it wasn't all smooth sailing along the way. That kind of insight can be unsettling. We are biologically programmed to interpret and project on our caregivers. I understand it; it was the way I looked at Carolyn.

But I've come to believe that the truth is more important than the illusion. Without the truth of our family history we find our own shortcomings overwhelming, because we are busy comparing ourselves to a chimera, not a flesh and blood human.

We can't help the biological imperative to assign perfection to our parents. It's their job to counterbalance it with some reality. Where this becomes difficult seems to revolve around the concept of secrets. And in particular, the hushed secret of shame. The disparity between the interpersonal and the solitary, between the face we have and the masks we wear. Who truly knows anyone? And to Carolyn, I think sexuality was a source of deep shame.

At one point when Carolyn was in her sixties and I was in my late twenties, she snapped at me because I was asking some deeper questions about her life than she felt comfortable fielding. She barked, "Do you think I never had sex after your father?" This came as a surprise, but of course it shouldn't have. This was my thesis here, rendered in 3D. Carolyn was a person, people like sex. Get over it. When she said it, though, over too much wine in a Fisherman's Wharf restaurant, the subtext was as unmistakable as neon; stop prying into my life.

But when? Where? With whom? I seem to remember the divorce lawyer taking her out to dinner a few times. She wasn't interested. She didn't date. She told me she didn't want to bring a man into my life.

But there was Tapan. He was around every weekend. They walked the dogs together, cooked together, gardened together. He went from being a student to a professor; Carolyn went from married to single. We moved houses. Things changed and Tapan remained a stony, taciturn constant.

One of the kids who my mother took in used to joke about overhearing Tapan and Carolyn having sex in the middle of the day. High comedy, primarily because of the absurdity of its underlying premise.

Now I'm not so sure. Consider this excerpt from a saved letter from India, hand-written with an engineer's precision on onion-skin thin airmail paper, dated January 30th, 1974:

> *I had met a lot of my old friends and they said **a lot regarding you**.*
>
> *Yesterday was a festive day in the sense that it was the day for worshipping the goddess of learning. So nobody reads that day and people enjoy themselves in different ways. I wish you could see such a gay (dirty!?!) Calcutta.*
>
> *There is positively something missing, which was there before. Not to mention I truly miss your company and your mere presence.*

It scanned as something more than friendly. But the secret of Tapan, if there was one, never spilled from her lips.

More paper she never thought I'd see extended the story for me, though. Other than notebooks and her paintings and sketches, there are probably fewer than twenty-five documents in the final toll of my mother's belongings. Birth certificates, report cards, diplomas, a few love letters, divorce documents, and a handful of news clippings (none of mine; I wrote features for her evening newspaper for a year). Now here we have one from an obscure publication – *The Asian Student* – dated January 20th, 1973 (the year my parents' divorce was finalized and a year *before* Tapan sent her that letter from Calcutta). It contained something meaningful to her beyond her vague interest in world cultures. From the "Customs and Manners" column is a full-page opinion piece. The title: "The Hindu Concept of Marriage."

"The Asian Student" Excerpt 1

Here's the question: did my mother find the strength to divorce my father because she thought she and Tapan would marry? *Were* they married, in some fashion that had never been made clear to us? Some way that Lisa, David, and I couldn't be privy to or understand?

This line that Carolyn underscored in the article really gets me: *Their love is a devotion, to be offered in secret.*

A secret indeed.

Whatever the relationship, a part of it was hidden. And that had to mean something.

Standing there in front of the Biosphere looking at their photograph, I couldn't help but wonder: do I have a step-father that I didn't know about?

There is one other way to interpret the saving of the article. Further down in the piece, Carolyn double-underlined another selection: *Hindus believe that running away from marriage is tantamount to running away from a battle*. Was Carolyn struggling with the idea of leaving her husband and researching the ideology of divorce across cultures? I don't buy it. There's no point in superimposing the keys to eastern ideas of marriage in a marriage of two Westerners. Once the divorce was final, why keep the article? And besides, the divorce decree was issued by the court in the summer of 1973, so the proceeding had been well underway by the time the article was published.

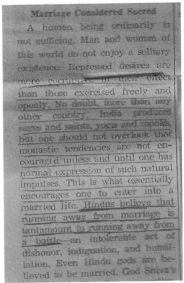

"The Asian Student" Excerpt 2

No, this was the work of someone studying a way of life they're considering adopting. The other line from the article Carolyn highlighted (albeit only a single underline) focused on the idea that in Indian matrimony, "Repressed desires are more corruptive in their effect than those exercised freely and openly... monastic tendencies are not encouraged." Was sex endorsed by the Indian culture, no matter what form it took? The article suggested it was the primary reason for marriage. So really, were we taking about an exploration of marriage or sex?

Now it became a question of whether Carolyn wanted Tapan physically and he was insisting on marriage first. Because perhaps she didn't underline anything. *Maybe it was him.* Maybe he gave her this article to say we can't be intimate unless we are married. Or maybe they *were* married in his eyes, simply due to the fact that they'd had intercourse.

Did I have a step-father I didn't know about?

I tried to imagine a situation where I believe my mother to be a single divorcee and that's what she wants me – and the world – to think, but inside she holds onto the truth: that she's actually married. Perhaps not in the legal sense, perhaps similar to the way nuns are "married" to Jesus Christ. Those who know *know*, but nobody's going around advertising it.

If the truth shakes itself loose years after the fact, who can predict what kind of collateral damage follows in its wake? Diving into a re-imagining of my fundamental perceptions, my anchor points on the way the world around me worked, was painful. The brain wanted to crack under the strain. Jack Nicholson was raised believing his mother was his sister and his grandmother was his mother. He didn't find out the real relationships until a reporter who was profiling him for a magazine piece told him. This took place a mere few weeks before Nicholson went before the cameras for the mental hospital drama *One Flew Over the Cuckoo's Nest,* and there was widespread speculation that the trauma of having to re-contextualize his family life in light of the revelation informed his Oscar-winning performance.

At least Jack got answers. He may not have liked them, and he may not have been asking any questions, but he learned the truth. I'd been left with puzzle pieces.

THESE DAYS, the entire park where the Expo '67 Biosphere was located had been turned into a museum complex dedicated to marine life and Canada's waterways. A large swimming pool area sat perhaps five hundred yards from Fuller's iconic dome. People were swimming while a construction crew roughly seven stories up worked with jackhammers, taking apart the enormous high dive platforms from the top down. It was like the dismantling of some sad Olympic village that had won the bid to host the games without understanding the costs that would put a strain on their economy years down the line. Perhaps they were merely being replaced, upgraded. I couldn't tell. To me, it seemed like the plowing under of history, one chunk of rebar-studded cement at a time.

Deconstruction.

I could dig that.

Harold Hill: *Mothers of River City!*
                 Heed that warning before it's too late!
                 Watch for the tell-tale signs of corruption!
                 The moment your son leaves the house
                 Does he re-buckle his knickerbockers below the knee?

                         – Meredith Wilson
                           "The Music Man"

SEVEN

∞

SORE EXCUSE
(AND SURROUNDING AREAS)

THRUWAY

Heading back across the border into New York State, it took significantly longer to get back into the United States than it did to leave it. There were more and heavier vehicles, and the border agents seemed less like toll collectors and more like soldiers itching for some kind of international incident. It was spitting rain when I finally approached the gatehouse. The woman who'd let me into Canada could have been a stunt double for the grandma in a Pillsbury biscuit commercial, but this guy – this clench-jawed solider – didn't have any softness about him. He flipped my passport open and shifted his glance between me and the photo several times.

"How long have you been in Canada?"

"About three hours."

The answer to the question regarding the length of my visit to our neighbor to the north didn't go over well. "Where are you headed?"

"Syracuse."

"Do you live there?"

"No, sir. I'm just visiting."

"How long will you be staying in Syracuse?"

"Four days."

"And the purpose of your visit?"

I didn't particularly want to say that I was bringing my mother's ashes back to dispose of them, because that might inadvertently bring up the slightly unclear question of whether it's legal to drive human remains across international borders. So I told the guard, "It's a homecoming."

He considered the data that I'd provided for a moment, then let me through. I was back on American ground and on my way back to Syracuse.

I LOOKED OUT over the St. Lawrence Seaway as I drove, catching just a sliver of the Thousand Islands. Despite the name of the region, there are actually *more* than one thousand islands along the habitable part of the St. Lawrence River that separates Canada from a cluster of northeast American states. It was one of the few examples of self-promotional restraint in our nation's history – possibly the Canadians were the ones who named the place. The Thousand Islands was an exclusive resort, a summertime playground community built around boat ownership. My brother, my sister and I all had friends whose families owned islands here, some going back generations. And my favorite college professor, whose philosophy was to only rent places to live so he could have the freedom to move anywhere in the world, owned only one piece of real estate: an island in the St. Lawrence. If you were from Central New York, the Thousand Islands was your Hamptons, your Gold Coast, your Santa Barbara.

There was a time when that river would've been my summertime backyard. The Connelly family was supposed to have a vacation home here. Early on after arriving in Syracuse, my father suggested to my mother that they buy one of the islands. At only a two-hour drive from home, Alexandria Bay, the gateway to the Thousand Islands right off Route 81, would've been a perfect summer getaway. And a hell of an investment, too. A $75,000 purchase in the early '60s could easily be worth three million or more today.

And if it's one thing I knew from my trip down memory lane thus far, it was that my mother loved the water. Beaches, waterfalls, streams, oceans. Even canals. All of it. Her idea of a good place for Thanksgiving was in the Virgin Islands. A beautiful river would seem to fit the bill nicely. It would've been her own Stillwater, following in Grandfather Black's footsteps. Water, I think, meant freedom to her. Nothing holding her back. An escape route. It was as if at any given time, if things got rough, she wanted the ability to simply untie and head downstream. There was a bit of Huck Finn in her, although she tried hard to keep that hidden.

That's why the Alexandria Bay decision had been such a mystery to me. Because Carolyn shot down the Thousand Islands house purchase. I would come to realize much later that the move was some kind of self-preservation. With my father's busy surgical schedule (real or created), he would only be available for a part of any given vacation – he'd "join you later," or "head back early" – and in the end, only a sliver of the ten days or two weeks would find him present. I didn't care, but Carolyn did. She didn't want to be on vacation without my father. She wanted him to want to be with her.

But even from a young age, I was under no such delusion. I can't speak for Lisa or David, but I dreaded the rare times I would see him in the house. (He was usually gone by 5:00 a.m. and not back until past my bedtime). Correcting my grammar with a sneer, poking a finger between my shoulder blades to force an improvement to my posture. I had felt my pulse tightening on the rare occasions I was told he'd be home for dinner. But of course, I hadn't fallen in love with him. I hadn't chosen him and then forced myself to find reasons to excuse his behavior. In other words, I didn't have to justify Dr. David in my life, so I could see him for what he was. And I didn't care for that.

I would've taken the island and the house on it, the latest Criss-Craft and sharp Canadian sun. And prayed for Dr. David to have back-to-back emergencies keeping him stuck in Sore Excuse all summer long.

But that was just me.

FUNDAMENTAL ISSUES

A STRAIGHT DRIVE SOUTH would've gotten me to my hometown in under two hours, but Syracuse would have to wait a bit longer for its prodigal no one. I headed southeast from the St. Lawrence border checkpoint instead, intent on a quick stop in Herkimer County first. Salisbury Center was nestled halfway between Syracuse and Albany, but the actual place I was looking for wasn't there anymore. The Pinecrest Bible Training Center closed up in 2010 and moved to Virginia, the entire enterprise a fugitive from northern climes. It was now a satellite campus for a private Manhattan high school, and looking all the lovelier for it. In 1988, when it had still been Pinecrest and the buildings all had the impermanent clapboard construction of a Catskills summer camp, Carolyn had spent three years living here. Now the grounds were better groomed, the masonry more solid, the lettering on the signs straighter. I wasn't sure how much bible teaching was done here these days, though.

Hand in hand with her love of the water, Carolyn had also always enjoyed communal living. In some ways a dorm worked better for her than her own house, possibly because it allowed her to abdicate maintenance and other homeowner responsibilities and just focus on herself and her relationship with the main man in her life by that point – Jesus.

∞ ∞ ∞

CAROLYN HAD BEEN RAISED Presbyterian, though her grand-mother on her mother's side took a few hard swings at turning her southern Baptist. Carolyn was a believer, but the temperance movement of the Baptists wasn't her speed. She liked dancing, cards, and drinking too much to fall into that. All three kids were baptized at St. David's off Maple Drive in DeWitt, our little bedroom community on the east side of Syracuse. I remembered going to that church semi-regularly when I was little, but there wasn't much religious activity in our house. A short recital of grace before dinner, church on Sunday, a before-bed children's book about Noah's Ark or Jonah and the whale rotated in among the Dr. Seuss classics. That was it as far as God was concerned.

I think my father was just keeping up small town appearances, but I couldn't swear to that. Somewhere he'd been quoted saying something like, "You can't be a doctor and not believe in the divine," but I knew him well. Nothing about the way he behaved was Christian. Carolyn hadn't seemed particularly devout to me then, but she clearly had a moral compass that had been passed down to me by osmosis. It was simple and definitely Christian, probably based around the Golden Rule: my mother was obsessed with fairness.

For a show-and-tell in second grade, a schoolmate brought in a toy Volkswagen. Bigger than a kid's fist, made of metal, detailed and cool. I loved its coppery paint job. The boy was a friend, where's-your-piano Ben, and I complimented him on the car.

"You really like it?" Ben asked.

I told him I thought it was great, and the next day Ben brought another one of those VWs to school. A brand new one, blue this time, still in its cardboard and cellophane display box. For me.

I was thrilled with the gift and asked him where – how –

he got it.

Ben told me. His house was an easy two-block walk to the P&C, a local supermarket chain. That's where he'd gotten it. Ben opened his Mighty Mac and replayed the transaction in pantomime. The circumstances snapped into focus for me. The kid had shoplifted the toy. Yes, as a gift to me. And yes, out of some sense of generosity. But still, the VW was hot merchandise. Ben was a thief. This insight both scared and pained me.

"I can't," I told Ben. My mother couldn't abide theft. Standing in the Moses DeWitt Elementary hallway I could hear her voice in my ears. It was a fundamental principle, predicated on fairness. She would've lectured me about the bond of trust between shopkeeper and customer if I'd brought the car home. She probably would've made me take it back to P&C. I'm not sure if she would've made me finger Ben as the man behind the crime, but it was possible. Not worth the risk, at any rate. I told Ben I couldn't take it.

I think he knew why.

Carolyn felt the world should be fair, and constantly seeing the world come up short, she at least expected the people with whom she interacted to act fairly. Among her papers, I found a letter written to Dr. David:

> *If anything in the past fifteen years means anything to you, please be kind enough to be fair. I can't seem to deal with unfairness in a Christian manner (maybe this is God's way of testing me).*

The last part was surprising, because over those years when my father was still around, I'd felt the family's commitment to religion receding. Church less often, grace becoming more *pro forma*. But that was before the divorce; afterwards something changed.

My father was far from fair. He calculated Carolyn's ability and stomach for retaliating and fought dirty. He hid assets, he used his upper-crust connections to get close to the bench, he played the aggrieved party. Every move pulled from the sociopath playbook and well-executed to boot. And when it came to paying alimony and child support, he made it as difficult as possible for Carolyn to collect. Her first job after the divorce, a job she had to take, was the circus ticket gig. The doctor's wife was reduced to taking in boarders, same as her grandmother. Two generations had passed without any tangible upward mobility.

Was it any wonder my mother felt rudderless? Was it any wonder she turned to God? She needed a source of hope, despite the facts in evidence. The salve of religion. She needed to believe that things would all work out, that there was a larger system in place in the universe that was going to tie everything together. That it wasn't all up to her to drag her three kids over the finish line.

In the midst of this stress and despair she became a Born-Again Christian. Studying the Bible in the beginning, then seeking the right church. It was a journey of self-discovery at first, but it wasn't long before she began to proselytize. To anyone whose attention she could lasso. Her non-believing son, for instance. Or her gentleman friend who happened to be Hindu.

IF I BELIEVED in God, I may have had some sense that Carolyn needed a funeral ceremony three years back. But I don't. As far back as I can remember, I would hear the religious stories, stories told solemnly and with authority... miracles and watchful loving God.

I was incapable of buying into the wish. That's how I saw Christianity; the it-would-be-nice-if-things-were-this-way wish. I kept my doubts a secret from Carolyn at first, but eventually it had to come out. I wasn't wired to swallow the Kool-Aid of any creation myth; perhaps life might be easier for me if I had been.

As I saw it (and still do) the actual problem with faith is

that it's antithetical not to how we treat the mundane but how we treat the crucial. The more important the proposition, the more we should embrace testing it with the rigors of logic and science. But religion says the opposite. Religion says unbelievable things are true despite the evidence of your senses.

Consider this example: the fate of your son who's running a low-grade fever isn't much in question. If a neighborhood psychic tells you to press cold spinach to his forehead overnight and the next day he'll be better, you might consider trying it. But if your daughter is bleeding from her eyeballs and her limbs are seizing, doesn't her fate seem more in play? Might you not call an ambulance rather than wasting twelve hours to see how the spinach works?

Why shouldn't we look at religion this same way? If you ask me to believe that your savings account balance totals $18,251.83, I have no reason to distrust you. It's an achievable sum, certainly. It's specific. But if you asked me to swear without a doubt that your number is the objective truth, I think it would be unreasonable to do so without further inquiry. We understand that implicitly. But if someone says there's a magic man in space who knows everything you or anyone else in the world has done and will ever do and you have to agree that that's true, there are plenty of people who sign on for that.

The demand for proof is the one thing that breaks it all apart. Faith is what you trust in despite the absence of evidence. It doesn't count unless there is mystery. Funny how that works. And convenient.

Born-Again Christians know their story as the truth and set out to save the souls of the people who don't see it. This is something I can understand: I'm not going to let one of my children stick their head in the roaring fireplace. If they don't believe me when I say that fire will burn them, I'll still prevent them from getting hurt. But the difference is, I can back up my belief on some plane of reality. If challenged about the properties of untouched fire, I could see my way clear to a demonstration with a candle or match that gives at least the suggestion that this invisible thing I'm claiming, this dangerously superheated air, actually exists. Furthermore, with a controlled and safe exploration of the process, I'd even be willing to let them attempt to prove me wrong. Let's see what's what. If it's a method at getting at objective truth, I'm a fan.

But I'm no fan of God.

By the time I was in ninth grade and the only child left in the house, Carolyn asked me to start attending church. I had no interest, and much of the fight was out of her by this point, so she came up with a deal. Some might call it a bribe, but to me it was a straightforward negotiation – what could she offer me in exchange for my commitment to attend services every Sunday through twelfth grade? I could pick the church, we would survey and sample until we found one that was a fit, and in exchange…?

The answer was at my fingertips: cable television. I even got her to throw in HBO as part of the deal. Soon enough the Cablevision "remote control," a brown box featuring a row of fifteen putty colored buttons with a wire running to the back of the television was sitting on the coffee table. Archaic technology now, it opened up a whole new world back then. Before long a 17-inch color TV appeared as well, the first new set in twenty years. At the Connellys it was black and white until I started tenth grade.

And I went to church, true to my word. I found one where I thought the pastor had some interesting things to say. I'd always maintained the part of the ceremony that changed week to week, the sermon, was the best part of any service. But it never changed my mind about God.

After I graduated high school and our deal was up, Carolyn went on to find another church. The one she felt suited her was far more fundamentalist, with the flock testifying from their seat or speaking in tongues as the Holy Spirit struck them. Some of the stories she told of that church made me feel she was walking the same path as the mother in *Carrie*.

I noticed all the clippings stuck to her refrigerator with magnets became Bible-related. Her hard turn into Christianity read like an act of self-preservation. Her qualities of mercy? She extended some, but needed far more from the universe in return. There was so much pain there, long plastered over with food and humor, but now even that wasn't enough. She needed additional solace, the cosmic kind.

"I'm an open book," Carolyn used to say, and it appeared so to everyone. Boisterous, merry, self-effacing, gregarious. But there was a hidden side as well, and actually *opening* her books started to shed light on the real story. Looking through her journals, it was clear that she had struggles she kept to herself. But she was definitely self-aware, and she wasn't so keen on letting people like me in on that fact. The journal proves it, though.

Among the entries:

> *I repent every day for a critical attitude, a lazy disposition, and not loving enough.*
> *I feel charged up but do not accomplish anything.*
> *We are all coming to the age of demise.*
> *I am consumed with myself (sin).*
> *I believe that my pride has brought into my life the isolation that I often feel.*
> *This wimp needs a sea of glass.*
> *My greatest sins are self-indulgence and a desire to be happy, content and to expect everything to go my way.*
> *Me, me, me – that combined with pride is a real affliction.*
> *In my heart I'm such a child.*
> *Thank you, God – what goes around comes around.*
> *Meaning my caring for my children and shelling out for them has paid off.*

NATIVE SOIL

SYRACUSE, NEW YORK... most of my formative memories spring from this anemic little city. I was an anemic little kid, so it all tracked. All of my friends from childhood had deep Syracuse roots. Bill's great grandfather was the chief of police sometime in the 1800s. Our friend Matt Bennett's father has been teaching at the University so long there might be a building named after him. But we were visitors. Out of my siblings, I was the only one born in the Salt City. Now I was really back in New York. Not the New York everyone pictured when you told them you were from New York, but the vast emptiness that totaled up the balance of the state. My destination and my goal, two overlapping but different concepts, were both within reach. The rubber was finally going to meet the road. Metaphorically, anyway. My wheels had literally been on the road for days.

The place was chosen as home base from a field of two – cities where my father had been offered a partner stake in a private plastic surgery practice. Syracuse and Washington, DC. This was before my time, and I wouldn't have had a vote even if I'd been around, but for the record, they should've gone with DC.

If they had, of course, everything would've been different. Geography may not exactly be destiny, but there is no possible way we can separate who we become from whence we came. I cannot imagine being from anywhere else. Period. That doesn't mean I like it, that doesn't mean I want to go back. But Syracuse is a part of me. For better or worse.

According to the family lore, my parents made this choice based on the quality of the Central New York school districts. Possibly. Knowing my father, it might have had more to do with; 1) the dramatically lower cost of living compared to the nation's capital, or 2) getting as far away as possible from my mother's family in Wilmington. Maybe a little from Column A and a little from Column B. There is also the slim possibility that, because my father specialized in reconstructive surgery, he believed he'd have a better supply of patients in Syracuse. Apparently, those suffering from a certain type or level of skin cancer around the country were encouraged to move to the Syracuse area because of its dependable lack of sunshine. I've always marveled at the ability children have to absorb any damn thing an adult tells them as fact. This has clearly been an evolutionarily advantageous brain function to keep little things from getting killed, but it has also created this unintended side effect: creating perfectly rational adults who have some tiny hidden brain distortions. A friend of mine was told by her father that the reason some cows face upslope while grazing and some face downslope was that some had shorter front legs and some have shorter back legs. These were known as north-facing and south-facing cows, respectively. It was all worked out by nature or God so that grazing took place facing uphill and downhill, so the herd could see danger coming from either direction.

This was absurd, just a little nonsense joke from a grown man who likely forgot saying it within moments. But my friend didn't know he was joking. It didn't come up again until the woman, by then in her thirties, was driving by a farm in California and looked out the window at some idling cows. She turned to her boyfriend. "Look, we got some north-facers."

"What?"

"North-facing cows."

"What?" he asked again, unable to connect the words to any concept.

She had to explain the *some cows* situation. "You know, some cows have shorter front legs and some have shorter back legs."

He looked over at her. "Who told you that?"

"My father."

"When did he say that?"

"When I was little."

After a long stare: "That's not a thing," the boyfriend told her. "There aren't... that doesn't make any sense at all."

And of course, as soon as he said it, the spell was broken. Some have shorter back legs? All of a sudden, as she processed the memory, she realized that for years she labored under this false belief. Not just wrong, but patently ridiculous. She wondered how many times she had mentioned it to others, people whose thoughts had run the same direction that her boyfriend's had but didn't bother to verbalize it, to correct her misperception. She had a blind spot, because a stupid trick had been pulled on a child too impressionable to understand or contextualize it.

And so it was with the skin cancer story in Syracuse, New York. I'd been telling the factoid to people for so many years that I was long past stopping to question it: Syracuse has so little annual sunshine that people stricken with severe skin cancer are encouraged to move there. It was certainly something I'd heard Carolyn repeating, and there wasn't any joke to it. And yet in the years since living there, I've been unable to dig up any evidence that it was "a thing."

In any event, Syracuse the town was what I knew growing up. All I knew. Huge snow drifts in the winter, muggy gray days of summer, not much to invite a kid outside. A city whose cultural significance begins and ends with a fluffy google-eyed orange in a ball cap and sneakers (an orange, by the way, that couldn't grow in the city's climate if you had Matt Damon's character from *The Martian* build a hothouse for it) has never meant all that much to me.

In fact, cutting Syracuse down has been a badge of honor, and it possibly may have been handed down genetically from at least one side of the family. Among Carolyn's meager saved clippings is a letter written by her mother-in-law to the local Syracuse newspaper, featuring this back-handed compliment: *Though some say Syracuse is a cultural desert, I don't completely agree.* Of all the hundreds of thousands of sheets of paper my mother dealt with in her life, I couldn't help but be continually surprised by which few she singled out as precious enough to keep. For a writer, it was simply a goldmine, a gift that kept on giving.

TO THIS DAY, nearly all my friends make the yearly pilgrimages back at Thanksgiving, Christmas time, or both. They might sleep in their childhood bedrooms in their parents' houses. If I went back, I'd have to get a hotel room. I'd been back only one time in this century, when a film I directed was chosen to screen in the Syracuse International Film Festival. It was the first time my children saw where'd I'd grown up, and it didn't disappoint. It was mid-April and it snowed.

Like nearly all of my friends, roots or no, I took the first chance I could to get the hell out of Dodge. Unlike most, though, soon enough I had no family ties to the area. Carolyn moved and once that happened, for me there was never much reason to head back. But here I was. It was a strange thing to need a hotel room in your hometown. It filled me with a profound sense of loss.

My first stop back was a trip to Lyndon Road, right on the border of two suburban towns that flank Syracuse, Fayetteville and DeWitt, to pay a visit to the house in which I grew up. I drove down the road where my first house sat, and accidentally went past it. It was, at twenty miles an hour, fundamentally unrecognizable to me. I circled back and pulled into the driveway. Same driveway I'd skateboarded down as a kid, back when the wooden boards were screwed to wheels that didn't have any rubber on them. It didn't look as steep as I remembered.

The mental timeline I'd carried around all these years didn't quite line up to the reality. I'd been telling myself we'd moved out of 51 Lyndon Road right after my parents' divorce 1972, but the divorce didn't get finalized until '73, and we'd stayed in the house for several years afterward. The terms of the split were hardly in favor of my mother (with her innate sense of fairness, she couldn't anticipate his pyrrhic need to win at any price, so of course he won), but among several poor choices, the most favorable was likely that she was allowed to stay in the Lyndon Road house in perpetuity.[34]

It turns out it was actually sold in 1976, so I'd lived there longer than I'd imagined. It shouldn't have been that hard to remember correctly. For one thing, in '73 I was either in third or fourth grade; my new house was walking distance to my elementary school, and I never walked to school. That meant I didn't leave Lyndon Road until I was in middle school, starting in the '75-'76 school year. The catch was, my memory of this house with my mother as a solo parent was

---

[34] My father was responsible for the mortgage payment, but upon the house's sale, any proceeds had to be split evenly between the couple. Dr. David resented Carolyn squatting there, sitting on the equity, and took to referring to Carolyn not by her name but the address. "What does Fifty-One Lyndon Road have to say about it?" This ugly pettiness, the smarmy depersonalization had a real Trump kind of feel to it. It was the "Low-Energy Jeb" of its time.

virtually a blank. I remember clear as day coming home from school when I was told that my parents were divorcing. That was the '71-'72 school year. (I heard about the impending divorce from another second-grader, Claudius Modesti, whose sister Militta was destined to watch me get first-time drunk at my sister's wedding). I went home and told my mother, of course insisting it wasn't true. She knelt down, held me by both my hands. and said that what I'd been told was the truth. The seven-year-old me burst into tears. But the thing was, what I actually felt was a sense of relief. I'd been pretty sure she didn't like my father around the house any more than I did. I was playing the role. I forced out the tears easily enough, but the truth was, I knew I'd be happier in this new reality. Like Carolyn, afraid of the unknown in our future, but quietly pleased not to have to deal with Dr. David any longer.

She moved houses for my benefit, not her own. It wasn't in her financial interest to leave 51 Lyndon Road, but there we were surrounded by mature families whose children were either older than me or already grown and gone. There were no neighborhood boys for me to play with, no potential to make friends. So we would leave Lyndon Road.

My FATHER DID NOT wear his wedding ring and watch on the right hand as a matter of course. Nor did his suitcoats have a right breast pocket. I'd found an 8x10 photograph of my parents holding my older sister as an infant that had been printed backwards, though no one through the years had apparently ever seemed to notice. This disconnect jumped out at me the first time I saw it, pulling it out from a jumble of my mother's other flat paper mementos. Though I'd read my share of mystery books, ("My good sir, clearly you didn't notice the way the tip of his belt angled off the buckle, pointing the way to a hideous discovery of the only left-handed suspect in the manse: our murderer!") and I wasn't looking for clues. No, it just looked weird.

The Mirror Image of Happiness

And to me it looked like an achievement in expressionism; we were an inverted family, and what you saw was likely the opposite of what you were going to get.

The fact that the mistake wasn't caught at the time of its printing (this was a mounted 8x10, certainly portraiture of a professional nature taken in 1957) spoke volumes to me about the viewers' state of mind. My sister was off the hook, too young at the time to critique the work. But the same could not be said for her parents. My sense was that David and Carolyn, Narcissus-like, were looking only at themselves, and even then only their chiseled features. Who would bother to notice what the hands were doing (or the hands of the watch for that matter)? It may've been nothing but a simple illustration of my parents' mutual self-centeredness, but digging a little deeper, I began to wonder if perhaps they just didn't care about the photograph at all. It came back from the photographer and it was put with the others. This was, after all, a time when perception of happiness seemed to rule the day. John Cheever, the dark underbelly heaving beneath the suburban landscape, *Revolutionary Road*, and that sort of thing. In which case, the picture was a metaphor for a '50s marriage: artificially posed, fundamentally wrong, and yet still unexamined.

There would come a time, though, when at least one of them would take a closer look, pick away at the veneer, and reflect – react – upon finding what lay underneath.

THE FIRST TIME I tried, no one was home at the Lyndon Road property. But I stood there on the porch regardless, struck with reverie.

I'd completely forgotten anything particular about the front door, but there was something to be remembered. Seeing it, the memories came to me; not so much in a deluge but with the bracing clarity of a clogged sink drain slowly backing up on you. The door: three giant circles carved into three stacked squares. Inside the wide circles were smaller concentric ones. Rings down to the center, which was a slightly protruding circle about five inches in diameter. I used to pretend to twist those center pieces as if I were cracking a bank vault door.

The sensation of child's play enveloped me, a longing as wispy and cool as dry ice fog. There was a time when there were no cares at all, when the external pressure and that internal voice of doubt didn't exist. I was accessing that state staring at the old door. That version of me that is so far gone. I wondered what Carolyn would've felt on a visit to 36th Street. Maybe the basement would've been the last thing on her mind.

Safe at Home

I jotted a note with my name and number and a quick sentence explaining what I was doing in Syracuse in general and at 51 Lyndon Road in particular and slipped it in the screen door next to a lawn services flier.

There were secrets inside. I could just tell. Maybe even answers. But apparently, they would have to wait.

STEP RIGHT UP

THERE WEREN'T MANY days left until my birthday, and I felt there were a lot of places to get to in Syracuse. I didn't want to waste any time. Even as night fell on that first day in town, I figured there was one thing on my checklist that would still be up and running. Since it was the last few weeks of summer vacation, I knew the New York State Fair was going on. It had run the last week of August and the first week of September as far back as I could remember.

When I was growing up I hadn't realized how special the State Fair was. Not special in the sense that it was amazing – it wasn't – but it was unique. As a child I considered it a local carnival, not realizing that it was the only one in all of New York State. This was a fact that one should've been able tell from the name alone, but through the lens of kid logic, because it was in Syracuse, I simply believed it was Syracuse's version. It seemed like Rochester and Albany and Ithaca all must have had their own state fairs. Even more amazing, and I didn't learn this fact until I'd already moved away, but New York was the first state in America to have a fair like this. The very first State Fair, king of them all, though the Midwest probably controlled most of the State Fair mindshare these days. But there were no other state fairs – not in Iowa, not in Wisconsin, not in Arkansas – until

New York showed the way. In retrospect, it seems like that might've been a bit of history worth promoting.

And there certainly was endless promotion. Billboards everywhere proclaimed, "The Great State's Old-Fashioned Fair." From the moment I'd stepped foot in Syracuse I'd realized – thanks to old time paste-up flyers – that the band Blondie had been at the fair a few days earlier, and I had the feeling that any and all the friends that I grew up with who still lived in Syracuse had probably hit that show.

After checking into the hotel, I headed to the fairgrounds in North Syracuse. The parking area was sprawling, elevated, and far enough away that the fairgrounds-at-night view looked pretty spectacular. The lights and sounds promised something I knew from experience the event couldn't really deliver.

CAROLYN HATED the State Fair. She found it depressing. And yes, depressing it was. Practically the mission statement of the endeavor.

The fair may have dredged up memories of those first harrowing days after the divorce, when she was dropping off thick packets of Shriner Circus tickets along Syracuse's panorama of low-slung office buildings. From doctor's wife to broke in six months, Carolyn made the best out of acting as a bagman for the Shriners. I went along on her circus tickets rounds one day; probably I was sick and too young (read: afraid) to stay home by myself. I remember the first stop, some insurance agent's place. Typically these people bought a block of tickets as a charitable donation and gave them to their employees as a little perk. The insurance man took the tickets and decided to hand me the money. The math was simple: tickets were five dollars, she'd given him twenty. I took the cash and, turning away from the man, quietly counted it. My instinct was not to offend by behaving as if I didn't trust this businessman. However, being a businessman, being a big fish in a small pond… hell, being a man in the 1970s, he took the opportunity to teach this woman and her kid a lesson.

"He should've counted that," the insurance agent told Carolyn. Then he looked at me. "You count money when someone gives it to you. So you know that you didn't get cheated."

Carolyn swiveled toward me, finger aimed in judgment. "Stuart, the man is right. You *always* count the money."

Now, it was one thing to get berated for something you didn't do, but to have your mother take the stranger's side? For a sensitive kid like me, this was disastrous. I didn't defend myself. I just stood there, head hanging, fury impersonating shame.

When we got back to the car, I erupted in tears of self-pity as I climbed in the passenger seat. "I *did* count it!" I shoved the twenties at her. "I did it so he wouldn't see. I'm not stupid! I was trying not to hurt his feelings!"

"Oh honey, I'm so sorry."

The drained shock playing on my mother's face told me the story. She *was* sorry. If I'd ever doubted that Carolyn had been a kid herself almost a century ago, one playback of this memory should've clarified things. Because she had the horrified look of a person who'd been humiliated by her own parent and knew just how it felt.

So, STIPULATED: the State Fair *was* depressing. But worse than that, it had lost a lot of the seediness that it had in the '80s. The freak show had fallen to more compassionate culture (*au revoir*, Human Nailhead and Otis the Frog Boy) and the outright cons of the midway games of "skill" were policed a bit more heavily these days. But the fair hadn't been much fun back when those things were around, either. We weren't looking for fun, exactly; it had been more of a late-summer time killer for teenagers.

There would usually be at least one decent band to see (even though it was outdoors and during the day) and since a ticket to the show got you into the fair, there would be one day spent there for certain. And because it took place around my birthday, my friends often took me to the show in question to celebrate. But the most indelible visit happened with Carolyn, when she brought the family to the State Fair.

I was afraid of the rides, naturally, and so we were somewhat split up, with my mother and I stuck together. Lisa and David went their separate ways, with my brother heading right for the midway.

At the time most of the carnival games were not completely rigged against the player, but engineered to be much harder to win than the barkers made it appear. On the knock-down-the-milk-bottles game, for instance, the bottles weren't glued into place, but they might be bottom-weighted to prevent them from tipping over very often. This meant that on occasion some sucker would actually win. This was the case with my brother David, maybe fifteen at the time, who had a pretty good fastball. Much to this particular carny's chagrin, David won the top prize. Pick anything you want, that had been the come-on. Step right up. Surrounding the game booth were dangling stuffed animals, but the one David wanted wasn't dangling; it was the biggest one they had, a six-foot-long long red snake with big happy eyes. There was one strung above the awning of the trailer, draped over the five floodlights pointed up to illuminate the booth's sign.

Technically it was a prize all right, but it actually was just bait – hypothetical winnings to attract players. To be seen from across the midway like a beacon. Never meant to be claimed. The man reached up with a stick and detached it from its perch.

When we reconnected with David later on, he was grinning and clutching his hard-fought prize. Everyone thought it was a tremendous achievement. Except...

"What's that?" Carolyn barked. She rotated the snake in her son's hands slightly. On the belly, there was a scorched mark, a thick ribbon of brown smudges.

"It's just a mark," David said, a little embarrassed. Because he knew what had happened.

"I can see. Did you notice it before just now?"

"Yes," my brother said. "I told the man it was burned. He told me that was what I won."

"Uh-huh."

"I could take it or leave it."

"Uh-huh." There was a long moment. Calculating. I'd seen Carolyn's pupils pinpoint down like this before. When a certain kind of "take no prisoners" emotion kicked in hard, her facial features changed. Through clenched teeth she said, "Show me where he is."

ONE THING I KNEW for sure about my mother, she had a real problem with people taking advantage of the weak. She had been a champion of the underdog as long as I could remember. Despite the fact that she was often the one outmatched, she rarely reacted to her own challenges with the same fury that with which she solved others' problems. Perhaps the solutions were clearer from a third-party perspective.

She'd done it for me before, when I was very young and she was trying to teach me how to make purchases in a store sometime after the Shriner Circus ticket fiasco. She wanted me to get experience with ordering, paying, getting change. Unbeknownst to me, the site chosen for the lesson was Snowflake Pastry Shoppe, an old-fashioned, from scratch kosher bakery on the east side.

The building was long and flat with nothing but glass for a front and all the parking spots lined up. We pulled in out front the way we always did, but this time Carolyn turned to me, handed me a five-dollar bill and said, "Get us a dozen bagels, Lollipop."

I got out of the car, went inside, and took my place at the end of a short line. Carolyn sat behind the wheel and waited, but she could see through the window wall that I wasn't moving with the line. People kept coming into the bakery and the person behind the counter kept waiting on them instead of me. Carolyn watched and waited for me to do something for myself. But she wasn't going to wait forever. And because this fairness thing was an issue with her, eventually she was forced to act. She got out of that car and yanked the door to the bakery open. I turned and saw her as she pushed past the crowd, went right up to the woman at the register, went face-to-face. "What's the matter? Isn't his money good enough for you?"

The woman flushed red and stammered. Carolyn looked at me like a stage mother – time to go on.

In my smallest voice, I managed to croak, "I'd like a dozen bagels…"

THE EMBARRASSMENT I had felt at Snowflake was the precise kind that I knew David was experiencing at the fair as we approached the midway. The feeling of loss of control over how strangers would perceive you.

My mother had the snake by its tail, dragging it across the asphalt. The lights across the bottom of the booth's sign were unadorned, and Carolyn could see exactly where the snake had been stationed and what had caused the burns along its furry body. She spotted the spindly carny behind a wide counter that had small trios of baseballs lined up across it, each a set up for a different sucker.

"Is that him?" she asked.

My brother nodded.

As Carolyn made her final approach, she wound up with her right arm, spinning the stuffed animal like a bola. She finished by snapping it down in front of David's carny. The head of the snake landed on the countertop with a surprisingly solid *thwap*. Its googly-eyes bounced around with the impact. The baseballs scattered, rolling back into the booth and out into the busy walkway.

Carolyn's lips parted, but her teeth remained zipper tight; she might've been doing her best Clint Eastwood if she'd ever seen one of his films. "I think there's been a mistake," she announced.

The carny looked to the snake, to my brother, then to Carolyn. No doubt he ran quickly through all the options in his head. Finally, he said, "Gosh, how did that happen?" innocent as a choirboy. Then to David: "Let me get you another one, kid." There was a smile, but his eyes were shooting hatred at the tattletale. The kid hadn't been cool; the con artist was.

Still, he bent underneath the counter, and out of a beaten cardboard box, the carny produced a replacement snake. This one was sheathed in a clear protective polyethene tube. It was deeper red, not the sun-bleached brick color. And of course, it was burn free.

I can't seem to deal with unfairness in a Christian manner, Carolyn had once written. In this Year of the Snake, in fact, she had probably jotted it quite recently. I would go on to tell this story at my mother's retirement party in the early nineties and get a lot of heads nodding in recognition. It wasn't my story to tell, really; it was my brother's. But when the call came for anyone in the crowd to say a few words on Carolyn's behalf, David and Lisa demurred.

Okay, that's reasonable enough. I'm the storyteller of the family.

But if so, then I get to pick the stories.

Fair is fair.

MOMMY'S ALRIGHT

SYRACUSE WAS SMALL, but there was never a shortage of places for teenagers to get into trouble.

As a member of the class of 1982, I grew up linearly, in an analog world. We were the last generation of kids forced to create our own fun that had no pixels. Broadcast TV programming had only a few things of any interest, which played at specific times, and when the shows we didn't like filled out the programing blocks, the only alternatives were making our own fun. Hence the Super 8 productions. RCR Productions, which stood for Rapp, Connelly, and Royce. I was fortunate to find a pair of friends who were smart, funny, and loyal. Maybe they had their own deep-seated issues, and that feeling of seeing yourself reflected in another was what brought us together. If so, their troubles weren't apparent. I know that I saw them in very kindly lit, broad strokes.

Mike Royce was the cautious one; whatever trouble he might get into, he was led down that path by me. He saved the money from his crappy afterschool jobs. He was raised Catholic and the values took root, even if the religion didn't. He did his homework, he told the truth. Out of the three of us, only Mike had both parents in the home. A fact that summed him up nicely: his self-assigned stage name in our band was Records and Research, off of the character from the not-great *Hardy Boys* rip-off book series *Alfred Hitchcock and the Three Investigators.*

Bill Rapp lived across the street from me after we moved out of the Lyndon Road house. He was more headstrong than Mike. A rebel down to the bone, Bill had a confrontational attitude and interest in trouble-making that would lock right into the burgeoning punk rock movement. The early '80s were free-range enough in general for kids, but for me and Bill, children of divorce, perhaps even more so. Bill was the son and namesake of a big-league businessman, a car dealer with commercials airing and his name plastered to the rear of one out of every ten cars driving around Syracuse.

We were each a different reading on the outcast scale – Mike had his tight connections to the theater kids and Bill was plugged into some of the sports – but basically, we had only each other for any meaningful friendship. And we made a childhood with all the adventure you could pack in. It was as if we were living out Netflix's *Stranger Things* the entire time, minus the alternate dimension with the interesting things going on. The sense of freedom was similar. No one knew where you were when you were gone. Gone meant freedom, gone meant the buzz of slightly dangerous fun.

What did I try to get away with? You name it, I tried it. Carolyn was stressed and distracted during my high school years, and I took full advantage of that situation. When she went out of town for the night, there was no question if I'd be throwing a party. If she went to bed early on a Friday night, I might be taking the car without asking.

Our Super 8 movies gave us good cover for breaches of the public trust. They acted like an umbrella for any odd thing we took on throughout the years. Weapons, drugs, all manner of contraband was hand-waved away under the heading of "Movie Props." Carolyn undoubtedly was too exhausted to investigate; she did not have the bandwidth to keep track of what I was up to in those years when I was the only child at home. We managed to hide the illicit in plain sight like Hollywood. This movie business papered over a lot of sins.

The evidence might paint a different picture, but I was a decent kid. Most of the trouble we got into was innocent enough. There wasn't a mean spirited bone in our three bodies. I think, because we'd been picked on (a softer term to describe bullying, no doubt, but one that felt closer to the truth) the three of us had real empathy. There was one exception, one that either proves the rule or calls it entirely into question. When Carolyn discovered the transgression, she was furious with me. She thought it was downright mean, but we thought we were providing entertainment.

PERHAPS BECAUSE WE could make movies, a form of magic in those days in many people's eyes, my neighbor Mark Petty might've thought we were capable of anything. Even spaceflight. Mark was the son of a single mother who it seemed was struggling to make ends meet. He was the classic version of the troubled kid, never looking particularly put-together or cleaned up. He was the same age as Bill's youngest sister Jill, and he craved attention and friendship from the kids in the neighborhood. We would put up with Mark for a while, but always wanted to be able to extricate ourselves when we grew bored of hanging out with him. The method we cooked up for this was convincing him there were evil *doppelgangers* of each of us, so at any given moment we could decide to reveal we were clones and chase him away.

One day we decided to take the craziness up a notch. And we had the perfect prop for the job. When Bill was a toddler his father had made a rocket ship for him out of various sized metal drums stacked together. This was how it looked the Christmas Day it arrived:

Apollo 17 Before the Launch

Bill's Apollo 17 had been sitting unused in his stepfather Bernie's workshop for years when we decided there had to be some way to have fun with it. We immediately thought of Mark. Could we convince him to take it for a test drive? It was a blend of our interest in storytelling and our deep love of the elaborate con.

It took a few days of planning to get hold of some walkie-talkies and the other gear we'd need. "It's for a movie," our standard refrain was spit out quite a bit. Finally, we were ready to approach the sucker. We told Mark Petty we had a mission planned, but after some careful new calculations, it was apparent that none of us three were light enough to do the job.

Did he want to volunteer for the sub-orbital flight to test our rocket? By god, he did.

He seemed to trust we'd be able to strap him in a rocket and safely launch it. Looking back, I would have to ask myself a question. Was it possible that Mark was simply playing along with us? I mean, he wasn't stupid. We may have been older than him, but he knew we were kids too. Did he pretend to believe? Or did he believe because he wanted to so badly?

The next day the Apollo 17 rocket was out in Bill's driveway. There was a hatch on the bottom drum, which we opened in solemn ceremonial fashion. We gave Mark one of the walkie-talkies and saluted him. Then we crammed him inside and sealed up the hatch with thick layers of duct tape.

There were no lights or windows in that tin can. Not even a fake wheel or a joystick. We hadn't promised him he could pilot the thing; we were Mission Control and would handle all that. Mark just had to take the ride.

This wasn't Disneyworld; our special effects technology was limited. We had a cassette playing rocket noises and two of us shook the capsule violently side to side, spinning it on edge while the third one radioed in with "How are you holding up, Mark?"

He said he was doing alright in a cracked voice, but he sounded panicky enough to make me think he believed.

It wasn't long before we had to warn him of an impending meteor shower. "It's looking like ninety seconds away." The anticipation was part of the effect.

"Is it going to be bad?" Mark moaned.

"We'll see." We counted down over the radio and then began lighting the variety of firecrackers we'd taped haphazardly around the edges of the fuselage – *pow pow pow!*

Then next phase was off-script – serendipity, as I remember it, Bernie walked past and saw what we were doing. We hushed him with a finger to our lips. He was used to this; we were always trying to keep people from walking into the shots of our movies. Bernie could often be found around the house on a work day as he was self-employed. Because he was a contractor who hauled around all kinds of equipment, he drove a pickup truck. The three of us locked eyes, sharing the same idea. While Mike and I were rattling Mark around by hand, Bill ran up to Bernie with the request: any chance he had a few minutes to help out?

Bernie was game. We let Mark know we were changing the trajectory of his flight and the four of us worked the rocket into horizontal position and into the bed of the pickup. Bernie headed slowly for our old middle school a couple of miles away while Bill, Mike and I stayed in the bed, working the capsule side to side and checking in with Mark on the radio the whole way.

"We're tracking you on mobile radar," I shouted into the walkie, "We have a chase car. We're not losing you." The very statement probably injecting a fear of being lost into him he hadn't previously had. "Repeat: we're not losing you."

It was summer, and we knew when we got to the Jamesville-DeWitt Middle School we'd find it a ghost town. Bernie backed up at the far end of the empty parking lot and we hoisted Mark's rocket out. Beyond the concrete parking blocks there was a steep grassy drop, perhaps thirty degrees, down to a drainage basin twelve feet or more below.

"Mark, you're heading in for a crash landing!" Bill shouted into the walkie. "Brace yourself!" And we pushed Apollo 17 down the hill. A kid that we had literally sealed inside a 55-gallon steel cylinder went spinning away from us, and we were all good with that decision. The rocket rolled smoothly at first, but as it picked up speed it developed a head-to-foot wobble like an out of balance washing machine. It was bobbling severely before it hit bottom and came to a hard stop on top of the drainage grate.

The three of us kids ran downhill after the rocket; Bernie moseyed behind. We ripped off the duct tape and yanked open the rocket's door.

There was Mark. He extended two arms and as he pulled himself out, it was as if the ship were birthing the kid. Mark was slathered in sweat, squinty-eyed and confused. He blinked in the brightness of the earthbound day.

Mark looked at the three of us, and then the adult right behind, grinning. Maybe it was the adult that sold it. Maybe it was the unfamiliar field where he found himself.

We smiled at him.

Mark grinned back. "Was I... in space?"

"Without a doubt."

I STOOD ON THE CREST of the hill where we'd crash-landed our young neighbor. It was summer again, a summer far removed from the Apollo mission. The parking lot remained empty, the grate over the drain still oxidizing in place. I remembered Carolyn being upset with me when she found out about the rocket launch, but I couldn't recall whether she'd forced me to apologize to Mark or not. I also can't remember if Bernie's involvement made her more or less angry.

But it wasn't like he was the only adult around to have a bit of mischief inside. Not every questionable endeavor of my childhood involved an end-run around on Carolyn. Many included her. In fact, she was the architect of some of them. I had to get the hell-raising gene from somewhere, and Dr. David was all about following the rules. Of grammar, of table manners... of everything except paying taxes. Carolyn wasn't a rule follower *per se*.

She didn't go out of her way to cause mayhem, but she let her own internal moral guidance system take precedence over any rule book. That led her into some interesting situations.

For example, my mother was the one who introduced me to Brickyard Falls.

She appeared in my room one day and told me to get my

bathing suit on. "I have something you're going to love," she told me. Her eyes sparkled the way they always did when she was misbehaving just a little bit.

We drove to the next town over, Manlius, and parked on a residential street. We walked between two houses and into the wooded area beyond. From there it was a half-mile hike down to a secret: an isolated swimming hole cut beneath a fifty-foot cliff upon whose face a hard curtain of water cascaded down. The spot was perfect in every way save one; it was all on private property. We'd passed a half dozen NO TRESPASSING signs on the way in, but Carolyn wasn't deterred. We swam together, and the time we spent there that first day was magical. I felt like Tom Sawyer frolicking on some hidden tributary of the Mississippi.

The next chance I got I showed my friends the secret place. And before long, Brickyard Falls became our go-to spot for swimming.

It was impressive how cool Carolyn could be, when the winds were blowing just right. (Cool as filtered through a teenager's perception of the world, naturally – a contemporaneous parent might have labelled her behavior irresponsible.) I'd be hard pressed to find another mom who would be the wheelman for this next kind of caper.

It all started with *Mission: Impossible*.[35] Bill and I were both tremendous fans. What we thought was so cool about the TV show was the patter, the act of talking your way into and out of danger. Getting in disguise and diving headlong into unpredictable. We thought it was smart. We thought

---

[35] For the record, mentions of *Mission: Impossible* refer to the syndicated re-runs of the hour-long late '60s-early '70s CBS Peter Graves spy show, not the Tom Cruise action movie franchise. There is an enormous difference. The show was entirely focused on the disguise-based con games with international stakes played out by the U.S. Government, while in the films, the cons are basically window dressing for a more traditional action-based spy thriller.

outsmarting people was smart. We wanted to try it in real life.

It should go without saying that there would be a vast difference between *Mission: Impossible* in reruns and *Mission: Impossible* in real life. Still, I had it in my head that, under the right circumstances, we could pull off something like what the Impossible Missions Force did every episode. The circumstances were nothing but a random opportunity; the band Cheap Trick was coming to Syracuse. The reason presented itself in the form of a bet. On impulse and without thinking it through, Bill and I bet our friend Gerry Vogler that we could talk our way into the concert without buying a ticket.

I don't know what it was about the idea of making a bet over something we had no idea if we could pull off that drew us in. It wasn't high stakes... at least, the terms of the bet were not. No money for the winner, just bragging rights if we succeeded, mockery if we didn't. And it wasn't because we couldn't afford admission. Tickets to national acts were likely in the eight-to-twelve-dollar range at the time. The money wasn't the issue; we liked the challenge. That would've had to have been the case, because in the process of saving the ticket fee, Bill and I spent all our free time for about a month working on our con game strategy. Even as low as minimum wage was back then, we could've earned the money in a single after-school shift. There may have been real stakes up ahead if things didn't go our way, but that wasn't how I thought at that age. The prefrontal cortex hadn't finished its job filling in its jigsaw position in my brain.

The grift we came up with was simplicity itself: Bill and I would pose as beer deliverymen and hit up the backstage door. "Where does the beer go?" Once inside, we would make a wrong turn and head into the crowd instead of back out the way we'd come in.

There were a few problems with this approach. First of all, we looked nothing like deliverymen. We were scrawny teenagers. We barely even had to shave. Then there was the transportation issue. Beer deliverymen had beer trucks. We weren't even old enough to drive, and even if we could, we had no access to a box truck. Beer deliverymen also had beer. This was key, non-negotiable.

But we were determined. We couldn't buy beer (and wouldn't have wasted the money if we could), but we had ready access to the empty bottle boxes. They threw them out at The Dark Room, a bar on East Genesee Street less than a quarter mile from where we lived. These were heavy cardboard and minimal printing, made for the trade and not the consumer. So we would be lugging empty boxes to the War Memorial, miming their weight. There was a product back then called a beer ball, which was a kind of disposable plastic draught beer system about half the size of a pony keg. They came in boxes that were supposed to be filled with ice when the ball was tapped, so when we got ahold of an empty beer ball box, we knew that was the crown jewel. It would sell the illusion. What self-respecting rock band wouldn't want to tap a beer ball after the show? Additionally, the beer ball box gave us some room. Inside it we had our change of clothes and, most importantly, Bill's 35mm Minolta camera and lenses. In that era, concert photos were a precious commodity, something the bands could monetize, and no cameras were ever allowed inside the venues. They frisked concert-goers at the door to keep cameras out. But Bill and I, we'd be able to shoot photos at the show.

Uniforms and transportation were the real problems at hand. But I knew who could solve them, if she were so inclined. So I explained our plan to Carolyn in detail over dinner one night and closed by asking for her help. Was it a criminal enterprise or just a couple of kids using their imagination? Either way, she was in. We'd purchased light blue chambray shirts and large Miller Beer patches, but we couldn't do a decent job of sewing them on. No problem,

Carolyn took a needle and thread to them.

And we had to have someone to take us to the stage door. We needed a drop off and a pick up a couple hours later.

"Or someone to bail you out," Carolyn offered.

The evening came, which was likely May 9th, 1980. I could pinpoint the year because the kid we made the bet with was a senior when we were sophomores and would've graduated in 1980. I could pinpoint the month and day because that's the birthday of Cheap Trick's bass player, Tom Petersson. The cool rock radio station 95X had made him a ten-foot tall birthday card that they left inside the entrance for concert-goers to sign as they made their way to their seats. Ticketless, Bill and I didn't get a chance to sign it there in the lobby though.

The OnCenter War Memorial Arena's stage entrance was just off the main road. Carolyn pulled up around the corner in the station wagon. Bill and I hopped out, our work shirts mushrooming out from our 22-inch waist Levis. We opened the back and took out our boxes, stacking them in our arms and holding them from the bottom. We strained as if they had some weight to them. The *pièce de résistance* was the clipboard. We'd tricked it out with a delivery form we'd made at the library Xerox machine – preprinted addresses on the left and a corresponding signature block on the right – and a pen whose clip dangled from a string. The form wasn't blank, we already had various signatures because, of course, we'd made other stops on our way to the War Memorial. I wedged the clipboard between my chin and the top box and Carolyn pulled away as we headed to the stage door.

It hasn't changed one whit since the '80s. Taken in August of 2018, this is exactly what the place looked like then, back when it was called the Onondaga County War Memorial:

Stage Door, War Memorial

Looking back, it was hard to imagine how we'd ever fool anyone with this gambit. Neither of us was exactly the twenty-five-year-old Orson Welles playing Kane as an old man. But when we kicked the door sharply, and one side swung open, things began to unfold. A huge bearded roadie eyed us up without saying a word. The thrashing of the opening band pushed at the air behind him.

"Where's the beer go?" Bill said, trying to make it nonchalant.

The roadie looked back in the cavernous space beyond. We could see only hints of the motion of people hustling around backstage. "Goes back there in the wings. To your left. Big table. With the liquor." He stood aside and held the door open for us with one massive arm.

Every nerve in my body was urging me to hustle past him while we had the chance, but I held my ground. I wanted to sell the authenticity, and it would work a bit better if we weren't in a crazy hurry to get inside.

Maybe I wanted to savor the moment a bit, too.

I shot my eyes down to the clipboard under my jaw. "We need a signature."

The roadie yanked the clipboard out, scrawled a real signature beneath the fake ones, and slid it back on top of my empty box. "You all set?"

We were. Inside, we dropped off all the boxes except the beer ball where we were told, then double-timed it across the walkway that ran parallel to the stage. We were moving fast because that roadie might be wondering why we hadn't returned. We had to stop once though, only long enough for the perfect capping moment. The DJs from 95X were coming in the other direction, fumbling with that massive birthday card. We stopped them asking if we could sign it.

"No pen," one of them said.

We had our own. We signed using the pen from our clipboard.

We exited the backstage area on the far side of the arena and headed for the men's room. We covered our deliverymen shirts with hoodies, broke down the box flat and slid it behind one of the toilets along with the clipboard, which had to be sacrificed.

We stood for the concert, finding where Gerry was sitting so we could celebrate together. He lost the bet, but he was happy for us. I recall Cheap Trick putting on a great show that night, but how much of the feeling might be attributable to the adrenaline, I couldn't say. About halfway through, the 95X guys presented Tom Petersson with his birthday card onstage. I shared a look with Bill – our signatures were up there among the hundreds of others, but we'd signed backstage, without a ticket, outlaw style.

There was no question about it: mission accomplished.[36]

IT'S NOT EVERY MOTHER who would go to the mat for their kid in this way. She may not visit you in the hospital, but if you needed a driver for your sting, she would be right there for you.

Of course, putting the pieces together all these years later, I could see there was a consistency in her behavior. Hadn't she helped with the Cheap Trick con because it was exciting for her? Hospitals are no fun and so they weren't on the list. But real-life *Mission: Impossible?* Yeah, that was something she could definitely get behind.

---

[36] I returned to the War Memorial for another concert, a band I didn't even really care to see (and maybe that made the difference). Same gag but different associate, Jay O'Connell this time. But we got caught. They were on to us immediately, almost as if there were some bulletin up back stage about the Cheap Trick event. We were lucky we didn't get arrested. This is why magicians will never do the same illusion twice in a row.

CITY OF LIMITS

HERE'S THE ONE important thing Syracuse once had: a canal. Here's what they did: they paved over it.

I refer here to the fabled Erie Canal. I'd learned the song about it when I was a child, but again – like the situation with the State Fair – I assumed anything as important as a song must have been written about some *other* Erie Canal. Not the one in my backyard. But our canal was world famous. It ran right from the Hudson River west to the Great Lakes and put sleepy Syracuse on the map nearly two hundred years ago, prompting some newspapers to refer to the city within a few short years as "the Venice of America." However, the moniker was short lived.

In 1920 the city fathers voted to fill in the section of the canal that ran through the center of downtown. The barge traffic had fallen off significantly. True, the canal was once considered a marvel of civil engineering, but paving over it may have made some economic sense. After a certain point, mules pulling boats right through the middle of your city center may not play like the beacon of progress it once did. In fact, it may well hamper progress. But with that decision, the idea of Syracuse as the Venice of America disappeared. Filling it in may have been considerably cheaper than maintaining it, but there would be a price paid for turning the Erie Canal into Erie Boulevard. With no barges coming through, no longer a crossroads, the city embraced its landlocked, subarctic nature. Syracuse was no longer special, and it steered right into that skid.

FROM MY PERSPECTIVE, with or without the canal, downtown Syracuse didn't have much to recommend it. The only reasons I had for spending any time there growing up was Dream Days, the comic book store that opened near City Hall, and Loew's, the city's grindhouse movie theater. Carolyn spent a lot of Saturdays driving me to one or the other. Dream Days was long out of business. Loew's had been converted from some kind of sticky-floored indoor drive-in to Central New York's premier concert venue – no more *Dr. Phibes Rises Again* playing there.

But I was downtown for the Onondaga County Bureau of Vital Statistics, which was still there after all the passing years. There are some things in this world you can count on… with birth, death, and real estate transactions near the top of the list. The Bureau of Vital Statistics offices were in the Civic Center but located on the basement level, which was not a promising sign. On the plus side, a sticker at the entrance proudly proclaimed, "No Appointment Necessary," which was right in my wheelhouse. The meandering nature of the trip didn't allow for me to schedule many appointments.

I wanted to get some information – confirmation really – on the story I'd been told about the Lyndon Road murder-suicide. Searching news records online armed only with the address and a rough idea of the time frame had gotten me nowhere. I needed the names of the deceased.

Vital Statistics kept county-wide death records and would help me cross reference place of death with names. But the woman behind the bulletproof glass in the basement had hard news for me.

"We only release information on death to next of kin," she told me sliding a photocopy of the procedural dos and don'ts of the department through the gap in the glass like a bank teller. I stood there, reading down the list. I was hoping for a loophole and, amazingly, found one.

"It's been more than fifty years." I held the sheet against the glass, printing facing in. Near the bottom it stated: If a record has been on file for more than fifty years, then anyone may request it. "I'm anyone," I said.

The woman nodded pleasantly and sent across another sheet of paper, a form. A form wrong in every conceivable way. For one thing, it required the name of the deceased. In fact, that was almost all it required. Secondly, there was no place for additional information such as where the person had died, which was the only piece of the puzzle that I had. And finally, it was going to take twelve to sixteen weeks to get the information. Vital Statistics was a bust six ways from Sunday.

I went back up onto the nearly empty downtown streets to consider my next move. My stomach had been cramping up on me all day, so the thought of walking wasn't appealing, but the Syracuse newspaper building was only about five blocks away. I thought I might charm my way into the morgue there, the archives. I'd spent some time working for the *Syracuse Herald-Journal* during college, and I figured I could drop a few of the old-timers' names and get somewhere. Maybe even get a crime reporter to point me in the right direction. So I walked, hand on my right side like my appendix had been returned to me in worse condition than it had been taken, and found… what used to be the newspaper building. It still had the name of the city's one remaining daily emblazoned on it, but there were thick chains with padlocks around the front doors.

This still from one of our films captured the building as I'd always known it:

Print Is Dead, and I Don't Feel So Well Myself

It turned out what's really left of the Syracuse newspapers was now encamped in a retrofitted bank building a few blocks behind me. It had the web address Syracuse.com plastered all over the soaring windows. But I didn't go in, partly because I knew there wouldn't be a morgue to dig through (the new owners never would've moved all that moldy newsprint over to the new building) and partly on principle. I had no problem embracing change and rolling with the new technology, but one thing, if anything, was sacrosanct: newspaper offices didn't have soaring windows.

WHILE I WAS DOWNTOWN, I figured there were two more places I should visit. It turned out both establishments were out of business these days. One I'd known was defunct, but the other took me by surprise. They were at opposite ends of the city, and when I lived here they were in very different industries. But they are bound together now in an unpredictable way.

847 James Street had been the final resting place of Careerco, a trade school my father had invested in against my mother's wishes. It was the Trump University of its time. The institution went down hard when the U.S. Justice Department discovered the school had "phantom enrollment," billing the government for student aid reimbursement using a roster of former and fake students.

Carolyn had been against the investment from the beginning, smelling trouble even though Careerco was run by Alan Apple, her cosmopolitan friend Joan's husband (as well as the father of the girl who taught me how to tie my shoelaces at the bus stop). My mother hadn't liked the pitch, the suggestion of easy money. My father's nose didn't work that way. He simply had a blind spot for getting hustled. My sister can't see it, either. For all their intelligence, they couldn't sense the basic flaws when the too-good-to-be-true opportunities cropped up.

Carolyn didn't start out as a told-you-so sort of wife, but the state of their relationship was such that she took some real satisfaction on those rare times when she saw my father laid low by his own hubris. They were still married when the investigation began, but she enjoyed his dread as the set-up was unraveling around him.[37] And the marriage was long in the rearview mirror in 1978, when Careerco collapsed completely. She saw Dr. David's investment blow up from afar, all over the front page along with everyone else in Syracuse.

(Final) THE POST-STANDARD

Charge Careerco Heads With Fraud

Bad Investment, Bad Publicity

---

[37] Dr. David would eventually be named as an unindicted coconspirator in the proceedings. He would testify and pay some fines while Alan Apple would earn a four-year federal prison sentence.

He should've listened to me, she thought. And though she'd probably never heard of the concept of *schadenfreude* at the time, she was marinating in it.

THE BUILDING AT 847 James Street was now home to Willow Inpatient Treatment Services, a rehab facility owned by Helio Health. I found this sublime, because coincidentally this line of work intersected partially with the other business I wanted to visit. The Benjamin Rush Center on South Salina Street was a psychiatric hospital, but my only experience with it had been related to LSD-induced psychosis. So it too was a drug treatment facility, after a fashion.

I parked in front of the building entrance, the doors of which were chained shut similar to those at the newspaper headquarters. Benjamin Rush was empty. I was looking at an abandoned mental hospital, the hoariest cliché of horror fiction. The place had been in financial turmoil in the late '90s. In 2001, new owners gave it a makeover that included a name change – Four Winds – and that new age rebranding and influx of cash may have kept them afloat a while longer, but it didn't work for the long haul.

I had a friend who wound up here after a psychotic episode, a brilliant guy named Jay O'Connell. These days he's an accomplished science-fiction writer. Those days, he was one of my best friends. Until the breakdown.

GROWING UP, JAY WAS one of the most interesting people I'd met. He read more books than any other four people I knew, he remembered everything, and his interests were varied and deep. He was kind of a genius, it seemed to me, but a tortured one. Jay was a year older than me and not really supposed to be my friend. I first slept over at his house when I was in sixth grade, but at the invitation of his brother John, who was a friend from my grade. The date was certain: Friday, April 2nd, 1976. I knew this because that was when part two of the Charles Manson miniseries *Helter Skelter* aired on CBS. What happened, naturally, I was forced to watch the Manson program. Most sleepovers had the problem wherein some kids would be ready to throw in the towel before others. In this case, my friend John was out like a light shortly after *Helter Skelter* ended, but I was too rattled by the real-life cult and home invasion murder story to close my eyes. Jay was wound up as well, though not scared. He was happy to stay up and talk… and talk… and talk. He told me about books I knew I had to read, shows I'd never seen. He opened up new worlds.

Somehow, the friendship switched in focus. I made it through the night without being victimized by a mass murdering cult. And Jay turned me on to a bunch of authors I would've never heard of, a substantial bonus. Jay was an artist, a talented one. This was something I'd always had more desire than skill for, but Jay just took his for granted. There was no real work involved, it seemed almost effortless for him. So he didn't take it seriously enough. Nobody does when things come easy.

Jay and I remained close for years. We'd go to the Egg Plant, DeWitt's all-night diner together, see movies, he even starred in one of our Super 8 films. But in the middle of high school Jay become seduced by another way of adolescent life. He began hanging out more and more with a crowd interested in experimenting with drugs. Different music, different parties, a whole different vibe. I thought either the drugs were a kind of self-medication (because he seemed to have one speed – cranked up) or an access point (because he was always hungry for more information and ideas). Either way, the result was the same: Jay changed. Later in life he would be diagnosed as bipolar.

A perennially frightened kid, I backed away from heavy stuff like mescaline, hallucinogens, speed, and LSD. Jay went the other way on all those and more. So what? As friends get older they can have a way of changing, drifting apart. Except here was the thing: Jay wasn't drifting, he was sinking. I saw it and did nothing. Jay was a great guy, an interesting young man with a lot of potential, with a lot to teach me. If he'd been Mary Jo's friend, she would've rescued him.

But all I did was pull out of his orbit.

Jay graduated a year ahead of me and ended up attending Syracuse University, where his father taught. On his own, living with our friend Gerry in the dorms, the freedom was too much. That's when things really started to go off the rails.

My senior year of high school the news came: Jay had been found – naked, gibbering – on someone's lawn in his parents' quiet neighborhood. Ranting. Out of it. On drugs. The Town of DeWitt police were called out. Handcuffs and backs of squad cars and all sorts of lunacy. I heard it on the rumor mill. I heard it through the grapevine. Jay O'Connell had gone crazy, everyone said. He was in the psych ward, strapped to a bed, they said. He was catatonic, said someone else.

My old friend, off the deep end. I found the idea chilling.

THOUGH ABANDONED, the place looked much the same as it had when Jay was confined here, give or take the broken glass and a handful of Styrofoam cups caught in the shrubbery. If you were looking for signs, as Jay was always happy to point out, you could do worse than the Benjamin Rush street address; 666 could have indicated, at least to those inclined to look deeply, that there was some diabolical shit going down there. Hell's area code, perhaps. Bad juju, at any rate. Pressured by his parents as a juvenile to sign his freedom away, Jay stayed in that psychiatric hospital, a steady diet of Haldol, Thorazine and Jell-O sluicing through his system. None of it making him any better.

I visited Jay at Benjamin Rush a few days after he was

admitted. Hovering by his bed I could see the fear in his dark eyes, the fear that helplessness mainlines into one's system. I made the most painful small talk to try to plow through it. Jay was quiet. Filled with tranquilizers but not tranquil. He would've had to have been a lot more dulled to miss the fact that I had one foot out of his hospital room door the entire time I was there.

At the end of the visit, I told him, "I'll come back when I can."

Anybody could write what happened next: he was in the hospital for another three long weeks, but I never went back. It was the practicality of the situation, a little of the Connelly pragmatism for which we were so well-known. It was too uncomfortable for me. Jay was already uncomfortable, I reasoned, but that didn't mean both of us should be. Never mind that another visit might have eased Jay's discomfort. Pragmatic and loyal, I was sure I was both, but somehow, Jay's situation had shown me those two traits are often in opposition.

Don't visit me at the hospital, Carolyn always said. *Because I won't visit you.*

OUR FRIENDSHIP WENT from a slow drift apart to full-on radio silence. We froze each other out. I did it out of a sense of shame, him out of… who knows? Pride? Or more likely, embarrassment.

I stood there out front by the frame of the illuminated sign. Its massive translucent plates were long gone, and I could see the florescent tubes and wires inside. It was impossible to know what this beige building had once been. I dialed Jay on my cell. We'd reconnected as adults, he knew about this trip, but I wasn't sure if I'd ever made it clear how I felt about my treatment of him during his trauma, my vanishing act.

"They changed Benjamin Rush's name to Four Winds," I told him.

"That sounds about right."

"I was afraid here," I said to him. "When you were a patient."

Jay told me that he understood. He was sanguine about his experience, but generous with his forgiveness. He would've been afraid visiting that place too, he said with a laugh.

But he *was* there, and not visiting. He was *held* there. For weeks. "I was afraid for me, not you."

"I know," he said. "You came once. That means something."

"It's the *Godspell* Syndrome," I said, reminding him of the year my good friend Mike won the lead in the school play. He played Jesus, basically, though the *Godspell* script goes out of its way not to name the character. I didn't go to the show. I told Mike why. I didn't like musicals. Nothing personal, I just didn't like musicals.

Jay laughed. "C'mon, Stuart. It's how you were raised."

I simply didn't do anything for anyone if it was outside my comfort zone. Like a greatest hits collection, the lessons in shame just kept on coming. Welling up inside, perhaps the force that was making my stomach cramp, I struggled to keep Jay from knowing how disappointed I was in myself. "I can't help but think, if the roles were reversed, you would have been there for me."

Jay didn't respond to that one way or the other. All he said was, "It's okay, buddy."

This trip was beginning to feel like what I imagine confession felt like to Mary Jo.

THE TOWN CRIER

It had become clear that I wasn't going to get the name of the former owner of 51 Lyndon Road through information on the alleged murder and/or suicide. But there's more than one way to skin a cat. If I couldn't get information about the death, I'd get information about the house.

I drove to the DeWitt Town Hall, hoping I wouldn't come up empty like I had with my visit to Vital Statistics. I'd never been in this building, it was only about fifteen years old, but coincidentally it had been built only about three-quarters of a mile from the Lyndon Road house. I couldn't remember if the old one had been in an existing business park or retail area, but DeWitt had built its new town hall on a marshy triangle of land where Butternut Creek joined the eastern part of the Erie Canal that still flowed. An odd choice, it seemed more like a spot where they'd put a ranger station in a wildlife reserve than the seat of local government. But on the plus side, there was no traffic and plenty of parking.

I headed up past the Police Department and found the Planning Department, a vast sprawl that included traffic court and what I was looking for, the Assessor's Office. This time there was no bulletproof glass. The set-up felt more like a Kinko's, with a long L-shaped counter dividing the visitor area from the town's assessors and tax collectors.

An elderly woman with a friendly smile approached. She

leaned across the counter, which was littered with large-scale printouts of tax parcel maps, and asked, "How may I help you?" A better attitude than I'd enjoyed at the Civic Center, certainly. This woman seemed happy to have a visitor.

I explained what I was looking for: the transaction record from when my parents bought the house on Lyndon Road. "I'm trying to learn about the history of the house where I was born."

"That shouldn't be a problem," she said. "Do you know when the purchase took place?"

I told her it was late '63 or '64.

She wrote down the address, then shuffled off and started digging for the information. While I waited, I glanced at the tax parcel map sitting there at my elbow. Oddly, the top sheet was the outline of DeWittshire, the neighborhood where our family had moved after the Lyndon Road house sold. I saw where Cornwall Drive met York Street and there was the property I'd grown up in. I wasn't a guy who looked for cosmic signs, but this seemed like something. In real life my house had a street address of course; this was its public face. But also this unfamiliar designation the powers that be used for it: I came of age in tax parcel lot 60-14-31. It made me think of what I was doing with my mother; how she too had an image she shared with the world and something different underneath, not for public consumption. I'd known her by society's designation, like a tax parcel number – **YOUR MOTHER** – but in the end I was searching for Carolyn on a different kind of map.

The clerk reappeared. I'd been expecting her to bring out a file folder, like a medical chart for real estate, but instead she clutched a small hinged box, like something in which someone would keep recipes. This was it. I could feel my pulse quicken as the woman flipped open the box and pulled out the document. "What did you say the name was?"

"Connelly."

Her bony finger ran down the entries that had been typed on a library-like card. "Okay, here it is." She turned the paper to me.

The name Connelly was there all right. The earliest entry, bottom of the sheet. The deed transfer record only went back as far as 1976, which meant the furthest back owners listed were my parents. Both of their names were on it. Tantalizingly, it showed them selling 51 Lyndon Road to the next owner. But the sale to my parents remained enshrouded in tax parcel mystery.

"And what about before this?" I asked.

"Oh, any records earlier than this are in the archives."

I let out a sigh. The positive momentum had seemed too good to be true, so I shouldn't have really been surprised at another roadblock. "Okay. And how does someone get to look at the archives?"

"Oh, we don't do that," the woman said, probably sensing something in me that made her drop the smile. "They're in storage."

"Yes, that's what an archive is: storage," I said, fighting not to raise my voice.

"No, I mean they're in a storage facility."

"Right, I get that," I assured her. "And where is the storage facility?"

"You can't get into it. There's no one there."

"But somebody can find something for me," I said, urging her to agree with the premise.

The clerk shook her head. "I don't believe so."

The pain in my abdomen by this point had been a low-grade needling that had kept me on edge, so I was already primed for an outburst. "But the archives exist to preserve the information, right?"

"I suppose."

"So... for whom?"

"Not for people just wandering in," the clerk let me know. A shot across the bow.

Time to get officious, an argumentative tone I no doubt received from my father's DNA strand with which I'd been known to bludgeon people. I took out my reporter's notebook and flipped it open. I needed to indicate I was a problem that wasn't going away. Why did I even care about this? I thought. But what I said was, "If the archives are not available to me, at my request right now, then please tell me for whom and under what circumstance they would be available."

The clerk, who'd been so happy to help a few minutes earlier, looked defeated. Her morning had been ruined by one of DeWitt's ex-citizens – a man who paid no taxes here, who didn't contribute a dime to her salary, to whom she owed nothing. "I'll get Linda," she told me. "She knows more about this than I do."

As IT TURNED OUT, a visit under the bridge where the troll held the golden keys to the Town of DeWitt Property Tax Archives would not be necessary. Linda was younger than the clerk I'd upset, nimbler and perhaps more experienced in the department. I explained the situation to her and she told me she thought she knew where to look.

After disappearing for a few minutes, Linda was able to produce another recipe box from somewhere in the building. This one older, dustier. It went further back, it was a time machine. It was a box that registered not transfers of deeds but the local taxes paid for real estate transactions. And Linda was able to give me a peek at the 51 Lyndon Road bill of sale. Pay dirt. A date and a price. The Connelly family had purchased the four-bedroom, two-and-a-half-bathroom place for $36,500 in April of 1964, four months before I was alive.

And there was a name of the seller: William Barry, Jr.

Now we were getting somewhere. The only thing left to do was to discover who this William Barry, Jr. was. And what he'd done in the house where I'd crawled around.

∞ ∞ ∞

PULLING OUT of the town hall visitor's lot, I passed the Erie Canal parking area on Butternut Drive. It was where Carolyn always parked when she took the dogs – whatever dogs were around at the time – for a walk. I'd always thought it was strange that she'd gather the dogs and get them in the car only to drive such a short distance when she could have simply made the walk to the canal part of the outing, but she didn't want to walk past other people's houses. Carolyn wanted to walk in a kind of peace that only nature could provide.

These days, when the weather's decent, I'll go for a two- or three-mile run, and I don't do it along my country road, either. I'll drive to a county park that's eight miles from our house and run the path that's been cut alongside the rocky waters of Brandywine Branch Creek.

Maybe I'm more like Carolyn than I thought.

THE SCHOOL OF PARTICULARLY
HARD KNOCKS

THE SYRACUSE UNIVERSITY CAMPUS had changed enough to
convince me that their alumni donation drives must've been
well-oiled machines. Whereas the time passage at Bowdoin
could be measured by the thickness of the tree trunks, at
SU it was brick and asphalt keeping track. New buildings
had sprouted since I'd last been there, areas that used
to be public streets had been clipped off and turned into
walkways. The quad's footprint had expanded with feverish
hunger, swallowing up my sense of permanence along with
the surrounding roads.

But I wasn't looking for the changes on campus, I was
looking for what remained from the past.

I walked into Crouse Hall, where most of the ground
floor was taken up by Gifford Auditorium. Gifford had been
the home of Film Forum, the student run cinema. During
the pre-home video era, classic and cult films were out of
reach to the average viewer, particularly in their pristine
condition, unedited for television. But Film Forum brought
that artwork to Syracuse – the whole city, because it was open
to the public. Looking back, it was a remarkable gift. The
Film Forum would distribute its schedule at the beginning of
the semester on a large card stock poster and Carolyn would
bring it home from work. She and I would sit at the table

and go through the fine print of the listings, highlighting all the must-sees for the next three months. Sunday nights were perfect for us, and the night tended to be particularly heavy on genre fare: films like *A Clockwork Orange* and *Carnival of Souls* were on offer in that time slot. But there were also gems Carolyn introduced me to like *Harold and Maude*, Hitchcock's *The 39 Steps*, and Wilder's *Sunset Boulevard*.

She had the kind of love of movies that was contagious. The kind that adhered to someone's psyche when they'd grown up before television, when movies were the only form of visual entertainment. She knew their power, loved their glamour. And mostly, because her life was adrift, I believe she needed to experience stories where there was clarity and concision by the end. In a life of uncertainly, she found solace in the three-act structure.

Carolyn would never have tolerated the mess my friends and I made of the house while working on our Super 8 productions if it weren't for her abiding passion for motion pictures. The house was never clean enough for the fastidious Dr. David, but he left before we started turning bedrooms into sets and the kitchen into craft services. That would've probably been enough to drive him out if other things hadn't already sent him packing.

I STOOD ON what used to be the plaza of the S.I. Newhouse School of Public Communications. My alma mater was now nearly unrecognizable. There used to be two I.M. Pei-designed buildings flagging this plaza, but now there was an unfamiliar new building there, Newhouse III. Glassy and ugly in a different way than the first two, which as exercises in the brutalist style had always felt right at home under Syracuse's leaden and brooding cloud cover. The new Newhouse stood out like a sore thumb and seeing it in person made me wish progress would sometimes actually make it to the finish line. Stop at two eyesores, know when enough was enough.

It was on this plaza that my hero, professor Jon Keats, and Carolyn finally met. It was graduation day, and my mother had a lot of duties of her own but had swung by for my convocation and I was able to introduce her to Keats for the first time, four years after I'd met him.

He was a mentor and she knew how much I respected him. He was also ancient, opinionated, and had a sense of humor so wry that his jokes sounded for all the world like no laughing matter when he spat them out.

"Keats, this is my mother, Carol," I said, bringing together two of the most formative people in my life. "Mom, Professor Keats, the one I've been telling you about."

Carolyn told Keats it was a pleasure to finally meet him as they shook hands. In return, Keats pulled her closer, not letting up on his grip. "This man, your son, is a *writer*," he hissed at her. "Your job is to take care of him while he writes. Feed him, put a roof over his head, and for Christ's sake don't make him get a job! Give him the time to work on the great American novel." It was a joke – one so dry it was in danger of fueling a forest fire, but a joke nonetheless.

And Carolyn understood that. But she also understood that she wasn't going to be part of any punchline. Moreover, to her it was a frightening idea that I might take even a part of the proposal seriously. She had to nip it in the bud. "Sorry, you got the wrong girl," she said, throwing a hand over my shoulder. "I can't afford that. Us administrators don't get tenure, you know. He'll have to make his own way."

At the time I had exactly two hundred dollars to my name.

Keats smiled in that way that turtles and old men do. My mother had lived up to her reputation.

NEWHOUSE HADN'T BEEN a foregone conclusion. At least from Carolyn's perspective. "Maybe you should apply to Arts and Sciences to start with," she had suggested when I was attacking my college application. "Then you can transfer over to Newhouse after your first year."

This approach went against my entire philosophy. I was only applying to one place; there was no safety school for me. There was one simple reason for that: though the divorce settlement clearly stipulated that Dr. David had to pay for each of the three children's college education, the writing had been on the wall for some time. There wasn't going to be money for college, not without a protracted fight. God's gift to plastic surgery had joined the ranks of the deadbeat dads. The one escape hatch to the problem was Syracuse University. One of the perks of Carolyn's work at SU was full coverage of my tuition if I attended. So my college choice had been made by circumstance. My opinion of Syracuse was mixed, though. They had a top tier communications program (which I luckily was interested in), and a so-so everything else. If I had to go to Syracuse, I'd go to the best college the university had on offer.

Carolyn was suggesting the Arts and Sciences strategy because she knew my grades, which were abysmal. I hadn't done a lick of work in high school. I was a zombie, shuffling through the halls but not really embracing my education. I didn't study. I would get my textbooks at the beginning of the year and stick them at the bottom of the locker, where they would remain until June. Test days snuck up on me, each one an unpleasant surprise. I read piles of books, but never the ones assigned in English. Was I boycotting something, was I in the grips of fear of failure? I couldn't say. Had the upheaval in my home unmoored me? Maybe. I'd hated my father being around, but I hadn't been crazy about Carolyn crying while she explained to me what the negative symbol in her check register represented once he left, either.

So Carolyn had real concerns about my getting into a competitive college like Newhouse. But I was engaging in some serious magical thinking, I've come to understand. I'd coasted through high school on attitude. Not great grades, but with teachers passing me because they could had a sense that I was intelligent. This was the brush I'd been painted with; smart but wouldn't apply himself. It didn't bother me in the slightest. In any event, Carolyn let me do it my way. And here was the logic I imposed over the entire process; we all knew that when many of the applicants to Newhouse are denied admission, they are offered the Arts and Sciences Program as a kind of consolation prize. Maybe you're not ready for Newhouse, but you're welcome to start in our farm club. The minor league. Arts and Sciences. So if you ask for first class you may get coach, but if you ask for coach... there's no way you're ever getting first class.

Perhaps there was a flaw in my logic. I applied to film school at Newhouse. The letter I received back months later left me stunned. I received a full rejection from the university. No offer of a slot in Arts and Sciences. No second place, no Miss Congeniality. I had no college. Me, the one who had cost a fellow senior a job because I assumed *everyone* went to college. I had already proclaimed it – "Newhouse School of Public Communications" – beneath my high school yearbook photo. I'd gone public, committed. What had I been thinking? The reality of my situation hit me squarely, so hard that I didn't know what to think, let alone do. Effort, as it turned out, seemed to be at the heart of every successful endeavor.

I knew I wanted to be an artist, and I couldn't help but wonder if fucking up badly was the price one had to pay to join that club? I might've thought so back then. Let the record reflect the answer was a resounding no. Mike Royce has gone a long way in the interim years following the rules. He's perfectly attenuated to it. He's won Emmys, Peabodys, you name it. And he's never missed a deadline, never broken a promise, showed up before everyone else and stayed in the office until the lights were extinguished. Records and Research is a successful artist, and he never would've found himself with his back against the wall like I did.

Of course, his parents seemed normal. So there was that.

We needed a plan, *I* needed one. Carolyn seemed to shrug the situation off. I'd never been one for taking her suggestions, and now that I desperately needed the help, no advice was forthcoming. Her demeanor came off this way: you made your bed, you lie in it. Looking back, I feel now that it was an act, that Carolyn was likely as anxious as I was but didn't want to let on for fear of further destabilizing me. But what it felt like back then was that I'd let her down for real this time.

I went for a run the day of the rejection, which was something I'd never done in my life. High stamina exertion wasn't part of my makeup. I wouldn't go running again for another thirty years. But that day, the day I realized I had nowhere to go after high school graduation, I hit the road and tried to scheme my way out of the problem I'd created with my own thoughtlessness.

Returning from the run, heaving for breath and sweating profusely, I sat there in my room and looked around. All the material of my life surrounded me. There was a play I'd written on a manual typewriter. There were drawings, sketches, and these puzzles and toys I'd built out of cut and scored index cards. There were cassettes with game show parody performances, props from Super 8 films Mike, Bill and I had made and even homemade movie posters for them. I saw the clutter of an energetically creative boy. The kind of person who'd be an asset to a student body, not a liability. And I realized my one shot at college didn't help explain me. If they knew me, they might just change their mind. What does a smart person do when no one realizes he's smart? He proves it.

As I write, there is a scandal about school admissions chewing up the headlines, an excoriation of the wealthy and privileged that have been caught using their money to fake test scores and bribe college faculty. Outrage in social media about cutting in line and taking someone else's valuable place and gaming the system. There's nationwide sensitivity around the subject. And yet I find myself having to explain my own run-in with the admissions process.

From her office, Carolyn called Admissions on an internal line at my request and asked for them to speak with me in person. As a courtesy, one of the Assistant Admissions Directors named Sal King agreed to a meeting. Carolyn picked me up from school and dropped me off on campus.

I met with Sal and pleaded my case, bringing in a portfolio to show him everything I had drawn, written, sculpted, or shot. I told him I could leave reels of film for him to review if he liked. He took it all in, surprised. I came clean with him; I hadn't lived up to my potential, I told him. The grades reflected a kid who wasn't trying, not one who tried and failed. I told him I didn't know why I'd been sleepwalking though the drudgery of the public education system, possibly fear of failure. Maybe I was trying out the *you can't fire me, I quit* ethos. But that only worked until people let you know they accept your resignation. The SU rejection letter had been a wake-up call. A much-needed slap in the face, and I now was on course correction, now I knew what I had to lose. If he let me in to the Arts and Sciences School, I would be doing the hard work and I would *earn* the transfer to Newhouse. I was dancing as fast as I could, but I wasn't giving him a line. I'd seen the limits of phoning things in, and I wasn't interested in a debris-field future.

The number one thing sales gurus teach about success is that salesmen must believe in their product. I've never been much of a salesman, but I was selling something I knew was gospel. My vast reserves of untapped potential. That was a product I knew top to bottom.

Sal suggested that if I thought applying myself would get results, I should be able to bring him a straight A report card as evidence. "If you do that, I'll let you in," he said.

The next report card was weeks away and would be the second to last of my high school career. The marking period was nearly halfway over, and I sure wasn't on track to get straight As. English was probably safe, and Art. Social Studies, Math and Physics were a different story. Never mind. I told Sal he could expect all As.

I was going to remake myself the way I'd seen myself all along, as a brilliant person. I went to each one of my teachers and laid out the situation. There were no do-overs, I knew that, but I just explained I was willing to do any extra credit, anything at all to work out my averages. And I think because deep down, my teachers knew I wasn't living up anywhere near my potential, they made the opportunity.

I went into turnaround mode. I was like a corporate raider that had just gotten a hold of Stuart Connelly's under utilized body at a fire sale, and I was going to swoop into that husk, pump up the numbers, put lipstick on the pig and get it back on the market for a tidy profit. Nothing else mattered, and it worked.

I set up the meeting when the report card arrived and brought it to Sal's in triumph a few days later. Sal looked at it. "This is good," he told me as he handed it back. "Do it again."

Again? That hadn't been the deal. I'd been expecting a handshake and a welcome to the university. What I got instead were moved goalposts. But I told him I'd deliver. I had one marking period left.

The phone rang about two weeks later. It was Carolyn, calling from work. "I'm sorry, honey," she said, "I have some bad news." She had just found out that Sal had quit his job in the Admissions Office. I felt the despair drape down over me. Sal had been the last hope.

About three days after that I received a letter from the Admissions Office. I'd been accepted to Syracuse University after all, and not Arts and Sciences. It was Newhouse welcoming me to the class of '86. It wasn't something that

I deserved, it wasn't even something I'd asked for. It was a rare moment of grace. Relief washed through me, cooling a central nervous system that had been jittery for months. But I didn't know why it had happened, and there was no way to find out. Not without asking questions of people who I didn't want poking around in my admission history.

SOMETIMES IN LIFE, mysteries got solved. Four years on, during my senior year at college, I interned on the features desk at the city's now defunct evening paper, the *Herald-Journal*. Of the two dailies, the *Herald-Journal* was my favorite, likely because they'd started carrying the syndicated Spider-Man comic strip when I was a kid.[38] I'd been assigned a story on a new trend in education, private guidance counselors. Looking over a list of locals in the field, I saw Sal's name. I called him first off, asked if he'd agree to be interviewed, and then reminded him of our paths crossing before.

"Of course I remember you, Stuart," Sal told me. "I quit my job because of you."

His story was a revelation: he'd gone to the Dean of Admissions with my situation after we'd met. I'd struck him as smart, motivated. The dean was a numbers man, which was why Sal gave me the report card assignment. My SAT score was strong, but my GPA was a disaster. Sal knew when I delivered the promised report card it probably wouldn't convince the dean to offer me admission, but his plan was to show the first one to his boss and let him know another one was on the way. He presented my report card with a flourish – "Remember that local kid I was telling you about?" – but it fell on deaf ears. Apparently not.

---

[38] This comic strip was abysmal, by the way. I knew it at the time; four black and white panels to try to get something going that resembled action was doomed to failure. But, along with the terrible '78 TV show, the newspaper comic represented the first mainstreaming of my chosen superhero. I had to show up and support, so we subscribed to the evening paper.

Sal started in with the old you-didn't let-me-finish routine: *There's another set of straight As right behind this one. This is a good story.*

The dean made it clear. He couldn't see a path to me attending the university. Despite the deal I'd been offered.

Sal believed that the staff should have more discretion in the admissions process. I was his pick, but it didn't matter to the dean. My case was the straw that broke the camel's back.

In the interview, Sal told me he'd tendered his resignation shortly after I'd handed in my shiny new report card. He didn't like the cookie cutter approach to the Syracuse's admissions decisions. My application was a reflection of my mother's future application to Foukleways; a dicey bet on paper, but something that might be good for the community if it broke just the right way.

Sal thought he might have more impact in children's lives in private practice. But before he cleaned out his desk, in one last act of defiance, he had slipped my folder into a pile of acceptances. There were thousands in the incoming class, the dean would never know. And for good measure, he put it in the Newhouse pile.

Sal straightened my life out. On the other hand, I made him look pretty good in the newspaper feature I wrote, so maybe we're even.

CAROLYN MAY NOT have wanted to ever visit hospitals, but between my father and Syracuse University's School of Nursing, she managed to get her life completely wrapped up in healthcare.

I made my way across the hill to nearly the outermost edge of campus. 426 Osterman Avenue was now home to the university's Department of Psychology Research Facility, but it used to be School of Nursing and my mother's office used to be inside.

In 1973, the circus left town, as they tend to, Carolyn was

jobless. The volunteer work at the World Affairs Council was fulfilling, but it didn't pay our bills. Fine while her husband was in the picture, but when that went belly-up and her *noblesse oblige* lifestyle dissolved, her practical side took over. Dr. David's child support and alimony checks came through erratically. My mother was desperate to find employment. She had an advanced degree but a twenty-year gap on work history and the search was an arduous one. Circus tickets was the low point, but I recall her struggling with a learn-to-type course, endless job interviews for which she had no qualifications. Finally, she was able to land a gig as an administrator, recruiter and guidance counselor at the School of Nursing. I would drive in to work with Carolyn every time I had any kind of medical appointment downtown; she didn't want to leave on personal matters too many times in a day. I would sit in a corner reading or play with the secretary's IBM Selectric until it was time to run out to the appointment.

Much of the work in the medical field has always been considered a trade, so Syracuse University had a hard sell in the world of nursing education, trying to squeeze four years' worth of tuition out of a student that would be able to become a practicing nurse after only two years of classes from just about any other nursing program. The SU brand did some of that work. My mother might've done the rest. You'll have better job opportunities, command higher salaries. Such was the promise, whether or not the data backed it up.

There was, however, a bigger problem than if the four-year degree was worth the cost, as the students who graduated from the four-year bachelor's program eventually discovered. At some point in the late '90s, SU's nursing program had improperly worked through the New York State Board of Education accreditation process. There were four-year graduates who were out in the world not with, as they'd been promised, something worth more than a two-year nursing degree, but something worth far less. Their degrees weren't legitimate.[39]

The esteemed School of Nursing had fallen so far there was no rising back up. It would shuffle its current classes of students and send them off with comparable degrees. It was all dried up within four years. One can no longer study to become a nurse at this enormous institution of higher learning.

I made my own mistake with the School of Nursing. It's where I learned something about human nature, about my own and my mother's. It was catastrophic – so tone deaf on friendship and on what constitutes humor vs. what constitutes cruelty.

One of my friends had been dating a nursing student. I mentioned the young woman to my mother, curious if they knew each other. They did.

"She's bad news," Carolyn told me.

Here was another lesson, another marcher in my own parade of shortcomings. I heard a thing, and I should've let it go. But I found it intriguing. Maybe because it seemed like an exchange between two adults, and that was fairly new in my life. Whatever the reason, this was the inflection point, the stumblingly bad move. Two people can keep a secret if one of them is dead, the saying goes. We were both alive then, and so the next time I saw my friend, I told him what my mother had said about his girlfriend. *My mom says your girlfriend's trouble, isn't that interesting? Isn't that funny?*

Now there was the chance that my friend looked at the world the way I did and told his girlfriend with the same how-about-that manner I'd told him. Equally possible was the notion that I'd offended him and that made him want to share the offense with his girlfriend. Either way he went ahead and told her. Better for me to have prefaced my story

---

[39] This was some coincidental connective tissue between my parents: both of them were involved in an education scandal where paying students were the collateral damage.

with, "Don't tell your girlfriend this, but…" Better still for Carolyn to preface her own comment with, "Don't tell your pal this, but…" I didn't think I needed to clarify, I believed that it was self-evident. So did Carolyn, I suppose.

We discovered that my friend had indeed shared Carolyn's comment. The nursing student stormed into her office the day after I'd told my friend. She was bold, didn't mince words and confronted Carolyn.

"I heard you're telling people I'm bad news," she said. It took more nerve than I had at that age. "Is that true, Mrs. Connelly?"

She leaned over my mother's desk, waiting for an answer.

GORDON LISH PUBLISHED a short story in the early '80s entitled "I'm Wide" that I think about more and more often as I get older. A lyrical character sketch, it tells a story of a man who was tired of constantly having to wax his shoes. Searching for a solution, he decides to shellac them. This, he believes, will give all his shoes a permanent shine. Disaster ensues, naturally, and the shellacking results in his ruining every single pair. When he ends up walking to the shoe store to get at least one pair he can wear to work, he's forced by the salesman to explain why he's wearing galoshes on a sunny day. The narrator is unable to take the public embarrassment and covers his culpability the only way he can conceive. Lish wrote:

> "Listen," I said. "I got this boy, God love him, he's seven, and all he wants to do is do for me. So what happens? So when I'm not looking, what happens? Listen," I said, now and raising my voice for them in that whole shoe store to hear, "that kid, that wonderful kid, he takes a can of shellac to every last one of my shoes to put a lasting shine on them!"
> I even laughed when everybody laughed.
> Do you understand what I am saying to you?
> I winked my goddamn head off – me, a man.

The narrator of the story blamed his child for his own stupid idea. That's how low fear of being found out can bring us. It can take us by the nose and lead us around, lead us away from our closest-held beliefs.

And what did Carolyn do when faced with her own cutting words, confronted by the subject of the derision herself? She denied saying it. Straight out of the guilty adolescent's playbook. Denied everything. Stuart's joking, Stuart made it up. "Oh, I never said anything like that about you, dear."

She blamed it on her child.

In a letter to Dr. David amongst her mementos, Carolyn had written years earlier, *I'm afraid that when I'm backed into a corner I will fight as an animal and I don't know to what length I will go.* I'd backed her into that corner with my lack of decorum. The fear of what an admission of truth would do if the student took the situation above Carolyn's head, to the dean, shook her moral compass right out of her grip.

The student didn't believe the excuse for one second. No, despite the protestations, she knew who the guilty party was. The two had had their share of run-ins before. In the mind of that nurse – now married to that same friend and far from a bad-news type – Carolyn would forever be enshrined as a terrible person. That wasn't how I knew her, of course, or how any of those kids she took into the house when they were lost knew her. But everyone's opinions of others are valid, forged from their unique set of interactions; no two people have the same field of view.

We make friends, we make enemies. Sometimes we throw our mothers under the bus, even if by accident. And sometimes our mothers have to throw us under, too.

THORN INSIDE

My STOMACH was starting to feel like it was trying to tell me something. It seemed unlikely that there was a psychosomatic element to it, but the pain and pressure were difficult to explain. Digestion was typically one of my strengths. I considered it could be traveler's constipation, but that doesn't fit the profile; I've spent weeks in East Africa and had no problems below the belt.

I walked down the hill from the university, wincing all the way. I'd decided I needed to see a doctor about this stomach pain, and I made my way to the ER of what is now called Crouse Hospital. This was the hospital where my father had surgical privileges – Crouse Irving Memorial was what I remember it being called around the house, but Carolyn also referred to it as Crouse Heinz, its name before a hospital merger in 1968.

I talked to the nurse at the registration desk about my abdominal pain, making sure he understood appendicitis was off the table. "But the pain's right in the same ballpark," I told him. "Location-wise and intensity."

He put me in the chairs.

If waiting to see a doctor is wasted time for most, it allows the writer an opportunity to hop on the Internet and follow-up on some nagging threads of research. Crouse's ER waiting room provided me with just that for the next few hours, a perfect time to dig around for information about William Barry Jr.

But the digging didn't go well. The degree of information searchable on non-notorious, non-infamous pre-1990 incidents had always had a disproportionately low hit rate on the Internet. In general, the stories tended to fall through the cracks, and the digitizing of print pages into searchable text isn't a priority for struggling second-tier newspapers.

Information on Mr. Barry Jr. was beyond scarce, but I was able to track down a couple of useful pieces. This included an article reporting on his death, which ran in the newspaper where, more than twenty years later, I would work:

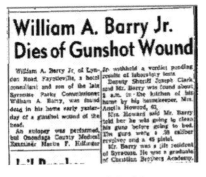

The Scene of the Crime

The facts came back half-matching the story. The truth of the matter isn't quite as gory as it had been presented. There was no murder, but there was a suicide.

It seemed, near as the pieces come together, that my father got the deal of a lifetime on the Lyndon Road place because the bachelor owner shot himself in the kitchen. The word "bachelor" in this context was coded language. The homeowner was gay in a time and place where that went unspoken, and in the apparent aftermath of the breakup with his lover, he must have felt he had no reason to go on living. This heartbreak was likely the catalyst that sparked the murder-suicide rumor.

The house sat on the market for half a year and my father low-balled the bank; bought it without even showing it to Carolyn, who was not happy with the decision.

My mother and I both grew up in homes nestled in the shadow of grisly death. That's going to leave some marks.

THE X-RAY MACHINE told of unseen worlds much more accurately than the Ouija board could. The pain on the right side of my abdomen wasn't related to my digestive system directly. A urologist eventually came to talk to me, and he let me know with a sympathetic sigh that I had a kidney stone. One unusual in its structure; six millimeters long and not even two wide. "Like a pine needle," the doctor told me. The vivid description didn't fill me with hope.

It had probably moved from the spongy insides of my right kidney into the ureter that night in Brooklyn. It had to hook around to follow bends of my internal piping, and this six-millimeter stone wasn't interested in doing any bending.

This was hardly great news. Trying to lead the witness, I said, "I don't need surgery though, do I?"

The doctor suggested because it was so slender there was a chance it would just move along the ureter, into the bladder, and then out of the body. But if he were a betting man, he wouldn't bet on it passing easily. Because the ends were so pointy, there was a much better chance it would get caught up in the soft tissue and stay put, irritating my ureter and eventually causing infection.

"We'd want to retrieve it before then."

I crossed my legs involuntarily. Like the word "bachelor" in 1963, I knew what "retrieve" meant to a urologist. I may've been born in that hospital, but I hadn't been born there yesterday.

FOR ALL YOUR RESTAURANT, ILLICIT DRUG, AND FUNERAL NEEDS

I NEEDED A PASTRY BAG and I knew exactly where to go. The place was just off Water Street[40] and under the shadow of the Route 690 elevated highway: Smith Restaurant Supply. Like many other establishments in Syracuse, the restaurant supply store had been upgraded since I'd last been there. What once was a rough-edged industrial supply company – selling aluminum tongs, chefs whites and cookie sheets by the gross – was now passing itself off as some kind of Salt City version of Williams-Sonoma.

The parking lot was empty, which illustrated how well that was going. No one in the patisserie today. I wasn't in the market for a croissant and an espresso, I was here for one thing only – that pastry bag – and it didn't matter if it were commercial grade or a fancier-but-flimsier version for the general public. It just needed a wide end and a thin one.

The nagging technical questions surrounding the disposal of Carolyn's remains were starting to feel like an incessant drum pattern in my head. It was one thing to imagine a hypothetical process, quite another to break it down into

---

[40] And why wouldn't Water Street be the name they bestowed on the road that, in another life, had been the Erie Canal? The name Erie Boulevard demonstrated a severe lack of imagination on the part of the city fathers.

the steps necessary to accomplish the job. So far, the plan included spreading Carolyn's ashes over a significant amount of space. In order to pull that off, I'd have to move the remains from the plastic box into something that had some level of dispensing control so that I could let them out at the proper rate. A kind of governor. So I figured the soft, cone-shaped pastry bag would fit the bill nicely.

I HAD BEEN a somewhat unlikely customer of Smith Restaurant Supply back in my semi-misspent youth. Like many stories, it related to drugs. The restaurant supply store might seem like an unlikely location to score, unless one was familiar with the narcotic euphoria induced by food-grade nitrous oxide. The little compressed gas cylinders were designed as a propellent for whipped cream canisters and seltzer bottles. They were sold under the brand name WhippIts in 18-count white and powder blue cardboard containers. In the '80s, Smith Restaurant Supply would sell those tiny G.I. Joe scuba tanks full of fun to anyone, whether you looked like you were in the restaurant business or not. A sale was a sale, after all.

The "cracker" was a simple mechanism you could buy at any head shop that fit around the canisters in two threaded sections. One end would be covered with a balloon, but not just any flimsy party balloon. They had to be strong enough to take the pressure. We used those punch balloons that came with a rubber band that kids whacked around like a paddle ball. When screwed together, the mechanism pushed a point against the aluminum air seal on the cannister and popped it. Untwisting the mechanism allowed the gas to escape, filling the balloon up with a whoosh. A frosty mist underscored the action, clinging to the rubber skin at first and then drifting into the ether.

Then it was a simple matter to remove the balloon, pinching the opening as you brought it to your lips. There was a medicinal taste to it all, between the latex, the gas, and even that oily residue from the knurled steel cracker. You drew the gas in the way you'd draw a breath, but of course it wasn't the air needed to properly fuel your system. These were other magic molecules that hitched a ride on to your brain, shaking serotonin and dopamine loose. Your lips went blue, a thundering roar started in your ears, you spit out a laugh that sounded like a foreign language to you, and the world fell away for a few surreal moments.

It was the very definition of getting a cheap thrill. I remember partaking and I remember observing, waiting my turn while Jay O'Connell or one of my other smart friends prepared the balloon. I watched them all at one time or another fall dumbstruck on their back, waiting for the train rushing though their central nervous system to fade toward the horizon. The party would end one of two ways: when we were out of Whippits, or when the balloon, made brittle by the cold, finally popped. It was like Russian roulette with that damn thing.

Not that my friends and I were drug addicts. What we were doing was trying to kill time; we were bored suburban kids.

Bored and off the grid. Out of the reach of any parental tracking. It's nearly impossible to imagine that kind of slack today. I've often thought that my mother's childhood and mine were more similar than mine and my childrens' were. Even though she grew up in the Great Depression, straight up *Little Rascals* style, I could understand the exploring, the building, the playing outside. Simple stuff, and no GPS.

So we had the freedom to wander, to experiment. And to stir up trouble.

My buddy Gerry – the one who'd bet with me and Bill about Cheap Trick – was two years older. He attended Syracuse University and lived the dorm life there. Even though he'd "gone off to college," he remained friends with some of us kids he'd left behind in high school. On a Sunday Carolyn might lend me the car or, if she needed it, she might drop me off and rendezvous with me later. Gerry and I would hang out, hitting the used record store or student bookstore, maybe grab some lunch at Hungry Charlie's and play a little pinball. Sometimes the Film Forum would be screening something incredible that I didn't know about, and it wasn't out of the ordinary to give her a call and ask if I could stay later, past dinnertime. This was usually not a problem. One particular time, however, it was. It sounded like a big problem.

"Is it okay if I stay?" I asked her, calling from the payphone in the dorm. "There's a –"

"No." she cut me off, her voice cold.

I knew something was up, but I didn't know what. "Is everything okay?"

"I have to talk to you," she said. "I'm coming to pick you up. Right now. Be waiting out front."

Fear shot through me. What did she know? What had she found? I wasn't a bad kid, but I had my secrets. Any one of them, if cracked, could definitely create a situation where we needed to "talk." I told Gerry I had to go and waited downstairs. My mother's car was there in a matter of minutes.

When I opened up the passenger door, I found something taking up a surprising amount of space. It was a home-made bong. *My* home-made bong. Man, it was an ugly thing; I think its ugliness may have been its charm, the initial aim in building it. Made with a two-liter soda bottle and some kind of long heavy-gauge cardboard tube, possibly from a bolt of fabric. Aquarium piping wrapped around it. The thing must've been four-and-a-half feet tall.

"I'm sorry," I told her.

I looked at Carolyn. Her eyes were rimmed with red. She was puffy from crying. "How could you do this to yourself?"

∞ ∞ ∞

I WOULDN'T KNOW it until later that day, but Carolyn had been struggling with her discovery for hours. I kept the stupid novelty bong in my closet, practically in plain sight (my closet was walk-in, with a door that had a clear glass window in its top half, like an office from a film noir). Carolyn had found it during a rare bout of housecleaning. She didn't know exactly what it was at first, but it scared her. Drugs terrified my mother, though I'm not entirely sure why. Yes, weed was illegal. And yes, it was something that could get you in trouble. But it wasn't heroin. She would go on to live into an era where marijuana became legal in many U.S. states. But she was shaken by her discovery of that contraption.

I had been out of reach, but Carolyn needed to discuss the drug situation immediately. I may have not been near a phone, but my friend Mike *was*. All my friends' numbers were written in the family's telephone directory, a gimmicky spring-loaded plastic affair. Carolyn called Mike and he was at home, much to his misfortune. She told my friend that she needed to see him immediately. Like it was a matter of life and death. Mike tried to figure out what the fuss was about, probably so he could talk his way out of meeting her. But when she hissed, "It's about drugs," he knew the situation wasn't going to go away, so he agreed to meet.

Carolyn pulled up in front of his house and Mike climbed in. I'm not sure if she had put the bong in the car yet, but she proceeded to cry and ask Mike for details about what I did when she wasn't around. It may have been because he was Catholic that she figured she could get the truth out of him, and perhaps she was clinging to the idea that such an upstanding kid wasn't involved with weed. The rationale behind grilling my comrade was hazy at best.

They sat in that car for what must've seemed like hours to poor Mike, trapped with someone else's mother half out of her mind and haunted by the specter of reefer madness.

Meanwhile, his own mother was peeking through the curtain from time to time, wondering what in the world it was all about. Mike spent the time trying to calm Carolyn down, trying to let her see that this was kid's stuff, that pot was fairly harmless, considering some of the other illicit alternatives. And that my use was infrequent, despite how the water pipe she'd found made it seem. Of course, it was a juggling act; he had to try to get all this across without implicating himself. He had to try to fix my problem – or at least minimize my potential damage – without creating collateral damage for himself.

He mostly succeeded, because by the time Carolyn picked me up in front of the dorm, she was more reasonable than I would've had any right to expect.

DRIVING HOME FROM the university, our discussion boiled down to one key. "Promise me you'll never smoke this stuff again," Carolyn said.

"Okay."

"Swear to me, Stuart."

"Okay, Mom. I swear."

Her relief was immediate and clear. I'd reassured her. The thing was, it was a promise I had no intention of keeping. I'd been caught, I said what I needed to say to move through it, to continue on behaving as I saw fit and keeping in pursuit of my own happiness. I could already anticipate a joint handed around at a party the next weekend. Or the one after that. Was I going to pass that up because I'd offered up to my mother some words of appeasement? Fat chance. Maybe Dr. David wasn't the only sociopath in the family.

But that party came, and I was there. Most of my high school friends were, too – many of them smoking. The lit bowl was passed to me. I shook my head and handed it to the next kid.

"No?" my friend Danny asked. Why not?"

I felt stupid explaining it, but I heard myself say, "I promised my mother I wouldn't."

Some of the guys already knew the story, some didn't. But none of them actually believed that I'd stop smoking pot just because my mother asked me.

"You're kidding," someone else chimed in. "You're not going to get high anymore?"

I thought about the notion. Keeping my word, as opposed to using it like a smokescreen. My promise had been made defensively, a flinch, me wriggling out of a tight spot with an act of cowardice. Like the line Carolyn gave the nursing student, it was expedient and knee jerk, but not the truth. Not then.

And if I turned it into the truth? What would that cost me? What would I gain?

"Are you really quitting?"

"I don't know," I said, "Maybe I am."

I took it one social event at a time. I never consciously decided to stop using marijuana for good, I left the door open. I figured I would indulge again, but each time the opportunity arose, I found the temptation didn't hold up, that the satisfaction of saying no actually outweighed that of the high. At a certain point I told myself, when I go to college, when I'm no longer under Carolyn's roof, I'll change the rule then. But by the time I moved into that same dorm Gerry lived in, that too felt like a cheat. I'd been fine without weed. I never smoked marijuana again.

Of course, Carolyn had expected me to keep my promise, so I didn't get any credit for doing so. This was a disappointment, her not understanding, because I certainly had no intention to when I'd made the vow. Why didn't people notice when I went above and beyond?

INSIDE SMITH'S, I FOUND the item I was looking for; a simple, reasonably priced funnel made out of what felt like very thin, wax-coated canvas. It came with several assorted tips, but those wouldn't be necessary. The ashes were not likely to form rosettes the way frosting or whipped cream did.

As I paid, the gentleman behind the counter gave me a look I remembered from long gone days. It was a look that seemed to be wondering what I was up to, judging the purchase. If a pastry bag could be used as drug paraphernalia, that information hadn't come my way. Still, in a certain sense the man wasn't wrong: I would not be using the pastry bag for food preparation. So I was still batting a thousand when it came to misusing restaurant supplies.

SALT IN THE WOUNDS

I DROVE BACK to Cornwall Drive, the house from the tax parcel map I'd seen in town hall. Thinking about Carolyn's discovery of the bong made me want to take a closer look at that strange closet of mine. It was what had sold me on the house.

Though the one we'd lived in was isolated with hardly any kids my age to play with, I still couldn't imagine moving. I cried about it. I wasn't up for any change beyond that the divorce and the carnival work had wrought. Carolyn brought me over to the new house and took me for a tour, trying to get me excited about the move. She showed me my future bedroom, which was in the front above the entrance. Due to the ceiling height and the slope of the rooflines of this new house, my room ended up having one of its two windows in the back of a deep closet. Necessity, always the mother of invention in design projects, created a situation where the closet door was designed to be more like an office door, with a glass pane set in the top half instead of a wooden panel. And that's how I saw it, as an office.

"That could be your reading room," Carolyn said.

Now there was an idea. I agreed it could be. I was warming up to Cornwall Drive.

The day we moved in, I brought in the bucket seat from the Triumph TR-7 that David had discovered at the local dump. I placed it under the exterior window of the closet, to become my reading chair. Carolyn had given me permission to paint on the door's glass. These were the words I carefully lettered on the glass along a slight arch:

THE COMIC BOOK ROOM

I was unflinching in my passions, I owned them. I had my precious comics all boxed up and held in their polyurethane protective sleeves. But I took it a step further; the sleeves weren't even interchangeable; each had a sticker along the bottom with the comic's title and issue number and each copy had to be returned to the same sleeve from which it had been taken. Mike did a fine job helping me, no surprise coming from the man who chose Records and Research for an alias.

The comic collection had grown since I took it over from my brother. The best part about being sick as a boy were the comic books. My mother always made a point of stopping at the university bookstore on her way home from work to pick up a handful of issues. She had no sense of the books that I actually followed and would pick somewhat at random. These were like a real-life extension of the fever dreams I was struggling with; a world with its own logic. I would be plopped down in the middle of whatever complicated story arc was entangling *Alpha Flight* or *Sgt. Rock* or the *Justice League* at the time, and never get any closure.

CAROLYN HAD PURCHASED the Cornwall Drive house on her own; there was hardly a whiff of Dr. David in the air on that street. Just the very occasional times he would pick me up for some awkward visitation my mother had forced upon him. Bill, my neighbor, may have seen him once through the car window. They never met. The house on Cornwall Drive may have been small, but it had been paid off and was sociopath-free.

Except possibly for me.

I knocked on the front door, but no one answered. I checked for the note I'd left in the mailbox with my cell number the evening before. It was gone. No call, though.

I looked across the street at Bill's parents' place. His stepfather may well have been inside and could probably have put me in touch with the homeowner. But I didn't want to ask for that favor. I was saving Bernie for my Plan B in the event I was unable to open Carolyn's funeral box. Bernie could build or take apart just about anything and had a full workshop of tools. I figured if I couldn't get at the ashes inside the plastic box, he could. If he were to play any role in my journey, that would be the one.

I stood there on the front steps, trying to feel if I could make my heart beat faster remembering the worst news of my childhood. From the distance of so many years, could I connect with the actual feelings, not simply the memory of them? It was from precisely this viewpoint, one floor up from my non-closet window, that I saw it. It was about this time of year, too – August of '85. Late in the morning, familiar cars were coalescing in front of Bill's house. Too many, arriving nearly simultaneously. People I knew. Something was going on I didn't understand.

By that time, Paul Doherty had moved over to the Bill's place and I understood inherently that people were speeding over to see him. Bill had been working for his father and driving a Pontiac demo that summer. I didn't see it among the other cars, and that suddenly had me worried. It wasn't Bill, but I was in the ballpark.

The phone rang and I answered. Bill was on the other end, just leaving the dealership. The receiver felt impossibly heavy. "J. Marc was hit by a truck," he told me.

"Jesus. He's... dead?"

"Yeah. He's dead. Everybody's meeting at my house."

That was how the news broke about the vanishing of our friend, J. Marc Patenaude. He was the guitarist and primary songwriter in Paul's band, The Trend. J. Marc was a prankster, a merry anarchist whose Québécois DNA was shot through with a manic energy that drove most people crazy. Not us though; there was too much punk rock in our own bloodstreams for that. J. Marc was our collective id. He'd been working for his father's construction company and was driving that morning to pick up some blueprints. On a rural two-lane highway, the driver of the cement mixer going the opposite way fell asleep at the wheel, drifted into J. Marc's lane, wiped the kid off the face of the earth.

When I told Carolyn, she didn't seem particularly shocked by the news. Or sympathetic. It could be that she didn't know how close we felt to J. Marc – like Paul, we hadn't met him until our senior year. Parents in general didn't enjoy J. Marc's particular brand of hellraising. People die, get over it, I could almost hear her thinking. But it was a real blow. A hole opened in all our lives. Life looked a hell of a lot more finite than it had when I learned that Grandmother Black passed away at Naaman's Manor.

I'd managed to pull myself out of the self-destructive streak in the wake of my college admission problem, but Bill was just about to start his. J. Marc's death lit that fuse as sure as we'd lit the fireworks taped to Apollo 17 on the very same driveway where the snarl of cars arrived heralding the death of a friend. Bill would spend the rest of college in a dark place.

J. Marc's was the first funeral I ever attended. Carolyn's won't be the last, but it was the one on deck now.

CONCERNING THE CHANCES of getting inside the Cornwall Drive house, perhaps my luck had finally run out, and something told me that was all right. I didn't want to push it, didn't want to go where I wasn't wanted. Not really. If I had to choose one house to get inside, it would be the other one. I may have come of age here on Cornwall Drive – had my friends, shot Super 8 movies, played in bands, got laid, drunk, stoned – but my personality, my neuroses, my *gestalt* – that all came from Lyndon Road across town.

HOMECOMING KING

THE THIRD TIME I drove over to Lyndon Road (and the first armed with real information about the house's history) the heavens smiled upon me. It was around three o'clock in the afternoon. My note was still pinched in the edge of the screen door with the lawncare information. Clearly, the owners didn't come in and out the front. It made sense; I remembered coming up through the basement from the garage. There was no way to tell if anyone was home, but I knocked on the flat section of the door between two of the three carved circles. In short order, a young man answered the door. A teen, friendly enough, said he'd just gotten home from school.

"I came by the other day, I left a note," I told him, handing the message over to him when I pulled open the screen door. "Which you guys clearly didn't get. I used to live here."

The teen read over my handwritten request to be contacted. "Uh-huh," he said.

I told him my name and he told me his – Andrew. The situation was not unlike my experience with Cachet a week earlier: I had family reasons that made me want to look around, and I had information on a death I really didn't want to share. Holding a secret while trying to be forthcoming once again created an odd static inside of me. Still, I gave this Andrew my best pitch, pulling out the photographs the same way I had back in Wilmington. I showed him a shot of the living room which featured a fireplace and what little resistance there was immediately crumbled. Its façade in the photo highlighted an unmistakable serpentine stone pattern.

"That's still here," Andrew said, his voice underscoring his vague amazement at this meeting in general and my photographs in particular.

"Could I see the fireplace, Andrew?" I asked. And then, pushing my luck: "I'd love to take a quick look around the whole place, if it's not asking too much."

Amazingly, the kid opened my old bank-vault door wider in invitation. "Sure."

I stepped across the threshold and back in time. Now was the moment, to use Dr. David's turn of phrase, to find out "What Fifty-One Lyndon Road has to say about things."

I had not seen the interior of Lyndon Road since 1976, and now that I was standing in the foyer, this journey was starting to feel like it was inching to completion. I'd been on the road for a full week alone, lost in thoughts about a relationship. I was starting to feel closer to Carolyn than ever before.

Directly in front of the door was the staircase landing. Two steps up to a large square landing, then a ninety-degree right turnout to the flight to the second floor. Upstairs, the hallway encircled the staircase. I told Andrew that I remembered climbing around the inside of the railing, starting where it met the top tread and shuffling along, holding on tighter and tighter as the steps dropped away behind and beneath me. He admitted to doing the exact same thing when he was younger.

"Could we start upstairs?"

Andrew said that was fine. He was accommodating in a way I was certain no adult would be, and I planned on taking full advantage of that.

We went up the stairs and around the long U-shaped open hallway. Past what had been my sister's room with the door always closed (my sister's secretive nature had always been obvious to me, while my mother's was a little bit harder to ascertain). We passed the hall bath where the squirrel met his Waterloo. I noticed something I'd completely forgotten, the interior version of those bank vault circles on the front door. It was a series of four tall cupboards in the hallway by the bathroom, built into the wall. For linens, I assumed. They had dangling pulls that looked like earrings, but I couldn't remember ever opening them. As soon as I laid eyes on them, though, I was certain I'd looked at them every day as a child.

I peeked into the next bedroom, which was on the end of the house opposite the stair egress. It was a small one, probably considered a nursery. As the baby, I'd originally had the smaller of the rooms, but for some reason my brother wanted to trade with me when I was very young. I went with it, happier for more space in which to play. I never understood why he preferred the small room with only one window.

The white-black-and-orange tiger wallpaper and Bruce Lee posters had been stripped away. There were no more wooden lacrosse sticks jammed in the corner. When David occupied the room, I only came in for one reason: the pink plastic laundry hamper kept here. I could close my eyes and see the tic-tac-toe grid etched into the hinged flip top. Three feet tall, when opened the surprise was it held no laundry at all. Comics were stacked inside, the tower of colorful superhero stories going down.

My old room next to David's didn't look as large as I'd remembered. It was hard to envision how the twin beds that had been in here fit when it was my room. As I considered the two beds, those other people who'd lived in the Lyndon Road house with us started to come back into focus. I couldn't say it was an actual memory, more of a feeling. I tossed it around as I stared at the spot where I used to sit on the floor and spin *The Music Man* cast album.

∞ ∞ ∞

WHEN I WAS very young, a Swiss *au pair* took care of me. Her name was Rosemarie, and her origin story was fuzzy. I could picture her well enough, I had a crystalline recall of her voice, which came in a lilting breath, a softer kind of French accent. I remember her sewing the blue Batman cape for me and red one for Cousin Craig's Robin, but I'm not sure why she was in the states, or why she would come to Syracuse to live with us. Or where she slept. Was it possible that as a little boy my female European *au pair* shared a bedroom with me? Was it possible that the reason David and I switched rooms wasn't because he wanted the smaller one as I was told, but because, at six-and-a-half years older than me, he was deemed too mature to be sleeping with the nanny?

And what about years after Rosemarie, when I was a bit more mature myself and we hosted a college girl from Bangkok named Phet (pronounced "Pet")? I remember her slinking around the Lyndon Road house, laughing with David, possibly even flirting with him. The only place she could've stayed was in my room. And there I was, undoubtedly a pre-sexual person at the time, but certainly on the cusp of puberty. How had that been allowed to unfold that way, and how had it been wiped from my memory?

There was one picture of Rosemarie in my mother's possession.

There were none of Phet.

MY ROOM CONNECTED to Carolyn's by way of the pass-through bathroom. It occurred to me just then that the house really had no master bedroom; mine and my parents were on equal footing, both roughly the same square footage occupying a corner of the house and sharing the full bath. This bathroom was primarily notable because I'd almost set fire to the house from there. I was alone playing the Jim West character from *Wild, Wild West* and I'd lit a match to pretend to melt the door lock. I extinguished the match but threw it hot into the wastebasket, which was brimming with tissues. They went up like magician's flash paper.

"How about we check out the first floor?" I asked Andrew. I didn't need to see my parents' bedroom. There was a closet where I used to dig for my Christmas gifts, a bed where I would find refuge from my plague of bad dreams. Nothing to see here, folks.

Downstairs, as we turned into the kitchen, I caught sight of the door that went down to the basement and the garage beyond. When I was home sick, it was almost always with a cold, the flu, or bronchitis. I often had a sore throat, and the idea that an ice-cold milkshake soothed sore throats was gospel to the family. Our kitchen had a full-size refrigerator, but the freezer was in the basement. The basement was just one more in the legion of places and things that scared me as a child. It was a damp, dark cinderblock space and it looked like the lair of a serial killer. When I was home sick, I was home alone. Carolyn had to go to work, so I just stayed in bed. I didn't love being alone on the second floor, but it was a party compared to the horrors of the basement.

Still, that lunchtime milkshake was a must. The trick was integrating these two opposing drives. How it would work was, I'd call Carolyn's office from the kitchen phone. She would promise to hold on while I went to get the ice cream. Phones had cords then, and she couldn't keep me company on my descent. I would creep down the stairs slowly, fighting my instinct to flee. I'd shout up to the receiver, "You're still there, right?"

Once my hand was on the ice cream carton, though, I shifted gears. It was as if I was ripping the Band-Aid off. On the way in it was about spotting the monsters, but now it was a matter of outrunning them. I'd fly back into the kitchen, snatching up the phone and panting, "I'm alright, I got it."

Being the person that I was, I wouldn't return the ice cream to the basement after I made my milkshake. The risk-to-reward didn't add up for me at that point. Carolyn would find it in the sink when she arrived home that evening. I'd tell her I forgot to put it away, but we both knew I was giving her a line. Occasionally, I'd run away from the freezer so fast that I hadn't been able to generate enough force to close its door. I knew it, I could see the light leaking out, but I wouldn't go back. Everything in the freezer would be defrosted and soggy. Useless.

I'd made the world's most expensive milkshake, but Carolyn wasn't the only one stuck with the tab. My fears were taking a hard toll on my self-esteem. I wasn't the kid I wanted to be. And I didn't know how to change.

The kitchen where William Barry Jr. wrapped up his affairs so untidily was nearly unrecognizable to me, mostly because the back wall had been cut out to make way for the addition of a sunroom, a somewhat optimistic approach to a house in Syracuse. Andrew's family had changed it, as our family had. We put up the barn wood to make it "rustic." Mr. Barry had made it rustic a different way; according to my sister, there was still a bullet hole in the wall when our family moved in. The bachelor had no one left behind to make the necessary repairs. The house had probably been sold "as is." It wouldn't surprise me to learn Dr. David had cleaned the bloodstain off the linoleum himself.

Some memories are seared in – tenacious, unshakable in the wake of some seismic event. They're almost never the good ones. I have no more vivid a memory of my parents together than here in this kitchen – a different kind of spilling, in fact. Not of blood but of coffee... and bile. A recollection of my fastidious father scrubbing away, of my mother showing her fangs. Standing in the actual space didn't goose the memory to life. It was always with me. If all the latest virtual reality, 3D and holographic projection, and computer rendering power were brought to bear on a recreation, it wouldn't hold a candle to the vivid nature of my memory of the Night of the Hammer.

It UNFOLDED LIKE a late-act Arthur Miller scene, from innocuous to red-lining in mere moments, seemingly out of nowhere. But run at half speed, slowed down and studied like Zapruder frames, the components were obvious. All there, just the far side of peripheral vision. It seemed like spontaneous combustion, but it was merely ignition. A kind of cruelty hung in the air, there was a pressure drop, the snapping of something that was never as strong as it looked. Cheap leather belt, a noose made of twine. My parents concern for one another…

I was sitting at the kitchen table working on a pencil drawing. The table was an octagon made of thick black slate with a webbing of white painted steel to support it. It was cold and ugly and looked like it should've been patio furniture. Carolyn was across from me, a cup of coffee hovering to the right of the master's dissertation she was writing. In my memories of the evening, this drawing – a space invasion tableau – was the best I'd ever done. It wasn't quite finished, but I was extremely proud of the progress so far and looking forward to hanging it on my bedroom door. At least, that's what I claimed in the wake of the incident. I probably made that up, a quick revisionist decision, as I went fishing for sympathy in the aftermath. Painting my hurt on a little thicker. Because the drawing would be destroyed. I wanted to make the participants feel badly about the collateral damage, as if in fact that was something they might be capable of feeling.

My father had just returned home from the hospital, still wearing his suit.

"I'd like you to read the introduction for me," Carolyn said.

"Fine."

"I'm having kind of a rough time," she said. Mistake number one; I was five and even I knew this wasn't a man to whom you offered up your weaknesses. Carolyn turned in her seat and held up three or four handwritten pages. "I just want to know it's going in the right direction."

Translation: just give me a "good girl" so my confidence will be boosted for me to continue this uphill slog.

He sidled up to the table. "Let me see it."

"It's rough," she said again as she handed him the pages. And then: "Don't laugh, okay?" Mistake number two.

I watched Dr. David's eyes play across the top of the first page. Within the time it would've taken to read the first two sentences, a sound escaped his nostrils. The thing she'd practically begged him not to do. A judging, condescending snort. A barely suppressed laugh of superiority.

Apparently, he thought it was rough.

Carolyn didn't let it go beyond that. She grabbed that cup of coffee and hurled its contents at my father, who was less than two feet away. The coffee sloshed out of the mug and splashed all over my father, then rained down on the table. I watched as the puddle of coffee overtook my pencil lines, turning the white paper sepia. I could've pulled it up, but I didn't. I let it all soak in.

My mother sat there, mug in hand, looking for a reaction.

It didn't happen. Carolyn's slavish work over her thesis had been reduced to her husband's snickering and that would stand regardless of what she did. My father's power came partially from the deadly calm he exuded in the face of calamity. Because everything was a game to him, as for every sociopath. And he had no intention of losing. Carolyn was going for a reaction, and so reactions were withheld. Unfazed, Dr. David stepped over to the sink and calmly began to blot at the coffee stains on his suit jacket.

He just wasn't going to give her the satisfaction.

And so my mother doubled down. She was going to inflict some sort of pain upon of him if it was the last thing she did on God's green earth. If making him feel love was off the table, she would take hate. It was better than his cruel indifference.

She pushed herself away from the table and headed out the basement door. Her footsteps faded as she went down the stairs.

I stared down at my wet drawing, crying now, trying to elicit emotion from my father myself. "It's ruined!" I shouted. Drawing or childhood? Take your pick.

We heard the faint sound of another door opening, directly underneath us. Carolyn had opened the door that connected the basement to the garage.

And then we heard a sharp pop, maybe the sound a champagne cork might make if, for some reason the cork took the top of the bottle off with it.

TIME IS FUNGIBLE in art, almost by definition. Directors can jump cut inside scenes to speed them up or use slow motion to underscore unfolding emotions and action. Nicholson Baker wrote an entire 142-page book in which the period of action takes place over the length of a one-floor escalator ride. Nothing happens in real time except real life.

And sometimes, not even then. Time slows down during accidents or trauma; the amygdala widens the bandwidth of incoming information, essentially creating a double exposure of the event. Upon remembering, the mind's eye plays the information back an illusion of slow motion.

It should've been the cloud of coffee shooting across my eyeline that seemed slowed beyond the grasp of physics, but it was not. It was my father's eyes.

We heard that champagne-cork pop, the tiniest little cracking sound from below, and we both knew what it meant. I looked at my father across the kitchen peninsula at the sink. It was the movement of his eyelids that dragged. Like a sheet shaken in the yard by a launderer before hanging on the clothesline, they fluttered up. His eyes glided over to meet mine and it felt like minutes had passed before they did. Something changed in him. I saw it. The catchlight was different. My mother – the lever, mechanism of the metamorphosis, didn't get to see that her final action achieved what she'd wanted.

I was the witness.

Time again ran normally after that. My father turned the kitchen faucet off and moved quickly down the stairs. I followed behind, as fast as my little legs would let me. Down into the basement. I had no fear of it then, not with both adults down in the monster's lair with me. We took the hard right at the bottom of the steps and crossed to the garage door. It was open and as we moved closer, the sight beyond the doorframe became clearer. The windshield of Dr. David's beloved Mercedes convertible had a spiderweb crack spilling out in all directions from the heavy gauge ball peen hammer that was still sticking out of it. It hung at an uncanny angle, like a hatchet left in a skull.

My mother stood next to the hammer with a take-that smile as icy as a Syracuse February. She knew her husband loved that car more than any member of the family. And if he didn't know it before, he did in that moment.

Here was this marriage's turning point, but I was the one that turned away. My memory ends there. Whatever came next happened in private.

AND WOULD HAVE stayed private, but for that letter. The one that read, *I'm afraid that when I'm backed into a corner I will fight as an animal*, which made the aftermath of the incident in the garage more public. Whatever words were thrown around in the garage, Carolyn ended up saying she was sorry. I was disappointed when I found that line in the letter. The one time she actually beat my father at one of his games, she apologized.

Elsewhere in the note Carolyn mentioned the car, so I believe this note is the follow-up from the Night of the Hammer, though I didn't have proof. The letter seemed to have been left for Dr. David to find the morning after the incident. In the opening, Carolyn had written:

> *I want to apologize for my behavior. It just shows what a person can do when deprived of sleep, pride and last but not least sex.*

That list matched up a little too well to the kind of treatments we've been giving war-on-terror detainees at black ops sites over the last twenty years. My father had been using psychological warfare his whole life. Though I had my share of battle scars, he left when I was quite young. My brother and sister have taken far more shrapnel.

ANDREW WAS ALL SET to show me the basement, but as we were opening the door, my cell phone rang. I glanced down at the screen and noted the 315 area code. It looked like the tour of the old house was over. Tapan was calling me.

What did Fifty-One Lyndon Road think of *that?*

OFFICE HOURS

TAPAN KNEW I was looking for him. His contact information was readily available on the Syracuse University website. I had tried the office phone number my first day in town, but it rang and rang and didn't click over to voicemail. I figured email might pay off, but it felt a little tenuous. I sent an urgent message about my availability in town along with my cell number and urged him to contact me, but I felt the need to be more proactive than that. Remembering Tapan had bought all his cars for forty years from the Bill Rapp dealership, I gave Bill a call. I was hoping I could convince him to find someone at the dealership to find Tapan's contact numbers. Being an upstanding citizen with more to lose than when he posed as a beer delivery man to crash a Cheap Trick concert, Bill suggested it was a longshot, particularly since his uncles had taken over the car dealership after his father's death. He agreed to be in backup position, but suggested I get in touch with Steve Bennett, one of our friends who'd just taken a high-level job at SU. Surely he'd have better access to contact information to one of the university's Electrical Engineering professors than a car dealer would.

"Okay," I told Bill, "but if I can't get anywhere with Steve, I'm circling back to you." As one of the Three Investigators, how could he refuse?

Steve Bennett was still on my list of people to reach out to when Tapan called my cell phone. He'd received the email. Standing on the lawn at Lyndon Road, I told him it was important that we get together. We hadn't spoken in years. I had no idea if he were even aware of Carolyn's death – would the university have clocked it? If so, would they have shared it amongst the faculty and staff?

Tapan sounded happy enough to talk over the phone but begged off on meeting me. "I'm flying out of the country tomorrow," he said. "Next time! Next time!"

I told him in no uncertain terms there wasn't going to be a next time. This was the last dance for me and Syracuse. "I just need five minutes," I said. "Is your office still at Skytop?"

It was. Skytop was a kind of SU annex to the west of the campus on the hill, sprawling parking lots connecting a maze of low-slung buildings that were built as temporary student housing after the Korean War.

What I didn't realize was that Tapan was only a mile away as we were talking, just on the other side of the new DeWitt Town Hall. He was living in the house my parents had kept as a rental property after they moved to Lyndon Road. My mother had sold it to him after the divorce.

But he didn't ask where I was, so we each assumed the other was near Skytop.

"How soon could you be at the office?" Tapan asked.

"Ten minutes," I told him, padding the time slightly; nothing in Syracuse was more than a seven-minute drive from anything else.

THE BUILDINGS in the Skytop complex were numbered haphazardly at best, and while some of them interconnected others just butted up against one another. I found myself wandering halls, trying different building entrances, and finally having to call Tapan again to have him talk me in. He made me get back in my car and drive to another parking area, that's how far off I was. He said he'd wait outside.

When I caught sight of Tapan, I had a hard time

processing what I was seeing. He was waving like one of those long-armed inflatables trying to get customers to pull into a used car lot. Grinning his gleaming white teeth from ear to ear, this Calcuttan scarecrow flagged me down. His hair wasn't that black crown any longer. A wispier ring had replaced it. He was balding. It had been a long time. I got out of the car and shook the hand of a man who had cast a shadowy presence over the first half of my life.

"Stuart, Stuart, it's good to see you," Tapan said through clenched teeth. "Follow me, follow me." I was thinking I had no idea where this was going to go.

I brought Carolyn's ashes with me inside. We sat down in Tapan's office, and I put the plastic box on my lap with a manila folder on top hiding the name plate and the dates.

"So tell me, why the urgency?" Straight to the point. In theory I'd interrupted his packing.

"I'm writing a book about Carolyn," I said.

"Yes, yes," Tapan said, all smiles.

I slipped the folder off the top of the brown box, revealing its cheap engraved plate. "I don't know if you've heard," I said in a reverent, low voice, "but Carolyn's dead."

Tapan's nod now turned solemn, his head straightening out on his neck. "Yes, I know. Paul told me."

Paul Doherty, the one friend that hadn't gone to college, worked at Bill's uncles' dealership. He probably saw Tapan every time he came in for warranty service on whatever he was currently driving. Paul knew Tapan well, was living at the Cornwall Drive house when Tapan was hanging around all the time. He was the one who used to joke about Tapan and my mother having sex, impersonating Tapan's awkward pillow talk.

I told Tapan my plans for the remains and waited to see if he'd ask if he could join me. He didn't. Then again, he'd told me he was leaving the country. Part of me wanted to ask for his itinerary, but I thought better of it.

"I've been going through Carolyn's papers," I said, "and

I've found a lot of pictures of you." I opened the folder and began handing over the shots I'd organized, one after the other. "You're in a lot more of the pictures she kept than my father is."

Tapan took each photo and studied it for a moment through his thick glasses. Each one made him smile and throw out noncommittal mutters, emotionless, before moving on to the next. "She was taking that photography class," he said. But these weren't compositions. They were snapshots. Around the dinner table, along the canal, in the backyard. Snapshots from a life she'd lived. With him in all of them.

I told Tapan that the book was an attempt at taking the full measure of my mother as a person, doing the work I'd failed to do while she was still alive. "I'm trying to set the record straight."

"Sure, sure," he said, still shuffling through the photos.

Looking at the pictures and seeing all the years they encapsulated made me think there must have been more between them than I knew. "To that end, I'd love to get some questions answered."

"Of course, of course."

And then I started to dig. I asked him if he ever met my father; he told me that he'd been at the same parties a few times, but they never spoke. That sounded about right.

"Would you say that you and Carolyn dated after the divorce?"

There was a long pause. His eyes were on a picture of the two of us standing in the Lyndon Road kitchen. I wore my pajamas. "We were very good friends only," was Tapan's answer.

"Did you love her?"

Now Tapan looked at me, seeing he wasn't going to brush off my questions easily. He said, "We loved each other the way good friends do."

"But you were around all the time," I said. "Every

weekend."

"We had similar interests," Tapan explained.

It was starting to feel like the Q&A was a game he planned on winning. Perhaps Prof. Sarkar and Dr. David shared some traits.

"Did you want to marry her?"

Tapan let out a half-laugh and shook his head.

"Did she want to marry you?"

"It wasn't like that."

"Did you sleep together?"

Tapan became animated. "Good friends, we were good friends!"

Not exactly a denial.

"Who stopped talking to each other," I pointed out. "That seems like more of a lovers' thing. Like a break-up."

Tapan tensed. "We disagreed on religion. She wanted to change my religion."

Well, there was *something*, anyway. I thought of the article I'd found on Hindus and marriage. It was from 1973, predating Carolyn's born-again fever. Predating her incessant proselytizing. That could've been a key; she could hang out with a non-Christian, maybe even engage in some casual intimacy, but *marrying* a non-believer? That wasn't going to happen. Unless the definition of marriage changed...

"There are some things I remember that paint a picture of a different kind of relationship." This guy had given me a car, no strings attached.

When I was a senior in college, I had that newspaper internship and needed to be able to get around to conduct interviews. Tapan was in the market for a new car, so he gave me the one he'd been driving instead of trading it in. This was a bird in the hand; worth real cash. Maybe not a fortune, but if my choice was to buy a car for $9,000 or buy it for $10,000 and help out a friend's kid, I was pretty sure I'd choose the former. But Tapan did the latter, and not because he was bad at math. I reminded him of the yellow Volaré.

"Well, you needed a car," Tapan said.

"You have nothing else to tell me about your relationship?" He said he did not.

I asked about the house he'd bought from my mother. He had been renting it from her for years, but Carolyn needed an infusion of cash for some reason and asked him if he would do her a favor and buy it from her. He did... in cash. It was the house in which he still lived. Tapan had owned one home in his whole life, and it was the one he bought at my mother's request.

"What are friends for?"

Right. She needed liquidity, or I needed some wheels, and the engineering professor was right there with a helping hand. "There's really no point in keeping secrets after all this time," I said, trying to coax something, anything, out of him.

"No point," Tapan said. "Yes, yes. I agree."

Who was this Tapan exactly? What was he to our family? Was he used by my mother for chaste companionship? As a boy toy? Did they use one another? Was there love there, maybe, but she bristled at the idea of a stepfather entering my life? Or perhaps she was just over the whole "couple" idea, which had defined her for so long?

And the big question, the one that strange article forced me to consider: Was there a way my mother could have believed she and Tapan were married?

But I didn't get an answer, and I was out of ammunition. I asked Tapan if there was anything he wanted to know from my end of things.

"How is your sister?" he asked.

I told him the hard truth; that Lisa has been a bit down on her luck for the past decade or so. She had gone all in on what I considered some real Nigerian Prince-level scams – getting hidden gold out of the country nonsense, currency trading. It all seemed to have taken her to the bottom. She'd lost her house in Virginia, which had put her on the path that ended in my brother's guest room.

Tapan nodded with wisdom. I could see something was adding up for him. There was a reason he'd only enquired about one sibling.

"Why do you ask about Lisa?"

He hesitated, as if unsure to share any further. But it was a bluff. Tapan wanted me to have the information, he couldn't help himself. "No, it's just… she called me a few years back. She said she needed…"

I braced myself, now really starting to feel like a detective. She needed. Needed, of course, the one thing. The money. Say it, friend of my mother's and nothing more. Say what you have to say.

He wouldn't, so I did. "She needed money?"

Tapan nodded.

"How much?" I waited for the figure.

"Fifteen thousand."

Fifteen thousand. "That's unfortunate," was all I could come up with.

"It's okay, no, it's fine. I was just wondering…."

Wondering if the sure-fire investment paid off? I thought. "If you were going to get your money back? No time soon."

"She said —"

I cut him off. "It doesn't matter what she said." Of course it was merely a loan, of course it was a sure thing. Of course there would be repayment, undoubtedly with a nice interest rate on top. Lisa had to convince herself of all that to make the ask. That didn't necessarily make it true, but hope does spring eternal.

HERE WE'VE AGAIN arrived at the doorstep of shame. This fifteen-thousand dollar-IOU was my sister's secret. One she undoubtedly dreaded anyone discovering. The difference between privacy and secrecy, to my thinking, lay in the degree of shame involved. "It's none of their business" and "They can never know" are a standard deviation apart. Because of shame, I seriously doubt Lisa will communicate with Tapan again until/unless she can repay him.

I'd like to know why the money was needed, but I probably will never learn. When the past is shrouded in secrecy, when it turns painful and shameful, it loses its shape. It dissolves like those pencil lines drowned in coffee. It gets buried. The ways to unearth it are basic: honesty works if you're alive and willing to talk, or – if you're neither of those – talismans and totems from the past, like this banker's box. Lisa's still around for now, but she's not talking. And something tells me she'll be a lot more careful about what she leaves behind than her mother. Just judging from the deadbolt on her bedroom door back in Alexandria.

I SUGGESTED TO TAPAN that he was perhaps financially secure enough that he could afford to write the whole thing off as helping someone close. Someone who apparently needed it. Tapan had been thinking the same way. You don't lend money and ever expect to see it again. But the critical factor remained, helping a long-gone friend's child to the tune of fifteen grand. Who did that?

I gave it one last try as I organized my notes and pictures. "Nothing else about Carolyn?"

"I would tell you," he said, "only there's nothing to tell." Tapan stood up and offered his hand. "It was good to see you after all these years, Stuart." And that was as far as it went. Just words on the wind. I got the head nods, the smiles, the signs that all communication here between us adults was perfectly direct. But there had always been a cultural aspect to Hindu social interaction that I couldn't quite understand. I wasn't plugged into the norms – not then, and not now – but I did know they were different enough from mine to resist a casual apprehending. And I knew this: in their culture it was sometimes perfectly acceptable to meet uncomfortable questions with lies.

No matter how long Tapan had been in the United States, he was Indian at his core. The affair with my mother would never be revealed to me. Perhaps because such a thing never existed, or perhaps simply because it was just for the two of them; a devotion offered in secret.

THE CHERRY JUBILEE

STEVE BENNETT WOULD end up coming to the rescue without compromising the employee records where he worked. He kept me from having to drink alone at Scotch N' Sirloin, which was perhaps an even higher calling than helping me get in touch with Tapan.

I would readily admit, from an objective perspective the name Scotch N' Sirloin sounded like a rube's version of a fancy restaurant. Something out of *The Simpsons*. But in reality, the place was as fine as dining got in a third-tier American city like Syracuse. They all have them, the Cincinattis and Burlingtons and Biloxies; three-star restaurants with one-star names. And the Scotch N' Sirloin near Shoppingtown Mall was ours. My parents would go often – after all, theirs was an era when red meat stood astride over the American diet like the Colossus of Rhodes. Occasionally they'd bring me along. Aside from the acid-drenched *bon mots* studded throughout my parents' grown-up conversation, there were two memories that have always stuck with me about dinner at Scotch N' Sirloin: the ice cream, which to me tasted exactly the way Christmas feels, and the cherry in my mother's Manhattan. Or more precisely, the cherry out of my mother's Manhattan.

The ice cream was merely a magic trick of the kitchen (*an ice cream parlor trick*, one could say). It was a privately manufactured mint chocolate chip, but the ice cream was white, not green – almost unheard of in the early '70s – and in place of the chocolate chips, the ice cream was studded with green and red sugar crystals used to decorate cakes, the kind that look like bits of shattered stained glass. So the sugar's colors and its reflective properties conspired with the wintergreen flavoring to pull on my synapses and created a Christmas experience inside my head.

The cherries, however... they were something special. Next level.

I'd come to believe the restaurant served the original Italian Luxardo brand back then, though there was no way of proving it. If they were the pale red things available in bars and grocery stores today, I was certain I would not have been nearly as excited to have her bestow them upon me.

Carolyn would order a Manhattan on the rocks after dinner, and when it came, she would look at me and say, "You want the cherry, Lollipop?" Excited, I'd nod and she would stab it with her stirrer and hold it out to me. Popping it into my mouth, I would taste just a little bit of the bourbon-vermouth mixture, which was somehow cold and warm at the same time, before letting my teeth sink into the sweet, exotic cherry flesh.

This was better than the bowl of ice cream because it was grown up. Literally forbidden fruit. There was something deeper going on there, though I didn't know it at the time. I found out many years later that my mother loved the cherries as much as I did. She didn't want to give them up, but she did for me. She even offered them, not waiting to see if I'd ask. A mother's sacrifice may have been assumed in late twentieth century America, a kind of standard operating procedure, but it wasn't really our family's style.

It was August 29th, the eve of my planned funeral service, and I met Steve in the bar of Scotch N' Sirloin. He was the younger brother of a good friend of mine named Matt. It wasn't that Steve and I weren't close, but we became genuine friends a bit later in life, so he didn't necessarily share the same history with Carolyn that some of my other friends did. This would prove fortuitous, because I could spend the evening regaling Steve with stories of Carolyn that he'd actually never heard. He was the perfect final audience.

Steve was happy to meet for a drink, regardless of the occasion. He'd been commuting to Syracuse from Washington, DC, weekly for a new job and didn't have much in the way of a social life here beyond his two sets of parents. When we first spoke, he'd mentioned that there were some cool spots near his apartment and my hotel in Armory Square (Syracuse's two-block gentrified hip section, a toy Williamsburg), but I told him there was work to do and it had to happen at the Scotch N' Sirloin. It was a Wednesday night during a Syracuse summer. He was in a pre-furnished apartment four hundred miles from his family and bored out of his mind. He was all in.

Steve and I sat at the bar and I explained the symbolic importance of Carolyn's Manhattan and her giving up the cherries for me. We would drink them in her honor.

The challenge was to figure out what bourbon might've made up that 1970 or '71 model Manhattan. What might have been all the rage at the time, the way Stolichnaya was the heavy hitting (or at a minimum the most heavily marketed) vodka of the era. We finally settled on Jim Beam. It sounded about right.

Josh, the bartender, stepped over to us. I ordered the two Jim Beam Manhattans up, "And this is important," I added. "I need a lot of cherries. More than you would think a person would want in a drink."

"Like, how many?"

Nope. The trick wasn't to tell this bartender how many cherries I wanted in the drink; the trick was to have him bring as many as he could. Fate played a role here. I decided upon a wholly new ritual for the departed; ask the bartender to bring us as many cherries as he could muster, and for each cherry I would list one unique and wonderful trait about Carolyn. A tone poem based on the connection we made over this iconic cocktail.

"Just bring me the number of cherries you think I'd want," I told Josh. "The number you think is appropriate for this situation."

"Which is?"

"A guy's about to sort of bury the woman who sort of raised him."

"The right number of cherries for the guy in that situation," Steve said.

The bartender stared at the two of us, not unkindly, then turned away to reach for the bottles. It was a challenge, and of course he didn't want to take up the space of the alcohol, that would leave him with a begrudged and stingy-with-the-tip customer. But Josh had the answer. When all the mixology was done, he delivered to me a pristine amber drink with no fruit in it at all. Then he produced a second rocks glass full of glowing maraschino cherries. They weren't Luxardo – they had stems – but he was working with the tools on-hand and the gesture filled me with gratitude.

Steve's drink contained one cherry, presumably because he wasn't burying anybody.

We dumped the rocks glass out on a cocktail napkin and counted: eleven cherries. Steve was kind enough to donate his lone cherry to the kitty, bringing the total to an even dozen. I'd decided to let fate fill that number in, and fate obliged. If I'd had the right to anticipate, maybe four would've been the maximum. But I didn't. Twelve, though? Was I really up for that? I suppose we'd pitched it to Josh full throttle. Who orders a drink with cherries on the side and expects eleven? Plus Steve's?

But I could make it work. If I'd learned nothing else on this trip, it was that discussing the details of a person's life brings the person into focus. If I didn't have twelve telling details about my mother by now, I wasn't half the writer Keats told her I was.

JOSH ONLY HAD enough Jim Beam for one more drink, so I had mine made with Old Grandad, the one with the garish orange label. I can't imagine Dr. David ever ordering that. The restaurant was closing soon, surprisingly early, so Steve and I took our second drinks into the dining room.

It was there he asked a few tee-up questions about Carolyn and I started on my roll. I probably spoke eighty thousand words that night. A whole book's worth, if I'd had a court reporter handy. The words were not fact-checked, of course. But remembered, deeply and perhaps even a little fondly. I told Steve of the funereal adventure thus far, probably recounted half the stories I've just written out.

Though Steve didn't get many words in edgewise, it wasn't as if I was performing a one-man show where there's a turning point for the audience to recoil and boo, and then a heartwarming third-act breakthrough that elicits an *awwww*. I'm no Mike Burbiglia, I merely talked about what happened. About my memories of life with a complicated spirit. The story arc, if there was one, couldn't be simpler: at first I didn't get my mother, then she died, and then I started to get her. A little bit. I put in the work post-mortem I should've put in pre-mortem. It was all a lesson in time management.

THE SECOND BIRTHDAY

IT WAS STRANGE, staying in a hotel room in my home town. There was nothing that could've done a better job of driving home the point that I was no longer connected to Syracuse in any meaningful way. If you have to pay to stay, then you almost certainly fall into the *persona non grata* category.

I'd rented a motel room a couple of times in college with a girlfriend, simply for privacy. It felt sketchy at the time, but the film noir kind of sketchy, so it worked for me. I chalked it up to an experience (on at least one level). But this hotel room offered none of that slumming exotica.

I sat at the desk and watched the bedside clock click over to midnight. It was now August 30th – the beginning of Day Eight, the start of Year 54. There was a nice bottle of chardonnay I'd put on ice for the occasion, but that was before I realized I was going to down two Manhattans. Well, technically those had been yesterday. However, at this point the only thing I was interested in uncorking was my right kidney. The awareness of the homegrown-yet-alien body inside unsettled me. I started to wonder if it had metastasized with my trip. It felt like this book had forced me to internalize and carry along some burden that I couldn't put my finger on. I was once inside my mother, pushing my way out, causing her pain at the time and probably unto death. And now beyond – picking away at the corpse, not leaving well enough alone. Eternal thorn in Carolyn's side. There was the metaphor, memoir as kidney stone.

I BEGAN THE LIST, writing by hand on a yellow legal pad. But I didn't get very far.

WHO ARE WE before our children eye us up, fix us in amber? Were we fully formed, or were we placeholders, cardboard standees awaiting the next generation to define us?

I sat there wishing my mother had written out her own list for me to transcribe. I suppose I could've just jotted down the Ten Commandments – those were supposedly important to her – and then added a couple of my own. But snide wasn't how this was supposed to go.

I FINALLY started writing. When it was done, the list looked like this:

Carolyn Connelly:

1 Loved to laugh more than almost anything else
2 Cared deeply for the less fortunate
3 Had her own set of acceptable behaviors that gave her a unique, personal moral compass
4 Listened deeply
5 Kept the judgement to a minimum
6 Loved the purity and guilelessness of animals
7 Stood up for what she believed
8 Almost never felt sorry for herself, choosing to focus on the small wins even when the big picture was looking grim
9 Didn't care that much about what others thought
10 Was always striving to improve herself
11 Focused on the abundance in her life, those non-economic blessings
12 Took responsibility for her own actions

I exhaled, recapped my pen, and studied the list I'd drawn up. It was immediately clear that I'd made Carolyn seem like at least fifty percent of the other mothers in the world. If every offspring of every mother in the United States was asked for a dozen thoughts on their mother, most of the lists would contain items from this one.

It was as trite as a eulogy, which was something I had strenuously avoided. It felt like an exercise, nothing more, and it didn't tell me or anyone else anything real about my mother. Alone in a hotel room on my birthday, my present to myself didn't measure up.

This trip was not about generalities. I was alone and tired and had tried my hand at the cherry list only to come up with tepid results. I hadn't come all this way for these twelve generic comments. The simple fact that Carolyn gave me those cherries to begin with said more about her character than the dozen baubles that I'd just scrawled out. The fact that I didn't know she wanted them, the fact that she didn't feel the need to point that out, to throw a spotlight on her sacrifice, that meant something special because it was specific. It also seemed out of character for Carolyn. But then again, maybe I had it backwards. Maybe the things she didn't say were the important things, but they weren't the ones I was noticing growing up. I registered text, not subtext.

And a mother that made me have to lean in closer for insight deserved a different list. The question was, could I grant that woman their unique place in the world, their unsolvable mystery? Twelve cherries worth? If not, I should not have undertaken this trip. I should've been using my writing ability in the nice squared-off boundaries of fiction. This was much messier than that.

3:00 A.M. A new top twelve formed. It came after a lot of thought. And a couple glasses of that white wine.

I'd even renamed the list itself. The film I'd started shooting the week following Carolyn's death had been dedicated to her, but I dropped her last name. I thought, at the end, that she wouldn't have wanted the continued association with Dr. David. I followed that logic with the new list:

Carolyn Black:

1   Adopted the next-door neighbor's dog because he seemed happier with her
2   Spent at least a year worrying that one of her infants was literally possessed
3   Mentioned, as we headed off on vacation, that she didn't care if the house burned down
4   Stopped making breakfast for my brother permanently after he ignored her single warning about criticizing her cooking
5   Kept a copy of *Fear of Flying*, the *Fifty Shades of Grey* of the '70s, in her bureau drawer
6   Crawled out on the frozen canal to rescue her dog, who had just fallen through the ice
7   Constantly used the phrases "Mean as cat dirt" and "You'll have fun whether you like it or not"
8   Would stop at my dorm on the way home from work to pick up my laundry and return it washed and folded the next evening
9   Would have friends over for secret cocktail parties despite her retirement community's strict ban on alcohol
10 Once tried to eat the crumpled cork foil from a bottle of cabernet off the table because she thought it was a piece of chocolate
11 Had my brother saw off a baseball bat and thread a rope through the handle so she could use it like a nightstick on her walks when the Canal Tow Path started attracting muggers
12 Was able to track down a missing dog named Blackberry three weeks after he disappeared by hearing of a family across town who'd found a dog and named him Raisin

Now with this list, Carolyn was starting to come into focus, starting to look like a unique individual. It wasn't comprehensive by any means, but it felt closer to the bullseye. Which came as no surprise. Writing, after all, is rewriting.

The ones who love us best
Are the ones we'll lay to rest
Visit their grave on holidays at best
The ones who love us least
Are the ones we'll die to please
If it's any consolation, I don't begin to understand them

– The Replacements
"Bastards of Young"

EIGHT

∞

THE DAY OF THE REMAINS

HITTING THE PAVEMENT

IT WAS LATER than I would have preferred on the morning of August 30th when the ringing phone woke me. This had been a meandering trip, and I wasn't a slave to a clock along the way, but I had shared the time I wanted to dispose of Carolyn's ashes with a few people in Syracuse plus my siblings in a thousand-to-one shot, and I thought it was only right to stick to the schedule in case anyone suddenly decided to participate.

On the other end of the line, my brother David was reaching out. This was a rare occasion. Not a birthday message – normally there would be no surprise there, but since I'd described my plans to him just a few weeks prior, including using the guideposts of Carolyn's birthday and my own as structural foundation, I would've thought the day's date might have been a little bit more in the forefront of David's thoughts this particular year.

No, he was calling about something else, and on behalf of someone else. My sister was apparently voicing some concerns to him about my writing this book. Specifically, her place in it. According to David, Lisa was beginning to get unnerved with my poking around in the past. Her past, as she saw it. Me at her college, me asking about the name of her horse (Prince, for the record), me texting her trying to get some details on a paranormal experience that was tangentially related to me. To her there was something deeply unsettling about these inquiries. Privacy had always been paramount to Lisa. I'd never stepped foot inside her bedroom on the third floor of her townhouse in Virginia; she really did keep the door at the top of the stairs locked. Exposure in a non-fiction book was likely one of the scariest things she could imagine.[41]

I tried to explain, telling David that the book was about my experiences and relationship with Carolyn, trying to process them, and that details of my childhood were a part of that. I meant no one any harm, but my siblings and I invariably had crossed paths growing up, and I wanted to get at the truth of my experience.

This struck David as ridiculous and the tone of the conversation shifted, the volume escalating. I gave him the checklist; it was my birthday, I was getting rid of our mother's ashes, and I didn't need the aggravation of my sister's paranoia right now.

"You know what, I've got work to do," he snapped and hung up on me. It was clear that work wasn't the issue. Fuck this, he must've thought. Fuck you. I'd rubbed him the wrong way, I'd pushed back on his request and as much as he didn't want to be the guy with the thin skin, that's who he was. A lot of tough guys are, I suspect. I may have shared a heavy dose of my father's DNA for better or worse, but David had always been like Carolyn's father. Generous but easily hurt and vicious in his retribution. And boy, did he hate the disloyalty. There are aspects of the Donald Trump personality in there; not the actions or intentions, but the soft self-hating aspects of the boy inside that allowed those kinds of behaviors to flourish. Him calling me was a generosity to Lisa. My pushback made him feel unappreciated and was like gaso-

---

[41] I, on the other hand, could never get enough attention. Lisa and I undoubtedly have different psychological issues.

line on the pilot light of his anger. I was Aunt Lana: who wants ice cream? Not me.

I called back a few times until David answered and tried to smooth things over, run him through my point of view again, but he was just exhausted by the whole thing. He knew it; I was going to do what I was going to do. Just like any Connelly. Couldn't hand one of us a glass of water if our face was on fire.

So be it.

Happy birthday to me.

THE SYRACUSE SUMMER wasn't known for its golden sun, but for its oppressive humidity. The morning was showing it off in full form. I decided to go for a quick run anyway, just to make sure the fifty-four-year old version of me could still hack it. I'd been running for more than ten years, yet three miles has hung in there at the far end of my comfort zone. I had not turned out to be a distance guy.

Tricked out in Dri-Fit, I left the hotel and headed for the canal. But before I started the run, I needed to make one last stop. This had always been a journey into the past, and in some ways the closer I got to my birth place, the earlier the memories. It made sense to me that on the last day, the celebration of my year zero, I would make the pilgrimage to the earliest memory I had of Syracuse, my earliest memory period, save Montréal.

I was driving on the road that appeared as a continuation of Lyndon, right at the spot where the Erie Canal opened up in a bend to its widest point. On the canal, the area was known as Cedar Bay, and likewise Lyndon Road changed names there, becoming Cedar Bay Road. It looked like a T, where Kinne Road deadheaded into Lyndon, but in fact, it was a dividing line, with the tail end of Lyndon pointing toward DeWitt and the south and Cedar Bay leading to Fayetteville and the north.

Something happened on Cedar Bay Road when I was a child. Though that statement resembles nothing so much as some forgotten volume of the *Hardy Boys*, it was no adventure.

I drove along Cedar Bay as slowly as I could, the Audi moving at the speed of a fast walk, really. I could feel where the road went up at a pitch, sudden and short to a plateau that curved around to the right. It was still the same, torqued like plastic Hot Wheels track. Once the road levelled off again, I turned around and headed down that little hill. I pulled over and got out of the car. This was the location, all right. Working over the calendar, this event seems to have happened the autumn after our ill-fated trip to Expo '67. I would've still been four at the time.

My mother had been on a fitness kick that included bike riding. She had a black and gold Raleigh bike that would eventually earn the sobriquet "The Black Widow" within the family. It hung around for years. The bike had a child seat mounted on the back, which consisted of a folding spring-loaded square platform and for a seatbelt the kind of canvas straps found on sleeping bags. I was on the back and Carolyn had taken me for ride. Not the tow path less than a mile from our house – which was perfect for biking, with its zero-rise grade and pulverized stone surface – but on the country road directly across from the tow path. It might have been that she considered the turn down Kinne Road that she would've had to take to gain entry to the canal too steep and dangerous. If so, that would turn out to be an error in judgment.

The town had been doing some drainage work on Cedar Bay, and on that bend a new galvanized steel culvert pipe had been installed on the shoulder. Loose gravel had been filled in surrounding the pipe to get all the work to grade.

I EXITED THE CAR and walked over to the culvert. The piping seemed ancient now. But still very solid. I wrapped my knuckles against it.

This thing, it had been built to last.

∞ ∞ ∞

MY MOTHER biked down Cedar Bay toward Lyndon on that rare sunny day in 1968. As she approached the short, steep decline at the bend, the loose gravel caught the front tire and the Raleigh skidded wildly. Our momentum took the whole thing sideways, with the wheels pushing out toward the shoulder. Those little canvas straps did nothing for me; I was untethered and tossed from the pancake surface of the child's seat like a stuffed animal.

Carolyn came down hard, with the new corrugated pipe having substantially less give than her skull. She was knocked out cold, crumpled on the shoulder, legs still tangled in the bike.

I landed in the street. Rubbery like any other four-year-old, I was unhurt and fully conscious, but likely in shock. Whatever I understood about the basics of traffic safety didn't stick at the moment of crisis. I was a toddler wobbling in the middle of this blind curve country road. I was a sitting duck.

ALL THESE YEARS LATER, standing where we'd gone down together, I stared at the solid yellow line that marked the border between road and drain field and I felt something new. I could only now, as a father, begin to imagine the abject terror that must overtake a parent waking up and realizing that they blacked out while they were signed onto guard duty for a tiny, helpless life. Carolyn wouldn't have been afraid for herself waking up in the hospital, but for me, for what had become of me while the Looney Tunes **NO SALE** rang up behind her eyelids. Any mother would, right?

I never asked.

Once when I told Dr. David my understanding was that a father would take a bullet for his child, there was a long pause before he muttered, "I guess I'd try to push you out of the way of one..." He trailed off and let his refusal to trade his life for mine remain unspoken.

∞ ∞ ∞

I'D SQUATTED THERE in the southbound lane fifty years earlier, shouting "Mommy… Mommy…" over toward the side of the road. I didn't want to approach Carolyn. I thought she might be dead, and nothing frightened me more than a dead body. Even my mother's. I didn't think I'd ever be the kissing-the-body type. The open casket.

I stood there now and realized I'd put my lips on my mother's slowly cooling forehead back at Foulkeways in the exact same spot she hit the culvert. First and last memories entwined of Carolyn and me alone, sealed with a kiss. Bookends of a sort; the fear that she'd left me on one side, the knowledge she had on the other.

At four I had no way of knowing the difference between concussion and death – stillness being a hallmark of each – and I was frozen helplessly in the street, convinced my mother was gone. "Mommy…"

There was a small house up on the ridge that overlooked the curve from the northbound side. Amazingly, someone was home and out on their lawn. A woman, who saw me standing there shell-shocked. In a heartbeat, she ran down the hill, grabbed me and pulled me to the safety of the shoulder where the wreck sat.

I COULD SEE the house from the spot, a little more overgrown in the yard, perhaps on purpose to dampen traffic noise.

If the accident happened today, it was likely no one would have noticed.

It was likely the little kid would have been ended.

MAYBE I DID HAVE a guardian angel, just not the one the Ouija Board offered. As the stranger who saved me knelt down to check on Carolyn, I just stood there next to the Raleigh, asking this over and over: *Is my mommy dead? Is my mommy dead?*

Is Mommy dead?

Not then, no. When I was finally able to give the good Samaritan my name, calls were placed and help arrived. My father showed up in the station wagon and hauled his wife off to the hospital, where she stayed for a week to recover from a severe concussion.

"Is Mommy dead?" No, she wasn't then.

SHE WAS NOW.

Is Mommy dead?

Indeed. Going on three years. Dead and in a box in my back seat.

It was time to put her to rest.

15 (DIVIDED BY 5) MILES ON THE ERIE CANAL

BY DESIGN, my planned morning run would accomplish more than just a bit of much-needed exercise. It also served as a kind of Erie Canal tow path reconnoiter. Hadn't I known that my mother had always been at her happiest by water? Even if I hadn't known, the photos would've told me. She seemed almost magnetically drawn to it. Even the street on which she grew up claimed to be very close to the Delaware River (the neighborhood cemetery was called Riverview, though I question what kind of view there really was).

She may not have been from Syracuse like me, but for as long as I could remember, when Carolyn lived here she'd taken daily three-mile walks along the towpath of the section of the canal that meandered not far from our old house... a mile and a half from the Butternut Drive parking lot, the same mile and a half back. My standard mileage for a run and my mother's daily walks came out to the same distance. Usually the walk was required in order to exercise whatever dog or dogs we had at the time, but even if there were no dogs around, the walks still happened. Rain, snow, nightfall, thunder, mudslide; none of it stopped Carolyn. I'd go with her once in a while, but most of the time it was Tapan who kept her company.

The Erie Canal was her space. It was ugly and half-forgotten, but it gave her something and she was loyal, there every day. It may have been her way of processing. Even when it started getting dangerous, when there were warnings of drug dealers and muggers down there, she remained undeterred.

This would be the spot; my mother's final destination. I'd known it the last time Mary Jo and I were thrashing out what to do with Carolyn's remains. My wife had asked me where I figured Carolyn would be happiest several times over the years, and I never took the question seriously until the idea of this trip erupted from my subconscious. But the answer came first. The trip was, in fact, reverse engineered from the answer to the question. The Erie Canal was the only place Carolyn could be. Once I'd realized it was the only place of significance where her ashes could rest, everything else fell into place. I hadn't let myself come to this simple understanding before because, like the best man speeches, like high school, I hadn't risked a real decision to protect myself from being truly accountable in the event of a mistake. I hadn't committed. In the final analysis, Carolyn had been in the closet for three years not because I didn't care about her ending, but because I cared too deeply – about my own self-image, that is. But my history offered nothing for me to lean on; no practice, no ritual, no roadmap. The truth was, it had been easier to ignore the ashes than to spend the rest of my life wondering if I'd screwed it up because I didn't know what to do with them.

With her.

But I did know, knew her well enough to make tracks to her final resting place at any rate. Learning whatever I could about her along the way, that helped the goose chase make some sort of sense. Even if what I learned was coming from within, it was still something I couldn't have achieved sitting at my desk. I needed to log the miles.

It was an imperfect experiment. Nature abhors a vacuum, writers a mystery without resolution. Yet in the face of these wide and general absolutes, there were still outstanding, concrete questions about Carolyn's life. Questions that more mileage on the Audi probably wouldn't answer. Vacuum and mystery to beat the band. I'd been picking up pieces and putting the picture together, but I didn't have all the pieces and worse, there was more to it than the one picture. At best, I was getting a better handle on the human being that people knew as Carolyn Black Connelly. Maybe I was glimpsing past the façade I'd helped erect. Maybe that was the best – all – that I could hope to do.

Fuck the eulogy. Give me the autopsy every time.

ON MY RUN I did my best to get a bead on the environment, make sure it could work the way I'd envisioned. I wasn't sure if security was a part of the park these days. I certainly wasn't sure if what I had planned was legal, so I just wanted to be as informed as possible. Call it a tech scout, or call it casing the scene of the crime.

So I ran, a mile and half down to the Cedar Bay parking area, and a mile and a half back to Butternut Drive. I worked up a sweat. I saw no cameras or security (maybe they were stationed outside the Salt Museum downtown), just a surprisingly large number of people. The canal had become a bit of a hotspot in the years I'd been away.

I saw a lot of people walking their dogs, and I thought about Carolyn's relationship with pets as I jogged along. She loved canines of every breed with a deep passion. Of course, the key was that the dogs' reciprocation was unconditional and constant. She found no judgement in a dog's eyes. Their needs were clear and minimal, their gratitude consistently enthusiastic. They made her feel good about herself. Passion in her life eventually boiled down to the simple pleasures.

My own love for animal life was mainlined into me by

the woman. I'd been a sucker for any mammal you put in front of me since I was two. It was probably an inconsistency of character, but then again, Dr. David the plastic surgeon started out planning on being a veterinarian, so maybe cold and animal-loving were on different axes and not at different ends along a spectrum.

Dogs were fixtures on Lyndon Road and Cornwall Drive. The one my brother brought home from the junkyard that would change his outlook and allow him to access a level of empathy he hadn't seemed capable of previously. There were the two thoroughbred standard poodles from the days of Dr. David (one that I grew up with and one that predated me from when the family lived in what would eventually become Tapan's house). The toy poodle Blackberry, the one that migrated from our neighbor's house to ours because Carolyn's table scraps were better than dry dogfood. Blackberry was the last of them.

As CAROLYN BECAME more elderly, she started to take perverse delight in spilling certain long-kept secrets. They tumbled out with a defiant "Ain't I a rascal?" smile that would've looked better on a seven-year-old than someone 87. They seemed like attempts to inflict pain on those closest to her. One secret that she let fly was that she'd always blamed me for talking her into euthanizing Blackberry. This perception created a resentment toward me which apparently had been quietly festering for years. I'd forced her hand when I was a college student, she claimed, insisting that she put the animal down. Somehow, according to her, I'd badgered her into it. The fact was, after fifteen years of walks along the canal, the little dog had contracted diabetes. His stomach was distended, he couldn't control his bowels, and he could barely get around. His skin and breath were producing a rank odor. His quality of life was awful. It was true that I discussed putting him to sleep. I did think it was time. It was my advice, no more than that. But somehow, though Carolyn was convinced that she alone would know when the time was right, she felt it wasn't time and yet put the dog down anyway. Because of my bludgeoning opinions on the matter, apparently.

I think she needed someone to blame as a way of alleviating her own guilt. The other side of her religion – the opposite of the comfort it gave her – was the responsibility. Again, I was bumping up against shame, and the lengths to which people will go to assuage it.

This and other late-in-life confessionals seemed like the start of some new aspect of Carolyn's ability to communicate more honestly, but of course it only extended as far as she chose. She required the freedom to say what was on her mind, but also wanted the privilege to keep information she felt shouldn't see the light of day hidden.

If we all are only as sick as our secrets, Carolyn certainly wasn't a terminal case. But neither could she have been given a clean bill of health.

I'D LIKE MY MOTHER to be the heroine of this story, I really would. It wouldn't be so bad a bonus if I came off looking good myself, but heroics didn't seem to be in the cards for either of us. Not when the commitment had been made to the truth.

The Christian-drenched America I'd grown up in had its effect on me: I've been led to believe that truth brought salvation.

Too late for Carolyn, of course. But maybe not for me. My list of sins was long, but I'd like to think not so deep. There are shallow transgressions – ankle deep, knee deep at most – where one just rolls up their jeans and takes off their shoes and wades along. That was mostly where I'd trafficked. And then there are other sins, the ones where you're in over your head.

Protestants don't do confession, and atheists have no rituals at all. I've tried to come clean on this journey, yet my admissions each seem to come with an asterisk. I'm unable to take responsibility for my mistakes and bad behavior without also indicting the one at whose knee I learned everything.

It was a package deal. Like the bike, we go down together, and we get back up the same way. Then perhaps forgiving Carolyn's mistakes as a mother had always meant forgiving myself for a son's transgressions.

Tolstoy wrote, "Every unhappy family is unhappy in its own way." That was hypothesizing a lot of complications for a lot of families throughout history. I personally considered it more of a cocktail. Family matters could be corrosive, scorching away physically right in front of your eyes, or erosive, slowly dissolving unnoticeably over the years. Different families had different mixtures of the two. We were WASPs, so metaphorically speaking, for every Night of the Hammer there were likely a thousand pets full of pentobarbital.

SACRED GROUND

BACK IN THE HOTEL, it was all drawing to a close. I had a narrow window to pack, shower, shave, and dress if I was going to keep to my timetable.

I'd never grown a full beard, but often, because I was self-employed, I'd be going through my day with Indiana Jones-style scruff. I suppose it was a look easy enough for me to pull off when I was younger, but as my facial hair started to go gray, it became less Hollywood and more Bowery.[42] I'd shaved the day before with the one beat-up razor blade I'd brought with me on the road, a kind of rough cut, so that I'd be able to get the smoothest shave today that I could achieve. Two shaves in two days was as rare for the self-employed as a meteor shower (or a traditional shower, for that matter), but it felt important to me.

I'd brought cologne, dragged it along every mile, but hadn't touched it until now. I'd packed it special for the day. Taberon, a scent by the House of Creed, sprinkled cool against my shower-hot skin. I spritzed on too much, really. But Carolyn liked it when men smelled nice – every time I wore cologne, she commented on it. It was a preoccupa-

---

[42] Carolyn was on a mission when my beard began growing gray, constantly asking me to dye it. There was always that shallow part of her, struggling against her better angels. Looks mattered to Carolyn, they had been her currency growing up. That was part of what drove her obsession over my sister's weight and whether David would go bald like her father had.

tion with her, and as a person with plenty of preoccupations of my own, I got it. So I did that for her. If I smelled too strong for most people, that was something I could live with. I didn't put the Creed on for most people. Not today.

I packed up – first the clothes, then the mementos – and then it was time to get dressed. Some actors have gone on record saying that a good costume does possibly half their job for them. I could believe it: when I put on the funeral suit, things started feeling pretty goddamn real. From time to time I'd had jobs that required wearing suits, but for the most part it wasn't part of my professional repertoire. When I did put one on, it usually dialed in on a feeling of excitement. In a suit I tended to be going to a show, a wedding, maybe an art opening or film premiere. But I slid that suit jacket on in the Syracuse hotel room and with that final sartorial gesture, something changed. The air in the room shifted, a weight – Poe's raven – arrived. Nothing on the trip so far had hit me so hard emotionally. But what was the sole pallbearer to do but soldier on?

I checked myself out in the full-length mirror and then I checked myself out of the hotel.

I PULLED INTO the wide gravel parking area at the tow path's Butternut Drive entrance and dropped the convertible into park. The air conditioning had been blasting, but my hands still remained stubbornly clammy. I held them up to the vents, which spit slight puffs of cool air, and splayed my fingers. After a few moments, I shut off the engine and climbed out of the Audi.

It had been more than a week that I'd been driving around with the plastic box of ashes on the floor behind the driver's seat, and I'd barely given it a thought. Carolyn, yes, much thought. The location too. But the object? The actual remains? No. Until now. By this time, the crematory's box was buried in the accumulated slurry that was the time-honored sign of a real road trip. I folded the driver's seat forward, and retrieved it.

The plastic enclosure that held the remains of my mother didn't seem designed to be opened. Mentally preparing for the worst case, I wondered if Bernie Gerthoffer would be home if needed. I imagined popping over to Cornwall Drive and getting him to force the box open with one of his ancient but perfect-for-the-job steel hand tools. *Hey Bern, haven't seen you in two decades... how about a hand opening up my mother's ashes?*

That request would not be necessary, as it turned out. Pressure from my thumbs on the short end of the box popped the plastic plate right off. I'd put Carolyn in a box my whole life, I suppose. And now I was taking her out of one. Opening her up. There was a lot more to you than mother, I thought. Motherhood might not even make the top ten.

Jammed tight inside was a bag with a wire twist tie around its opening. Threaded through the wire was a simple tag with Carolyn's name and the date of the cremation. It was like a gift tag. Once, when I was living in DC and Carolyn ended up in the hospital here, I'd sent Bill Rapp to her room to make a delivery on my behalf. Instead of flowers I had him bring a cactus. On a tiny card, faking my handwriting just like a good *Mission: Impossible* devotee might do, Bill had written what I'd requested, **BE TOUGH**, and pierced the note on a cactus needle. This tag reminded me of that, it had the same perverse simplicity. Carolyn hadn't liked Bill's hospital visit, of course. So she said. But she kept the note, which might indicate a slightly different reaction in private.

Counterfeit Sentiments

Here in my hand was the toughest part of Carolyn; after a lifetime of antics big and small, impactful and insignificant, this was what there was to show for it. Atoms too tough to get turned into gas, even at 1800 degrees. The remains were both whiter and finer than I'd expected. Not snow white, but still not the fireplace ash I'd expected. I started getting a little paranoid, wondering if passersby were going to think I was spreading anthrax all over the tow path.

Now that I realized the ashes were sleeved in plastic, it appeared that the pastry bag might have become irrelevant. I could make my own out of the bag inside the box without having to move the ashes at all. I had a pair of toenail clippers in my luggage and thought if I simply cut one corner off the bottom of the plastic bag, I'd have what I needed to get the job done. The plan I had was to walk the first mile and a half to the turnaround point at Cedar Bay carrying the ashes along without letting any of them go. On the return leg, I would slowly leak the ashes behind in a kind of smoky stream. Carolyn's final resting place would be the entire length of her usual walk.

As I was digging through my suitcase looking for the nail clippers, a vehicle drove up directly behind me. My ears picked up the slow crunching roll of the tires getting closer, too close. I looked up, half expecting to see that Tapan had decided to show up. Instead, I caught the reflections off the massive chrome-plated grill of a black Ram pickup, just like the one I drive. There was no front license plate, which is required in New York. But not, it was dawning on me, in Pennsylvania...

Three doors opened at once. Mary Jo and our kids, Callie and Wesley, climbed out of my RAM. They were dressed for the occasion, resplendent, with my son wearing a linen blazer, my daughter in a pale green sundress and Mary Jo, in a white and blue one.

My wife met me at the convertible with a deep hug. "You want some company?" she asked.

My family knew what I was doing with Carolyn's remains and they knew when it would happen. Nothing was going to keep them away, apparently. Mary Jo had never agreed to miss the ceremony, she'd merely stopped arguing with me about it. They'd woken up insanely early and driven to Syracuse that morning to help me.

And somehow, despite what I'd been saying all along about doing this entire trip alone, despite my misgivings over how my ceremony would come across to others, I had never been so happy to see three people in my entire life.

BURYING CHILD

THESE DAYS I COULDN'T HELP but be amazed at the fact that, as a little boy, I never imagined that my mother held onto the feelings of her childhood, contained those memories of her own life inside. It's laughable now, because when I spend time watching my children get into whatever they're getting into at the moment, I'm always keenly aware of how it felt to be a child. Such a clear, attenuated awareness came easy; the sense of being able to put myself into both the body and the mindset I'd had at their age. It wasn't all that long ago, although a teenager would never believe that. More importantly, for me anyway, childhood was a crucible so intense its intricacies were tattooed upon my psyche. There was nothing that had been lost, and I understood it all; the fear, the joy, the anxiety, the humor, the embarrassment, the self-righteousness. It was all glorious.

I saw it in the faces of Callie and Wesley. They had already had a long day by the time they arrived at their grandmother's unorthodox funeral. It was the very end of their last summer before high school. They had every reason to be annoyed by the drive and the task at hand. I would've been at their age. But then, my mother wouldn't have brought me to something like this. Or showed up herself. Wesley and Callie were being raised differently than I had been. They willed themselves to be happy in supporting me with the oddball ritual I'd concocted. They will see their friends in *Godspell* even if they don't like musicals; they will visit relatives in their hospital rooms, despite the lighting and the smell.

THERE WASN'T A LOT of talk between the four of us. There would be time for that later, over a birthday dinner in Armory Square. For now, it was quiet time.

Relative to how the weather had been the previous few days, the morning was on the cool side, but I was still sweating through my worsted wool suit. I found walking the gravel path in my dress shoes uncomfortable, and Mary Jo's fabulous Fluevog footwear wasn't any more practical. I hadn't anticipated all the people on the canal in the middle of the day. The four of us walked the mile-and-a-half along the tow path trail, slowing the progress of passing Spandex-ed runners, power walkers and cyclists who couldn't help but stare at this well-dressed, somber crew. We just nodded and kept moving, not allowing any strangers' curiosity to encroach on the magic of Carolyn's day.

No one had turned on the waterworks; not yet. I hadn't spread any ashes on the way in, so at the turnaround, I cut the corner off the plastic bag. As we headed back the way we'd come, I began to sprinkle ashes here and there on the bank side, along the water's edge. We sauntered along and I kept sprinkling as we talked a bit about the best aspects of Carolyn. We even managed a little laughter here and there, like those dogs that urinate every couple of hundred feet along their walk.

I noticed a cluster of snapdragons waving in the warm breeze and felt my pulse quicken.

I'D WAGER that not many heterosexual bridegrooms care all that much about the flowers at their wedding. The food, the music, these could be bones of contention. But flowers?

They may have a lower-case opinion here or there, but basically, if the bride's happy, they're happy. I was slightly different regarding our wedding's floral plan, though. I had a favorite flower, the snapdragon, and I wanted it to be a part of the service. This was no small concession on Mary Jo's part, because snapdragons aren't particularly elegant flowers. But it was important to me. It was about the flower itself, but it was also about my story of the flower. Maybe more about the story, writers being what they are.

They were my favorites because they *did* something, and because I had an association with what they did. They may not have been the prettiest, but they worked for your attention. Nature's free miniature puppet show. And they grew wild along the banks of the Erie Canal. Carolyn had picked them for me when I was a baby, had taught me how to manipulate their tiny jaws with my equally tiny fingers.

No question, I had to commit a significant portion of Carolyn's remains to this stand of snapdragons.

THERE WERE NOT TOO MANY pictures of the Erie Canal in Carolyn's mementos. The reasons were legion: it doesn't photograph well, it was often dark when she was there, she was often alone, and carrying a baseball bat for protection. And she walked this tow path in an era when you had to *bring a camera* in order to have a camera with you.

But there was one shot I liked. It seemed to sum up quite a bit about this story. Her story. No dog in it, which was a major oversight. But yeah, if I were going to share a picture of Carolyn along the canal, I could do a lot worse than sharing this one:

The Erie Canal, Circa 1975

THE LAST BITS of the remains were the hardest.

I'd gone the entire way looking at the near-stagnant water and referring to Carolyn's "view," even though I believe such considerations are pure magical thinking. I know one thing: if my mother's eyes are anywhere, they were everywhere in that ash. There aren't parts of the burnt-up body that could be separated out. It was all her view, or none of it was. Still, one last bit of her for the final act of the ceremony was called for. I was looking for the grace note.

At the end (beginning, really) of the trail, over by the stone aqueduct just this side of the parking area, I took stock. I had just enough of the ash left for one last dusting. It wasn't the placement of the last bit that would give this one-time ritual that extra something, though. It was me. I had to say something. Out loud.

I managed to choke out, "You were one of a kind." And then, turning over the plastic bag from the crematorium, shaking out the last bit of chalky ash, I could only add, "Welcome home."

Well, not Shakespeare, but true enough.

My children flanked me, hugged me around the waist as if they were much littler than they are. Mary Jo lay a hand on my right shoulder. Tears came for everyone.

I now know what a funeral is for, what it gives back to you after so much has been taken. Now I know. I suppose I had to learn it the hard way.

I always have.

What man really fears is not so much extinction,
but extinction with insignificance.

– Ernest Becker
"The Denial of Death"

EPILOGUE

∞

THIS GIRL'S LIFE

THE HOTEL SYRACUSE was a better joint than it had any right to be. Pulled out of bankruptcy on more than one occasion, sold more times than anyone could remember, it made a soft landing when Marriott decided to purchase it and restore it to its former historic glory.

I took the elevator down to the street level and slipped into Eleven Waters, the hotel's restaurant. The young lady behind the bar looked over as I entered and announced, "We're closed." But she was talking to her friend across the bar, not actually doing the work of closing up for the night. And the doors had been open.

"A couple of drinks, that's all," I told her with a plea in my voice. "I'm just going to take them up to my room."

"Shaughnessey's across the way. They're still open."

She was referring to the hotel's sports bar on the other side of the lower lobby. No good. My rule on sport bars is inviolate. Plus, the fucking place was called Shaughnessey's. I told the bartender mine wasn't a sports bar type of order.

"Anything I can make they can make," she told me with a Central New York smile. I was getting shut down. In no uncertain terms.

And yet…

I'd talked myself into enough places on this trip. What was one more? It was my birthday. I'd just buried my mother. My children and wife had crossed two states to be with me in this moment of finality. Will to power. This was not going be a Shaughnessey's kind of nightcap. I let out a soft sigh. "It's my birthday," I told her, often a magic key in these kinds of situations.

She was not impressed. Nothing back from her but a stare. Her friend said, "Happy birthday," though.

Not one to take pity on birthday boys, eh? Okay. How about this: "And I just buried my mother."

"On your birthday?"

A nod. "On my birthday."

The bartender frowned. "I'm sorry to hear that."

"She didn't want a big thing done, but when she was alive, she told the family when she went… died… she wanted us to get together, have a drink, and tell funny stories about her."

"She said that?" The bartender studied me, trying to figure out if I was levelling with her or full of shit.

I was *not* full of shit. Carolyn had said exactly that, though I left out the part where she imagined my sister and brother would be involved. "She did. Her name was Carolyn, and she liked a *good* cocktail." I said this in a low voice, wanting to convey the import of the celebration including her favorite drink. And not one from a sports bar. Sports bars made me want to revoke my citizenship.

"What did she drink?"

"Manhattans," I said. "It was her favorite, and she used to give me the cherries."

The bartender shook her head, disgusted at herself for giving in. "If you had said any other drink…" But she took pride in her skills behind the bar. "They can't make a proper Manhattan over there."

What, at Shaughnessey's? You don't say. "Rye, best you have." I'd left the bourbon behind at Scotch N' Sirloin.

"Quite a tribute," the woman said as she reached for the stemware and started on the drinks.

You have no idea. If I told you I brought my mother's remains to the Erie Canal and dusted them over the snapdragons there, I'd still be leaving out eight days of the service.

I watched as the bartender went to spear the cherries from a large glass container. She was doubling up, two per toothpick. And they were the goddamn Luxado cherries, the good, blood red ones from Italy. How about that? Quality was making a comeback in downtown Syracuse.

Even so, I'd never be stepping foot in this town again.

So a postscript to Mary Jo and my twins: the Book of the Dead, Syracuse edition, is officially closed. Find a different dumping ground for Daddy's ashes when the time comes, gang.

And wouldn't it be nice to see everyone again on the other side?

Wouldn't it be nice to believe?

The book's creator and the author's creator, circa 1964

ABOUT THE AUTHOR

Stuart Connelly has been writing professionally for more than thirty years. A graduate of Syracuse University's prestigious S.I. Newhouse School of Public Communications, Stuart has written speeches for Fortune 500 executives, reported for daily newspapers, edited a national magazine, and – at a career low point – once wrote a handful of jokes for the White House.

His work has been taught at the Algonkian Art of Fiction Writer's Workshop alongside such luminaries of the craft as Mark Twain, Flannery O'Connor, Franz Kafka, and Raymond Carver.

Stuart is a National Educational Press Association Award winner for his work with Scholastic Publishing and was the founder of the San Francisco-based advertising agency Topeka.

He has co-authored two award-winning non-fiction biographies of Martin Luther King, Jr. and Clarence B. Jones – *Behind The Dream* and *Last of the Lions*.

In addition, his journalism has appeared in *New Yorker, USA Today, Washington Post, Boston Globe, Huffington Post* and *Al Jazeera America*.

He made his feature film directorial debut with the 2013 thriller *The Suspect*.

He currently divides his time between New York City and rural Pennsylvania, which is of course not as useful as multiplying it.

Made in the USA
Middletown, DE
26 July 2024

58019031R00203